A PROMISING NEW START

With expert readings and forecasts, you can chart a course to romance, adventure, good health, or career opportunities while gaining valuable insight into yourself and others. Offering a daily outlook for 18 full months, this fascinating guide shows you:

- The important dates in your life
- What to expect from an astrological reading
- How the stars can help you stay healthy and fit
  And more!

Let this sound advice guide you through a year of heavenly possibilities—for today and for every day of 2008!

SYDNEY OMARR'S® DAY-BY-DAY
ASTROLOGICAL GUIDE FOR

ARIES—March 21–April 19
TAURUS—April 20–May 20
GEMINI—May 21–June 20
CANCER—June 21–July 22
LEO—July 23–August 22
VIRGO—August 23–September 22
LIBRA—September 23–October 22
SCORPIO—October 23–November 21
SAGITTARIUS—November 22–December 21
CAPRICORN—December 22–January 19
AQUARIUS—January 20–February 18
PISCES—February 19–March 20

IN 2008

SYDNEY OMARR'S®

DAY-BY-DAY ASTROLOGICAL GUIDE FOR

CANCER

JUNE 21–JULY 22

2008

By Trish MacGregor
with Carol Tonsing

A SIGNET BOOK

SIGNET
Published by New American Library, a division of
Penguin Group (USA) Inc., 375 Hudson Street,
New York, New York 10014, USA
Penguin Group (Canada), 90 Eglinton Avenue East, Suite 700, Toronto,
Ontario M4P 2Y3, Canada (a division of Pearson Penguin Canada Inc.)
Penguin Books Ltd., 80 Strand, London WC2R 0RL, England
Penguin Ireland, 25 St. Stephen's Green, Dublin 2,
Ireland (a division of Penguin Books Ltd.)
Penguin Group (Australia), 250 Camberwell Road, Camberwell, Victoria 3124,
Australia (a division of Pearson Australia Group Pty. Ltd.)
Penguin Books India Pvt. Ltd., 11 Community Centre, Panchsheel Park,
New Delhi - 110 017, India
Penguin Group (NZ), 67 Apollo Drive, Rosedale, North Shore,
Auckland 1311, New Zealand (a division of Pearson New Zealand Ltd.)
Penguin Books (South Africa) (Pty.) Ltd., 24 Sturdee Avenue,
Rosebank, Johannesburg 2196, South Africa

Penguin Books Ltd., Registered Offices:
80 Strand, London WC2R 0RL, England

First published by Signet, an imprint of New American Library,
a division of Penguin Group (USA) Inc.

First Printing, June 2007
10 9 8 7 6 5 4 3 2 1

Copyright © The Estate of Sydney Omarr, 2007
All rights reserved

Sydney Omarr's is a registered trademark of Writers House, LLC.

Sydney Omarr® is syndicated worldwide byLos Angeles Times Syndicate.

 REGISTERED TRADEMARK—MARCA REGISTRADA

Printed in the United States of America

PUBLISHER'S NOTE
While the author has made every effort to provide accurate telephone numbers
and Internet addresses at the time of publication, neither the publisher nor the
author assumes any responsibility for errors, or for changes that occur after publication. Further, publisher does not have any control over and does not assume
any responsibility for author or third-party Web sites or their content.

CONTENTS

INTRODUCTION

Put Astrology in Your Life

This year marks a time of transition as our personal universe opens up with possibilities we never imagined. Thanks to the Internet, we have a command-control center from which we can travel the globe at warp speed. We can meet friends and lovers in cyberspace, gather information from remote sources in moments, and manage the details of our daily lives online. But, as the saying goes, the more things change, the more they stay the same. In our personal lives, we are still searching for the same things that have always made life worth living: love, meaningful work, and fulfilling personal relationships.

Astrology is an age-old tool that can guide us in our search, one that works as well today as it has for several millennia. It can be a support system, career coach, and guide through difficult times. It can help you find your own strengths or assess your marketable talents to land the perfect job. Like links in the Internet, astrological clues can speed you from where you are now to where you'd like to be. But just like many of the newest high-tech laptops, there's a learning curve before you can use it to best advantage. It will take some practice and familiarity to operate effectively in your life. Fortunately a little knowledge can get you up and running quickly.

In this year's guide, we give you basic information to help you get hands-on with astrology. We tell you what you need to know about your sun sign and how to decipher the mysterious symbols on a horoscope chart. Then you can look up other planets in your horoscope to find out how each contributes to your total personality.

Many readers are fascinated by astrology's insights into

relationships. This leap year, find out who you're most likely to get along with and why, then how to attract the right sign. You'll see the celebrity combinations with your sign that made romantic history—and some that didn't.

Whether it's wealth-building advice, fashion tips, or help finding the perfect gift for a hard-to-please relative, astrology has something to say. Astrology can even guide you to the best place to take your vacation. For those who like to surf the Web, we recommend astrology-savvy sites where you can get your chart calculated free. Connecting with other astrology fans is a breeze with the reputable conferences, clubs, and even an accredited college that we list.

There are so many ways to put astrology into your life. Redecorating your home? Follow your sun sign's colors and styles to create the perfect environment. Share your birthday with a celebrity. Design a fitness program according to your sign's preferences.

So here are the year's picks and predictions, along with eighteen months of on-target daily horoscopes to make 2008 your best year ever.

CHAPTER 1

It's A Year of Change: What This Means for You

Astrologers judge the trends of a year by following the slow-moving planets, from Jupiter through Pluto. A change in sign indicates a new cycle, with new emphasis. The farthest planets (Uranus, Neptune, and Pluto), which stay in a sign for at least seven years, cause a very significant change in the atmosphere when they change signs. Shifts in Jupiter, which changes every year, and Saturn, which changes every two years, are more obvious in current events and daily lives. Jupiter generally brings a fortunate, expansive emphasis to its new sign, while Saturn's two-year cycle is a reality check, bringing tests of maturity, discipline, and responsibility.

Does Pluto Still Count?

At this writing, astronomers have demoted tiny Pluto from being a full-fledged planet to a dwarf planet, outranked by its celestial siblings. However, astrologers have been tracking its influence since Pluto was discovered in 1930 and have witnessed that this minuscule celestial body has a powerful effect on both a personal and a global level. So Pluto, which moves into the sign of Capricorn this year, will still be called a planet by astrologers and will be given just as much importance as before.

Capricorn Is the Sign to Watch

This year, we will be moving from a fire-sign emphasis to an earth-sign emphasis as Jupiter, Saturn, and Pluto all take up residence in earth signs. Until January 2008, Pluto had been emphasizing everything associated with Sagittarius to prepare us philosphically and spiriturally for things to come. Perhaps the most pervasive sign of Pluto in Sagittarius over the past few years has been globalization in all its forms, re-forming boundaries, creating new forms of travel, interacting with exotic cultures and religions as never before.

As it passed through truth-telling Sagittarius, Pluto shifted our emphasis away from acquiring wealth to a quest for the meaning of it all, as upward strivers discover that money and power are not enough and religious extremists assert themselves. We search the cosmos for something to believe in when many lies and scandals are exposed to public view, exposing leaders in the corporate, political, and religious domains. When ideals and idols are shattered, it becomes time to reevaluate our goals and ask ourselves what is really important in our lives.

Sagittarius is the sign of linking everything together; therefore, the trend has been to find ways to interconnect on spiritual, philosophical, and intellectual levels. The spiritual emphasis of Pluto in Sagittarius has filtered down to our home lives, as religion—and religious controversy—has entered local communities. Vast church complexes are being built to combine religious activities with sports centers, health clubs, malls, and theme parks. Religious education and book publishing have expanded as well.

Sagittarius is known for love of animals, especially horses. It's no surprise that horse racing has become popular again and that America has never been more pet happy. Look for extremes related to animal welfare, such as vegetarianism as a lifestyle. As habitats are destroyed, the care, feeding, and control of wild animals will become a larger issue, especially when deer, bears, and coyotes invade our backyard.

The Sagittarius love of the outdoors combined with

Pluto's power has already promoted extreme sports, especially those that require strong legs, like rock climbing, trekking, or snowboarding. Expect the trend toward more adventurous travel to continue, as well as fitness or sports-oriented vacations. Exotic hiking trips to unexplored territories, mountain-climbing expeditions, spa vacations, and sports-associated resorts are part of this trend.

Publishing, which is associated with Sagittarius, has been transformed by global conglomerates and the Internet. It is fascinating that the online bookstore Amazon.com took the Sagittarius-influenced name of the fierce female tribe of archer warriors.

Capricorn Brings Us Down to Earth

This year, both Pluto and Jupiter will meet in Capricorn, which marks a major shift in emphasis to Capricorn-related themes. Until 2024, Pluto will exert its influence in this practical, building, healing earth sign. Capricorn relates to structures, institutions, order, mountains and mountain countries, mineral rights, and issues involving the elderly and growing older—all of which will be emphasized in the coming years. It is the sign of established order, corporations, big business—all of which will be accented. Possibly, it will fall to business structures to create a new sense of order in the world.

Starting this year, you should feel the rumblings of change in the Capricorn area of your horoscope and in the world at large. The last time Pluto was in Capricorn was the years up to and during the American Revolutionary War. Therefore this should be an important time on the United States political scene, as well as a reflection of the aging and maturing of American society in general. Both the rise and fall of the Ottoman Empire happened under Pluto in Capricorn.

Jupiter in Capricorn

During the year that Jupiter remains in a sign, the fields associated with that sign are the ones that arouse excitement and enthusiasm, usually providing excellent opportunities for expansion, fame, and fortune.

One place we notice the Jupiter influence is in fashion, which should veer away from the flamboyance and sexuality of recent years to a more conservative look. Capricorn is concerned with quality, status, and prestige, and should elevate our collective taste level.

Those born under Capricorn should have many opportunities during the year. However, the key is to keep your feet on the ground. The flip side of Jupiter is that there are no limits. You can expand off the planet under a Jupiter transit, which is why the planet is often called the Gateway to Heaven. If something is going to burst (such as an artery) or overextend or go over the top in some way, it could happen under a supposedly lucky Jupiter transit. So beware.

Those born under Cancer may find their best opportunities working with partners this year, as Jupiter will be transiting their seventh house of relationships.

Saturn in Virgo: The Maturing of the Baby Boomers, Reforms in Care and Maintenance

Saturn, the planet of limitation, testing, and restriction, is now transiting Virgo. This is a time when Virgo issues—health care and maintenance and moral standards and controls—will come to the fore. For the next two years, we will be adjusting the structures of our lives, making changes so that we can function at an optimal efficient level. We'll be challenged with a reality check in areas where we have been too optimistic or expansive.

Continuing Trends

Uranus and Neptune continue to do a kind of astrological dance called a mutual reception. This is a supportive relationship where Uranus is in Pisces, the sign ruled by Neptune, while Neptune is in Aquarius, the sign ruled by Uranus. When this dance is over in 2011, it is likely that we will be living under very different political and social circumstances.

Uranus in Pisces

Uranus, known as the Great Awakener, tends to cause both upheaval and innovation in the sign it transits. During previous episodes of Uranus in Pisces, great religions and spiritual movements have come into being, most recently Mormonism and Christian Fundamentalism. In its most positive mode, Pisces promotes imagination and creativity, the art of illusion in theater and film, the inspiration of great artists. A water sign, Pisces is naturally associated with all things liquid—oceans, oil, alcohol—and with those creatures that live in the water—fish, the fishing industry, fish habitats, and fish farming. Currently there is a great debate going on about overfishing, contamination of fish, and fish farming. The underdog, the enslaved, and the disenfranchised should also benefit from Uranus in Pisces.

Since Uranus is a disruptive influence that aims to challenge the status quo, the forces of nature that manifest will most likely be in the Pisces area: oceans, seas, and rivers. We have seen unprecedented rainy seasons, floods, mud slides, and disastrous hurricanes. Note that 2005's devastating Hurricane Katrina hit an area known for both the oil and fishing industries.

Pisces is associated with the prenatal phase of life, which is related to regenerative medicine. The controversy over embryonic stem cell research should continue to be debated. Petroleum issues, both in the oil-producing countries and offshore oil drilling, will come to a head. Uranus in

7

Pisces suggests that development of new hydroelectric sources may provide the power we need to continue our current power-thirsty lifestyle.

As in previous eras, there should continue to be a flourishing of the arts. We are seeing many new artistic forms developing now, such as computer-created actors and special effects. The sky's the limit on this influence.

Those who have problems with Uranus are those who resist change, so the key is to embrace the future.

Neptune in Aquarius

Neptune is a planet of imagination and creativity, but also of deception and illusion. Neptune is associated with hospitals, which have been the subject of much controversy. On the positive side, hospitals are acquiring cutting-edge technology. The atmosphere of many hospitals is already changing from the intimidating and sterile environment of the past to that of a health-promoting spa. Alternative therapies, such as massage, diet counseling, and aromatherapy, are becoming commonplace, which expresses this Neptune trend. New procedures in plastic surgery, also a Neptune glamour field, and anti-aging therapies are restoring the illusion of youth.

However, issues involving the expense and quality of health care and the evolving relationship between doctors, drug companies, and HMOs reflect a darker side of this trend.

What About the New Planets?

Our solar system is very crowded; astronomers continue to discover new objects circling the sun. In addition to the familiar planets, there are dwarf planets, comets, cometoids, asteroids, and strange icy bodies in the Kuiper Belt beyond Neptune. The newest object at this writing is a planetlike orb slightly larger than Pluto, discovered in 2005, which was tentatively named Xena, after the TV series heroine. Recently this dwarf planet was christened with a permanent name by its dicoverer, Dr. Michael E. Brown of the California Institute of Technology. He dubbed the new planet Eris, after a goddess of discord and strife. In mythology, Eris was a troublemaker who made men think their opinions were right and others wrong. What an appropriate name for a planet discovered during a time of discord in the Middle East and elsewhere! Eris has a companion moon named Dysnomia for her daughter, described as a demon spirit of lawlessness. With mythological associations like these, we wonder what the effect of this mother-daughter duo will be. Once Eris's orbit is established, astrologers will track the impact of this planet on our horoscopes. Eris takes about 560 years to orbit the sun, which means its emphasis in a given astrological sign will affect several generations.

CHAPTER 2

Put Time on Your Side

"Do not squander time, for that is the stuff that life is made of," said Benjamin Franklin, our practical Founding Father. Yet many times your best-laid plans run amuck, your schedule is upset by sudden events, or your projects stall. On the other hand, there are days when projects get done effortlessly, people respond to you favorably, and perhaps you have some extra sex appeal.

Astrology offers many explanations why this might happen. For instance, when mischievous Mercury creates havoc with communications, it's time to back up your vital computer files, read between the lines of contracts, and be extra patient with coworkers. When Venus passes through your sign you've got extra sex appeal, time to try a knockout new outfit or hairstyle, and the nerve to ask someone you'd like to know better to dinner. Venus timing can also help you charm clients with a stunning sales pitch or make an offer they won't refuse.

In this chapter, you will learn how to manage your time by working with natural astrological cycles. You can find your best times to do specific projects as well as which times to avoid them. You will also learn how to read the moods of the moon and make them work for you. Use the information in this chapter and the planet tables in this book and also use the moon sign listings in your daily forecasts.

Here are the happenings to note on your agenda:

- Dates of your sun sign (high-energy period)
- The month previous to your sun sign (low-energy period)

- Dates of planets in your sign this year
- Full and new moons (Pay special attention when these fall in your sun sign!)
- Eclipses
- Moon in your sun sign every month, as well as moon in the opposite sign (listed in daily forecast)
- Mercury retrogrades
- Other retrograde periods

Your High-Power Time

Every birthday starts off a new cycle of solar energy for you. You should feel a new surge of vitality as the powerful sun enters your sign. This is the time when predominant energies are most favorable to you. So go for it! Start new projects, make your big moves (especially when the new moon is in your sign, doubling your charisma). You'll get the recognition you deserve now, when everyone is attuned to your sun sign. Look in the tables in this book to see if other planets will also be passing through your sun sign at this time. Venus (love, beauty), Mars (energy, drive), and Mercury (communication, mental sharpness) reinforce the sun and give an extra boost to your life in the areas they affect. Venus will rev up your social and love life, making you seem especially attractive. Mars amplifies your energy and drive. Mercury fuels your brainpower and helps you communicate. Jupiter signals an especially lucky period of expansion.

There are two downtimes related to the sun. During the month before your birthday period, when you are winding up your annual cycle, you could be feeling especially vulnerable and depleted. So at that time get extra rest, watch your diet, and take it easy. Don't overstress yourself. Use this time to gear up for a big "push" when the sun enters your sign.

Another downtime is when the sun is in a sign opposite your sun sign (six months from your birthday). That's when the prevailing energies are very different from yours. You may feel at odds with the world. You'll have to work harder for recognition because people are not on your wavelength. However, this could be a good time to work on a team, in cooperation with others, or behind the scenes.

Plan Your Day with the Moon

The moon is a powerful tool to divine the mood of the moment. You can work with the moon in two ways. Plan by the *sign* the moon is in; plan by the *phase* of the moon. The sign will tell you the kind of activities that suit the moon's mood. The phase will tell you the best time to start or finish a certain activity.

Working with the phases of the moon is as easy as looking up at the night sky. During the new moon, when both the sun and moon are in the same sign, begin new ventures—especially activities that are favored by that sign. Then you'll utilize the powerful energies pulling you in the same direction. You'll be focused outward, toward action, and in a doing mode. Postpone breaking off, terminating, deliberating, or reflecting—activities that require introspection and passive work. These are better suited to a later moon phase.

Get your project under way during the first quarter. Then go public at the full moon, a time of high intensity, when feelings come out into the open. This is your time to shine—to express yourself. Be aware, however, that because pressures are being released, other people will also be letting off steam. Since confrontations are possible, take advantage of this time either to air grievances or to avoid arguments.

About three days after the full moon comes the disseminating phase, a time when the energy of the cycle begins to wind down. From the last quarter of the moon to the next new moon, it's a time to cut off unproductive relationships, do serious thinking, and focus on inward-directed activities.

You'll feel some new and full moons more strongly than others, especially those new moons that fall in your sun sign and full moons in your opposite sign. Because that full moon happens at your low-energy time of year, it is likely to be an especially stressful time in a relationship, when any hidden problems or unexpressed emotions could surface.

Full and New Moons in 2008

All dates are calculated for eastern standard time and eastern daylight time.

New Moon—January 8 in Capricorn
Full Moon—January 22 in Leo

New Moon—February 6 in Aquarius (solar eclipse)
Full Moon—February 20 in Virgo (lunar eclipse)

New Moon—March 7 in Pisces
Full Moon—March 21 in Libra

New Moon—April 5 in Aries
Full Moon—April 20 in Scorpio

New Moon—May 5 in Taurus
Full Moon—May 19 in Scorpio (second full moon in Scorpio)

New Moon—June 3 in Gemini
Full Moon—June 18 in Sagittarius

New Moon—July 2 in Cancer
Full Moon—July 18 in Capricorn

New Moon—August 1 in Leo (solar eclipse)
Full Moon—August 16 in Aquarius (lunar eclipse)
New Moon—August 30 in Virgo

Full Moon—September 15 in Pisces
New Moon—September 29 in Libra

Full Moon—October 14 in Aries

New Moon—October 28 in Scorpio

Full Moon—November 13 in Taurus
New Moon—November 27 in Sagittarius

New Moon—December 12 in Gemini
Full Moon—December 27 in Capricorn

How to Schedule Activities by the Moon Sign

To forecast the daily emotional "weather," to determine your monthly high and low days, or to synchronize your activities with the cycles of the moon, take note of the moon sign under your daily forecast at the end of the book. Here are some of the activities favored and the moods you are likely to encounter under each moon sign.

Moon in Aries: Get Moving!

The new moon in Aries is an ideal time to start new projects. Everyone is pushy, raring to go, rather impatient, and short-tempered. Leave details and follow-up for later. Competitive sports or martial arts are great ways to let off steam. Quiet types could use some assertiveness, but it's a great day for dynamos. Be careful not to step on too many toes.

Moon in Taurus: Lay the Foundations for Success

Do solid, methodical tasks like follow-through or backup work. Make investments, buy real estate, do appraisals, do some hard bargaining. Attend to your property. Get out in the country or spend some time in your garden. Enjoy creature comforts, music, a good dinner, sensual lovemaking. Forget starting a diet—this is a day when you'll feel self-indulgent.

Moon in Gemini: Communicate

Talk means action today. Telephone, write letters, fax! Make new contacts, stay in touch with steady customers. You can juggle lots of tasks today. It's a great time for mental activity of any kind. Don't try to pin people down—they, too, are feeling restless. Keep it light. Flirtations and socializing are good. Watch gossip—and don't give away secrets.

Moon in Cancer: Pay Attention to Loved Ones

This is a moody, sensitive, emotional time. People respond to personal attention, to mothering. Stay at home, have a family dinner, call your mother. Nostalgia, memories, and psychic powers are heightened. You'll want to hang on to people and things (don't clean out your closets now). You could have shrewd insights into what others really need and want. Pay attention to dreams, intuition, and gut reactions.

Moon in Leo: Be Confident

Everybody is in a much more confident, warm, generous mood. It's a good day to ask for a raise, show what you can do, dress like a star. People will respond to flattery, enjoy a bit of drama and theater. You may be extravagant, treat yourself royally, and show off a bit—but don't break the bank! Be careful you don't promise more than you can deliver.

Moon in Virgo: Be Practical

Do practical down-to-earth chores. Review your budget, make repairs, be an efficiency expert. Not a day to ask for a raise. Tend to personal care and maintenance. Have a health checkup, go on a diet, buy vitamins or health food. Make your home spotless. Take care of details and piled-up chores. Reorganize your work and life so they run more smoothly and efficiently. Save money. Be prepared for others to be in a critical, faultfinding mood.

Moon in Libra: Be Diplomatic

Attend to legal matters. Negotiate contracts. Arbitrate. Do things with your favorite partner. Socialize. Be romantic. Buy a special gift, a beautiful object. Decorate yourself or your surroundings. Buy new clothes. Throw a party. Have an elegant, romantic evening. Smooth over any ruffled feathers. Avoid confrontations. Stick to civilized discussions.

Moon in Scorpio: Solve Problems

This is a day to do things with passion. You'll have excellent concentration and focus. Try not to get too intense emotionally. Avoid sharp exchanges with loved ones. Others may tend to go to extremes, get jealous, overreact. Great for troubleshooting, problem solving, research, scientific work—and making love. Pay attention to those psychic vibes.

Moon in Sagittarius: Sell and Motivate

A great time for travel, philosophical discussions, setting long-range career goals. Work out, do sports, buy athletic equipment. Others will be feeling upbeat, exuberant, and adventurous. Risk taking is favored. You may feel like taking a gamble, betting on the horses, visiting a local casino, buying a lottery ticket. Teaching, writing, and spiritual activities also get the green light. Relax outdoors. Take care of animals.

Moon in Capricorn: Get Organized

You can accomplish a lot now, so get on the ball! Attend to business. Issues concerning your basic responsibilities, duties, family, and elderly parents could crop up. You'll be expected to deliver on promises. Weed out the deadwood from your life. Get a dental checkup. Not a good day for gambling or taking risks.

Moon in Aquarius: Join the Group

A great day for doing things with groups—clubs, meetings, outings, politics, parties. Campaign for your candidate. Work for a worthy cause. Deal with larger issues that affect humanity—the environment and metaphysical questions. Buy a computer or electronic gadget. Watch TV. Wear something outrageous. Try something you've never done before. Present an original idea. Don't stick to a rigid schedule—go with the flow. Take a class in meditation, mind control, yoga.

Moon in Pisces: Be Creative

This can be a very creative day, so let your imagination work overtime. Film, theater, music, ballet could inspire you. Spend some time alone, resting and reflecting, reading or writing poetry. Daydreams can also be profitable. Help those less fortunate. Lend a listening ear to someone who may be feeling blue. Don't overindulge in self-pity or escapism, however. People are especially vulnerable to substance abuse now. Turn your thoughts to romance and someone special.

Retrogrades: When the Planets Seem to Backstep

All the planets, except for the sun and moon, have times when they appear to move backward—or retrograde—as it seems from our point of view on earth. At these times, planets do not work as they normally do. So it's best to "take a break" from that planet's energies in our life and to do some work on an inner level.

Mercury Retrograde: The Key Is in "Re"

Mercury goes retrograde most often, and its effects can be especially irritating. When it reaches a short distance ahead of the sun several times a year, it seems to move backward from our point of view. Astrologers often compare retrograde motion to the optical illusion that occurs when we ride on a train that passes another train traveling at a different speed—the second train appears to be moving in reverse.

What this means to you is that the Mercury-ruled areas of your life—analytical thought processes, communications, scheduling—are subject to all kinds of confusion. Be prepared. Communications equipment can break down. Schedules may be changed on short notice. People are late for appointments or don't show up at all. Traffic is terrible. Major purchases malfunction, don't work out, or get delivered in the wrong color. Letters don't arrive or are delivered to the wrong address. Employees will make errors that have to be corrected later. Contracts don't work out or must be renegotiated.

Since most of us can't put our lives on "hold" during Mercury retrogrades, we should learn to tame the trickster and make it work for us. The key is in the prefix *re*-. This is the time to go back over things in your life, *re*flect on what you've done during the previous months. Now you can get deeper insights, spot errors you've missed. So take time to *re*view and *re*evaluate what has happened. *Re*st and *re*ward yourself—it's a good time to take a vacation, especially if you *re*visit a favorite place. *Re*organize your work and finish up projects that are backed up. Clean out your desk and closets. Throw away what you can't *re*cycle. If you must sign contracts or agreements, do so with a contingency clause that lets you *re*evaluate the terms later.

Postpone major purchases or commitments for the time being. Don't get married (unless you're *re*marrying the same person). Try not to *re*ly on other people keeping appointments, contracts, or agreements to the letter; have several alternatives. Double-check and *re*ad between the lines.

Don't buy anything connected with communications or transportation (if you must, be sure to cover yourself).

Mercury retrograding through your sun sign will intensify its effect on your life.

If Mercury was retrograde when you were born, you may be one of the lucky people who don't suffer the frustrations of this period. If so, your mind probably works in a very intuitive, insightful way.

The sign in which Mercury is retrograding can give you an idea of what's in store—as well as the sun signs that will be especially challenged.

Mercury Retrogrades in 2008

Mercury has three retrograde periods, which fall in the air signs (Aquarius, Gemini, Libra) this year. This means it will be especially important to watch all activities which involve mental processes and communication.

January 28 to February 18 in Aquarius
May 26 to June 19 in Gemini
September 24 to October 15 in Libra

Venus Retrograde: Relationships Move Backward

Retrograding Venus can cause your relationships to take a backward step, or it can make you extravagant and impractical. Shopping till you drop and buying what you cannot afford are problems at this time. It's *not* a good time to redecorate—you'll hate the color of the walls later. Postpone getting a new hairstyle. Try not to fall in love either. But if you wish to make amends in an already troubled relationship, make peaceful overtures at this time.

Venus Retrogrades in 2008

There are no Venus retrograde periods in 2008.

Use the Go Power of Mars

Mars shows how and when to get where you want to go. Timing your moves with Mars on your side can give you a big push. On the other hand, pushing Mars the wrong way can guarantee that you'll run into frustrations in every corner. Your best times to forge ahead are during the weeks when Mars is traveling through your sun sign or your Mars sign (look these up in the tables in this book). Also consider times when Mars is in a compatible sign (fire with air signs, or earth with water signs). You'll be sure to have planetary power on your side.

Mars Retrogrades in 2008

Mars is retrograde in Gemini until January 30, 2008.

When Other Planets Retrograde

The slower-moving planets stay retrograde for months at a time (Jupiter, Saturn, Neptune, Uranus, and Pluto).

When Saturn is retrograde, it's an uphill battle with self-discipline. You may not be in the mood for work. You may feel more like hanging out at the beach than getting things done.

Neptune retrograde promotes a dreamy escapism from reality, when you may feel you're in a fog (Pisces will feel this, especially).

Uranus retrograde may mean setbacks in areas where there have been sudden changes, when you may be forced to regroup or reevaluate the situation.

Pluto retrograde is a time to work on establishing proportion and balance in areas where there have been recent dramatic transformations.

When the planets move forward again, there's a shift in the atmosphere. Activities connected with each planet start moving ahead, plans that were stalled get rolling. Make a special note of those days on your calendar and proceed accordingly.

Other Retrogrades in 2008

The five slower-moving planets all go retrograde in 2008.

Jupiter retrogrades from May 9 to September 7 in Capricorn.

Saturn retrogrades from December 19, 2007, until May 2, 2008, in Virgo. It turns retrograde again on December 31.

Uranus retrogrades from June 26 to November 27 in Pisces.

Neptune retrogrades from May 26 to November 1 in Aquarius.

Pluto turns retrograde from April 2 in Capricorn, then returns to Sagittarius on June 13. It turns direct in Sagittarius on September 8 and reenters Capricorn on November 26.

CHAPTER 3

Planetary Shake-Ups This Year

When the planetary weather is stormy, it's best to be prepared. Fortunately we can predict certain times when there are more likely to be shake-ups in your world, such as eclipses and Saturn transits, two events that could slow you down or make you change direction. With some basic astrological knowledge, you can find out where these events are likely to impact your life and what to expect when they happen.

Eclipses Clear the Air

Eclipses can bring on milestones in your life, if they aspect a key point in your horoscope. In general, they shake up the status quo, bringing hidden areas out into the open. During this time, problems you've been avoiding or have brushed aside can surface to demand your attention. A good coping strategy is to accept whatever comes up as a challenge that could make a positive difference in your life. And don't forget the power of your sense of humor. If you can laugh at something, you'll never be afraid of it.

What Is the Best Thing to Do During an Eclipse?

When the natural rhythms of the sun and moon are disturbed, it's best to postpone important activities. Be sure to mark eclipse days on your calendar, especially if the eclipse falls in your birth sign. This year, those born under Aquarius, Leo, and Virgo should take special note of the feelings that arise. With lunar eclipses, some possibilities could be a break from attachments or the healing of an illness or substance abuse, which had been triggered by the subconscious. The temporary event could be a healing time, when you gain perspective. During solar eclipses, when you might be in a highly subjective state, pay attention to the hidden subconscious patterns that surface, the emotional truth that is revealed at this time.

The effect of the eclipse can reverberate for some time, often months after the event. But it is especially important to stay cool and make no major moves during the period known as the shadow of the eclipse, which begins about a week before and lasts until at least three days after the eclipse. After three days, the daily rhythms should return to normal, and you can proceed with business as usual.

This Year's Eclipse Dates

February 6: Solar eclipse in Aquarius
February 20: Lunar eclipse in Virgo
August 1: Solar eclipse in Leo
August 16: Lunar eclipse in Aquarius

Saturn Gives You a Reality Check

When Saturn hits a critical point in your horoscope, you can count on an experience that will make you slow up, pull back, and reexamine your life. It is a call to eliminate what is not working, to shape up, to set priorities, to examine the boundaries and structures in your life (or lack of them) and set new ones. During this process, you may feel restricted, frustrated, or inhibited—not a fun time, but one that will serve you well in the long run. You may need to take on more responsibilities that will test your limits.

By the end of its twenty-eight-year trip around the zodiac, Saturn will have tested you in all areas of your life. The major tests happen in seven-year cycles, when Saturn passes over the angles of your chart, which means your rising sign, the top of your chart or midheaven, your descendant, and the nadir or bottom of your chart. This is when the real life-changing experiences happen. But you are also in for a testing period whenever Saturn passes a planet in your chart or stresses that planet from a distance. It is useful to check your planetary positions with the timetable of Saturn or prepare in advance, or at least to brace yourself.

When Saturn returns to its location at the time of your birth, at approximately age twenty-eight, you'll have your first Saturn return. At this time, a person usually takes stock or settles down to find his mission in life and assume full adult duties and responsibilities.

Another way Saturn helps us is to reveal the karmic lessons from previous lives and give us the chance to overcome them. So look at Saturn's challenges as much-needed opportunities for self-improvement.

Outwitting the Planets

Second-guessing Saturn and the eclipses this year is easy if you have a copy of your horoscope calculated by a computer. This enables you to pinpoint the area of your life that will be affected. However, you can make an educated guess, by setting up a rough diagram on your own. If you'd like to find out which area of your life this year's Saturn change is most likely to affect, follow these easy steps.

First, you must know the time of day you were born and look up your rising sign listed on the tables in this book (see chapter 7). Set up an estimated horoscope by drawing a circle, then dividing it into four parts by making a cross directly through the center. Continue to divide each of the parts into thirds, as if you were dividing a cake, until you have twelve slices. Write your rising sign on the middle left-hand slice, which would be the nine o'clock point, if you were looking at your watch. Then write the following signs on the dividing line of each slice, working counterclockwise, until you have listed all twelve signs of the zodiac.

You should now have a basic diagram of your horoscope

chart (minus the planets, of course). Starting with your rising-sign slice, number each portion consecutively, again working counterclockwise.

Since this year's eclipses will fall in Aquarius, Leo, and Virgo, find the number of these slices, or houses, on the chart and read the following descriptions for the kinds of issues that are likely to be emphasized. Saturn is now traveling through Virgo, so check this house in your chart for Saturn-related events.

If an eclipse or Saturn falls in your FIRST HOUSE:
Events cause you to examine the ways you are acting independently and push you to become more visible, to assert yourself. This is a time when you feel compelled to make your own decisions. You may want to change your physical appearance, body image, or style of dress in some way. Under affliction, there might be illness or physical harm.

If an eclipse or Saturn falls in your SECOND HOUSE:
This is the place where you consider all matters of security. You consolidate your resources, earn money, acquire property, and decide what you value and what you want to own. On a deeper level, this house reveals your sense of self-worth.

If an eclipse or Saturn falls in your THIRD HOUSE:
Here you reach out to others, express your ideas, and explore different courses of action. You may feel especially restless or have confrontations with neighbors or siblings. In your search for more knowledge, you may decide to improve your skills, get more education, or sign up for a course that interests you. Local transportation, especially your car, might be affected by an eclipse here.

If an eclipse or Saturn falls in your FOURTH HOUSE:
Here is where you put down roots and establish a base. You'll consider what home really means to you. Issues involving parents, the physical setup or location of your home, and your immediate family demand your attention. You may be especially concerned with parenting or relationships with your own mother. You may consider moving your home to a new location or leaving home.

If an eclipse or Saturn falls in your FIFTH HOUSE:

Here is where you express yourself, either through your personal talents or through procreating children. You are interested in making your special talents visible. This is also the house of love affairs and the romantic aspect of life, where you flirt, have fun, and enjoy the excitement of love. Hobbies and crafts fall in this area.

If an eclipse or Saturn falls in your SIXTH HOUSE:

How well are you doing your job? This is your maintenance department, where you take care of your health, organize your life, and set up a daily routine. It is also the place where you perfect your skills and add polish to your life. The chores you do every day, the skills you learn, and the techniques you use fall here. If something doesn't work in your life, an eclipse is sure to bring this to light. If you've been neglecting your health, diet, and fitness, you'll probably pay the consequences during an eclipse. Or you may be faced with work that requires much routine organization and steady effort, rather than creative ability. Or you may be required to perform services for others.

If an eclipse or Saturn falls in your SEVENTH HOUSE:

This is the area of committed relationships, of those which involve legal agreements, of working in a close relationship with another. Here you'll be dealing with how you relate, what you'll be willing to give up for the sake of a marriage or partnership. Eclipses here can put extra pressure on a relationship and, if it's not working, precipitate a breakup. Lawsuits and open enemies also reside here.

If an eclipse or Saturn falls in your EIGHTH HOUSE:

This area is concerned with power and control. Consider what you are willing to give up in order that something might happen. Power struggles, intense relationships, and desires to penetrate deeper mysteries belong here. Debts, loans, financial matters that involve another party, and wheeling and dealing also come into focus. So does sex, where you surrender your individual power to create a new life together. Matters involving birth and death are also involved here.

If an eclipse or Saturn falls in your NINTH HOUSE:

Here is where you look at the big picture. You'll seek information that helps you find meaning in life: higher education, religion, travel, global issues. Eclipses here can push you to get out of your rut, to explore something you've never done before, and to expand your horizons.

If an eclipse or Saturn falls in your TENTH HOUSE:

This is the high-profile point in your chart. Here is where you consider how society looks at you and your position in the outside world. You'll be concerned about whether you receive proper credit for your work and if you're recognized by higher-ups. Promotions, raises, and other forms of recognition can be given or denied. If you have worked hard, Saturn can give you well-deserved rewards here. Either your standing in your career or in your community can be challenged, or you'll be publicly acknowledged for achieving a goal. An eclipse here can make you famous or burst your balloon if you've been too ambitious or neglecting other areas of your life.

If an eclipse or Saturn falls in your ELEVENTH HOUSE:

Your relationship with groups of people comes under scrutiny during an eclipse: whom you are identified with, whom you socialize with, and how well you are accepted by other members of your team. Activities of clubs and political parties, networking, and other social interactions become important. You'll be concerned about what other people think.

If an eclipse or Saturn falls in your TWELFTH HOUSE:

This is the time when the focus turns to your inner life. An especially favorable eclipse here might bring you great insight and inspiration. On the other hand, events may happen that cause you to retreat from public life. Here is where we go to be alone or to work in retreats, hospitals, or religious institutions, or to explore psychotherapy. Here is where you deliver selfless service, through charitable acts. Good aspects from an eclipse could promote an ability to go with the flow or to rise above the competition to find an inner, almost mystical strength that enables you to connect with the deepest needs of others.

CHAPTER 4

Blame It on Moon Glow:
The Moon's Effect on Emotions

In some astrological systems, the moon sign is considered just as important as the sun sign. It adds many levels of meaning to a horoscope, because it reveals how a person reacts to life's problems, what makes the person feel comfortable, secure, romantic. The moon reveals secrets like what you really care about. It's the emotional factor in the horoscope, representing the receptive, reflective, female, nurturing self. It also reflects who you were nurtured by— the mother or mother figure in your chart. In a man's chart, the moon position describes his receptive, emotional, yin side, as well as the woman in his life who will have the deepest effect, usually his mother. (Venus reveals the kind of woman who will attract him physically.)

The moon is more at home in some signs than others. It rules maternal Cancer and is exalted in Taurus—both comforting, home-loving signs where the natural emotional energies of the moon are easily and productively expressed. But when the moon is in the opposite signs— Capricorn and Scorpio—it leaves the comfortable nest and deals with emotional issues of power and achievement in the outside world. Those of you with the moon in these signs are likely to find your emotional role more challenging in life.

Since detailed moon tables are too extensive for this book, check through the following listing to find the moon sign that feels most familiar.

Moon in Aries

This placement makes you both independent and ardent. An idealist, you tend to fall in and out of love easily. You love a challenge but could cool once your quarry is captured. Your emotional reactions are fast and fiery, quickly expressed and quickly forgotten. You may not think before expressing your feelings. It's not easy to hide how you feel. Channeling all your emotional energy could be one of your big challenges.

Moon in Taurus

A sentimental soul, you are very fond of the good life, and you gravitate toward solid, secure relationships. You like displays of affection and creature comforts—all the tangible trappings of a cozy, safe, calm atmosphere. You are sensual and steady emotionally, but very stubborn, possessive, and determined. You can't be pushed, and you tend to dislike changes. You should make an effort to broaden your horizons and to take a risk sometimes. You may become very attached to your home turf. You may also be a collector of objects that are meaningful to you.

Moon in Gemini

You crave mental stimulation and variety in life, which you usually get through either an ever-varied social life, the excitement of flirtation and/or multiple professional involvements. You may marry more than once and have a rather chaotic emotional life due to your difficulty with commitment and settling down, as well as your need to be constantly on the go. (Be sure to find a partner who is as outgoing as you are.) You will have to learn at some point to focus your energies because you tend to be somewhat fragmented—to do two things at once, to have two homes or even two lovers. If you can find a creative way to express your many-faceted nature, you'll be ahead of the game.

Moon in Cancer

This is the most powerful lunar position, which is sure to make a deep imprint on your character. Your needs are very much associated with your reaction to the needs of others. You are very sensitive, caring, and self-protective, though some of you may mask this with a hard shell, like the moon-sensitive crab. This placement also gives an excellent memory, keen intuition, and an uncanny ability to perceive the needs of others. All of the lunar phases will affect you, especially full moons and eclipses, so you would do well to mark them on your calendar. Because you're happiest at home, you may work at home or turn your office into a second home, where you can nurture and comfort people. (You may tend to mother the world.) With natural psychic, intuitive ability, you might be drawn to occult work in some way. Or you may get professionally involved with providing food and shelter to others.

Moon in Leo

This warm, passionate moon takes everything to heart. You are attracted to all that is noble, generous, and aristocratic in life (and may be a bit of a snob). You have an innate ability to take command emotionally, but you do need strong support, loyalty, and loud applause from those you love. You are possessive of your loved ones and your turf and will roar if anyone threatens to take over your territory.

Moon in Virgo

You are rather cool until you decide if others measure up. But once someone or something meets your ideal standards, you hold up your end of the arrangement perfectly. You may, in fact, drive yourself too hard to attain some notion of perfection. Try to be a bit easier on yourself and others. Don't always act the censor! You love to be the teacher and are drawn to situations where you can change others for the better, but sometimes you must learn to accept others for what they are—enjoy what you have!

Moon in Libra

Like other air-sign moons, you think before you feel. Therefore, you may not immediately recognize the emotional needs of others. However, you are relationship oriented and may find it difficult to be alone or to do things alone. After you have learned emotional balance by leaning on yourself first, you can have excellent partnerships. It is best for you to avoid extremes, which set your scales swinging and can make your love life precarious. You thrive in a rather conservative, traditional, romantic relationship, where you receive attention and flattery—but not possessiveness—from your partner. You'll be your most charming in an elegant, harmonious atmosphere.

Moon in Scorpio

This is a moon that enjoys and responds to intense, passionate feelings. You may go to extremes and have a very dramatic emotional life, full of ardor, suspicion, jealousy, and obsession. It would be much healthier to channel your need for power and control into meaningful work. This is a good position for anyone in the fields of medicine, police work, research, the occult, psychoanalysis, or intuitive work, because life-and-death situations don't faze you. However, you do take personal disappointments very hard.

Moon in Sagittarius

You take life's ups and downs with good humor and the proverbial grain of salt. You'll love 'em and leave 'em—take off on a great adventure at a moment's notice. Born free could be your slogan. Attracted by the exotic, you have wanderlust mentally and physically. You may be too much in search of new mental and spiritual stimulation to ever settle down.

Moon in Capricorn

Are you ever accused of being too cool and calculating? You have an earthy side, but you take prestige and position very seriously. Your strong drive to succeed extends to your romantic life, where you will be devoted to improving your lifestyle, rising to the top. A structured situation where you can advance methodically makes you feel wonderfully secure. You may be attracted to someone older or very much younger or from a different social world. It may be difficult to look at the lighter side of emotional relationships. Though this moon is placed in the sign of its detriment, the good news is that you tend to be very dutiful and responsible to those you care for.

Moon in Aquarius

You are a people collector with many friends of all backgrounds. You are happiest surrounded by people and may feel uneasy when left alone. Though you usually stay friends with lovers, intense emotions and demanding one-on-one relationships turn you off. You don't like anything to be too rigid or scheduled. Though tolerant and understanding, you can be emotionally unpredictable and may opt for an unconventional love life. With plenty of space, you will be able to sustain relationships with liberal, freedom-loving types.

Moon in Pisces

You are very responsive and empathetic to others, especially if they have problems or are the underdog. (Be on guard against attracting too many people with sob stories.) You'll be happiest if you can express your creative imagination in the arts or in the spiritual or healing professions. Because you may tend to escape in fantasies or overreact to the moods of others, you need an emotional anchor to help you keep a firm foothold in reality. Steer clear of too much escapism (especially in alcohol) or reclusiveness. Places near water soothe your moods. Working in a field that gives you emotional variety will also help you be productive.

CHAPTER 5

Hands-On Astrology for Beginners

After you learn all about your zodiac sign (and those of your friends), you may be ready to delve more deeply into astrology. This chapter can get you up and running. It's a quick owner's manual, your fast track to getting hands-on with astrology. You'll learn the difference between a sign and a constellation (they're not the same). And what happens in a house. You'll be able to define a sign and figure out why astrologers say what they do about each one. When you look at your astrological chart, you'll have a good idea of what's going on in each portion of the horoscope. Here's your key to understanding the basic principles of this fascinating, but often confusing subject.

Signs and Constellations: What's the Difference?

Most readers know their signs, but many often confuse them with constellations. Signs are actually a type of celestial real estate, located on the zodiac, an imaginary 360-degree belt circling the earth. This belt is divided into twelve equal thirty-degree portions, which are the signs. There's a lot of confusion about the difference between the signs and the constellations of the zodiac. The latter are patterns of stars that originally marked the twelve divisions, like signposts. Though a sign is named after the constellation that once marked the same area, the constellations are no longer in the same place relative to the earth that they were many centuries ago. Over hundreds of years, the earth's orbit has shifted, so that from our point of view here on earth, the constellations seem to have moved. However, the signs remain in place. (Most Western astrology uses the twelve-equal-part division of the zodiac, though there are some other methods of astrology that still use the constellations instead of the signs.)

Most people think of themselves in terms of their sun sign. A sun sign refers to the sign the sun is orbiting through at a given moment (from our point of view here on earth). For instance, "I'm an Aries" means that the sun was passing through Aries when that person was born. However, there are nine other planets (plus asteroids, fixed stars, and sensitive points) that also form our total astrological personality, and some or many of these will be located in other signs. No one is completely Aries, with all astrological components in one sign! (Please note that, in astrology, the sun and moon are usually referred to as planets, though of course they're not.) Pluto is also still called a planet by astrologers.

As we mentioned before, the sun signs are places on the zodiac. They do not do anything (the planets are the doers). However, they are associated with many things, depending on their location.

How We Define the Signs

The definitions of the signs evolved systematically from four components that interrelate. These four different criteria are a sign's element: its quality, its polarity or sex, and its order in the progression of the zodiac. All these factors work together to tell us what the sign is like.

The system is magically mathematical. The number 12—as in the twelve signs of the zodiac—is divisible by 4, by 3, and by 2. There are four elements, three qualities, and two polarities, which follow each other in sequence around the zodiac.

The four elements (earth, air, fire, and water) are the building blocks of astrology. The use of an element to describe a sign probably dates from man's first attempts to categorize what he saw. Ancient sages believed that all things were composed of combinations of these basic elements—earth, air, fire, and water. This included the human character, which was fiery/choleric, earthy/melancholy, airy/sanguine, or watery/phlegmatic. The elements also correspond to our emotional (water), physical (earth), mental (air) and spiritual (fire) natures. The energies of each of the elements were then observed to be related to the time of year when the sun was passing through a certain segment of the zodiac.

Those born with the sun in fire signs—Aries, Leo, Sagittarius—embody the characteristic of that element. Optimism, warmth, hot tempers, enthusiasm, and spirit are typical of these signs. Taurus, Virgo, and Capricorn are earthy—more grounded, physical, materialistic, organized and deliberate than fire-sign people. Air-sign people—Gemini, Libra, and Aquarius—are mentally oriented communicators. Water signs—Cancer, Scorpio, and Pisces—are emotional, sensitive, and creative.

Think of what each element does to the others. Water puts out fire or evaporates under heat. Air fans the flames or blows them out. Earth smothers fire, drifts and erodes with too much wind, becomes mud or fertile soil with water. Those are often perfect analogies for the relationships between people of different sun-sign elements. This astrochemistry was one of the first ways man described his relationships. Fortunately, no one is entirely air or fire. We all have a bit, or a lot, of each element in our horoscopes. It is this unique mix that defines each astrological personality.

Within each element, there are three qualities that describe types of behavior associated with the sign. Those of cardinal signs are activists, go-getters. These four signs—Aries, Cancer, Libra, and Capricorn—begin each season. Fixed signs, which happen in the middle of the season, are associated with builders, stabilizers. You'll find that sun signs Taurus, Leo, Scorpio, and Aquarius are usually gifted with concentration, stamina, and focus. Mutable signs—Gemini, Virgo, Sagittarius, and Pisces—fall at the end of each season and thus are considered catalysts for change. People born under mutable signs are flexible, adaptable.

The polarity of a sign is either its positive or negative charge. It can be masculine, active, positive, and yang like air or fire signs. Or feminine, reactive, negative, and yin like the water and earth signs.

Finally, we consider the sign's place in the order of the zodiac. This is vital to the balance of all the forces and the transmission of energy moving through the signs. You may have noticed that your sign is quite different from your neighboring sign on either side. Yet each seems to grow out of its predecessor like links in a chain and transmits a synthesis of energy gathered along the chain to the following sign, beginning with the fire-powered, active, positive charge of Aries.

How the Signs Add Up

SIGN	ELEMENT	QUALITY	POLARITY	PLACE
Aries	fire	cardinal	masculine	first
Taurus	earth	fixed	feminine	second
Gemini	air	mutable	masculine	third
Cancer	water	cardinal	feminine	fourth
Leo	fire	fixed	masculine	fifth
Virgo	earth	mutable	feminine	sixth
Libra	air	cardinal	masculine	seventh
Scorpio	water	fixed	feminine	eighth
Sagittarius	fire	mutable	masculine	ninth
Capricorn	earth	cardinal	feminine	tenth
Aquarius	air	fixed	masculine	eleventh
Pisces	water	mutable	feminine	twelfth

Your Sign's Special Planet

Each sign has a ruling planet that is most compatible with its energies. Mars adds its fiery assertive characteristics to Aries. The sensual beauty and comfort-loving side of Venus rules Taurus, whereas the idealistic side of Venus rules Libra. Quick-moving Mercury rules two mutable signs, Gemini and Virgo. Its mental agility belongs to Gemini while its analytical, critical side is best expressed in Virgo. The changeable emotional moon is associated with Cancer, while the outgoing Leo personality is ruled by the sun. Scorpio originally shared Mars, but when Pluto was discovered in this century, its powerful magnetic energies were deemed more suitable to the intense vibrations of the fixed water sign Scorpio. Though Pluto has, as of this writing, been downgraded, it is still considered by astrologers to be a powerful force in the horoscope. Disciplined Capricorn is ruled by Saturn, and expansive Sagittarius by Jupiter. Unpredictable Aquarius is ruled by Uranus and creative, imaginative Pisces by Neptune. In a horoscope, if a planet is placed in the sign it rules, it is sure to be especially powerful.

The Layout of a Horoscope Chart

A horoscope chart is a map of the heavens at a given moment in time. It looks like a wheel divided with twelve spokes. In between each of the spokes is a section called a house.

Each house deals with a different area of life and is influenced by a special sign and a planet. Astrologers look at the house to tell in what area of life an event is happening or about to happen.

The house is governed by the sign passing over the spoke (or cusp of the house) at that particular moment. Though the first house is naturally associated with Aries and Mars, it would also have an additional Capricorn influence if that sign was passing over the house cusp at the time the chart

37

was cast. The sequence of the houses starts with the first house located at the left center spoke (or the number 9 position, if you were reading a clock). The houses are then read counterclockwise around the chart, with the fourth house at the bottom of the chart, and the tenth house at the top or twelve o'clock position.

Where do the planets belong? Around the horoscope, planets are placed within the houses according to their location at the time of the chart. That is why it is so important to have an accurate time; with no specific time, the planets have no specific location in the houses and one cannot determine which area of life they will apply to. Since the signs move across the houses as the earth turns, planets in a house will naturally intensify the importance of that house. The house that contains the sun is naturally one of the most prominent.

The First House: Home of Aries and Mars

The sign passing over the first house at the time of your birth is known as your *ascendant,* or *rising sign.* The first house is the house of "firsts"—the first impression you make, how you initiate matters, the image you choose to project. This is where you advertise yourself, where you project your personality. Planets that fall here will intensify the way you come across to others.

The Second House: Home of Taurus and Venus

This house is where you experience the material world—what you value. Here are your attitudes about money, possessions, finances, whatever belongs to you, and what you own, as well as your earning and spending capacity. On a deeper level, this house reveals your sense of self-worth, the inner values that draw wealth in various forms.

The Third House: Home of Gemini and Mercury

This house describes how you communicate with others, how you reach out to others nearby, and how you interact with the immediate environment. It shows how your thinking process works and the way you express your thoughts. Are you articulate or tongue-tied? Can you think on your feet? This house also shows your first relationships, your experiences with brothers and sisters, and how you deal with people close to you such as your neighbors or pals. It's where you take short trips, write letters, or use the telephone. It shows how your mind works in terms of left-brain logical and analytical functions.

The Fourth House: Home of Cancer and the Moon

The fourth house shows the foundation of life, the psychological underpinnings. At the bottom of the chart, this house shows how you are nurtured and made to feel secure—your roots! It shows your early home environment and the circumstances at the end of your life (your final "home") as well as the place you call home now. Astrologers look here for information about the parental nurturers in your life.

The Fifth House: Home of Leo and the Sun

The fifth house is where the creative potential develops. Here you express yourself and procreate in the sense that children are outgrowths of your creative ability. But this house most represents your inner childlike self who delights in play. If your inner security has been established by the time you reach this house, you are now free to have fun, romance, and love affairs and to give of yourself. This is also the place astrologers look for playful love affairs, flirtations, and brief romantic encounters (rather than long-term commitments).

The Sixth House: Home of Virgo and Mercury

The sixth house has been called the "care and maintenance" department. This house shows how you take care of your body and organize yourself to perform efficiently in the world. Here is where you get things done, look after others, and fulfill service duties such as taking care of pets. Here is what you do to survive on a day-to-day basis. The sixth house demands order in your life; otherwise there would be chaos. This house is your "job" (as opposed to your career, which is the domain of the tenth house), your diet, and your health and fitness regimens.

The Seventh House: Home of Libra and Venus

This house shows your attitude toward partners and those with whom you enter into commitments, contracts, or agreements. Here is the way you relate to others, as well as your close, intimate, one-on-one relationships (including open enemies—those you "face off" with). Open hostilities, lawsuits, divorces, and marriages happen here. If the first house represents the "I," the seventh or opposite house is the "not-I"—the complementary partner you attract by the way you come across. If you are having trouble with partnerships, consider what you are attracting by the energies of your first and seventh houses.

The Eighth House: Home of Scorpio and Pluto (also Mars)

The eighth house refers to how you merge with something or someone, and how you handle power and control. This is one of the most mysterious and powerful houses, where your energy transforms itself from "I" to "we." As you give up power and control by uniting with something or someone, two kinds of energies merge and become something greater, leading to a regeneration of the self on a higher level. Here are your attitudes toward sex, shared resources, taxes (what you share with the government). Because this house involves what belongs to others, you face issues of control and power struggles, or undergo a deep psychological transformation as you bond with another. Here you transcend yourself with dreams, drugs, and occult or psychic experiences that reflect the collective unconscious.

The Ninth House: Home of Sagittarius and Jupiter

The ninth house shows your search for wisdom and higher knowledge—your belief system. As the third house represents the "lower mind," its opposite on the wheel, the ninth house, is the "higher mind"—the abstract, intuitive, spiritual mind that asks "big" questions like "Why are we here?" After the third house has explored what was close at hand, the ninth stretches out to broaden you mentally with higher education and travel. Here you stretch spiritually with religious activity. Since you are concerned with how everything is related, you tend to push boundaries, take risks. Here is where you express your ideas in a book or thesis, where you pontificate, philosophize, or preach.

The Tenth House: Home of Capricorn and Saturn

The tenth house is associated with your public life and high-profile activities. Located directly overhead at the "high noon" position on the horoscope wheel, this is the most "visible" house in the chart, the one where the world sees you. It deals with your career (but not your routine "job") and your reputation. Here is where you go public, take on responsibilities (as opposed to the fourth house, where you stay home). This will affect the career you choose and your "public relations." This house is also associated with your father figure or the main authority figure in your life.

41

The Eleventh House: Home of Aquarius and Uranus

The eleventh house is where you extend yourself to a group, a goal, or a belief system. This house is where you define what you really want, the kinds of friends you have, your political affiliations, and the kind of groups you identify with as an equal. Here is where you become concerned with "what other people think" or where you rebel against social conventions. Here is where you could become a socially conscious humanitarian or a partygoing social butterfly. It's where you look to others to stimulate you and discover your kinship to the rest of humanity. The sign on this house can help you understand what you gain and lose from friendships.

The Twelfth House: Home of Pisces and Neptune

Old-fashioned astrologers used to put a rather negative spin on this house, calling it the house of self-undoing. When we undo ourselves, we surrender control, boundaries, limits, and rules. The twelfth house is where the boundaries between yourself and others become blurred and you become selfless. But instead of being self-undoing, the twelfth house can be a place of great creativity and talent. It is the place where you can tap into the collective unconscious, where your imagination is limitless.

In your trip around the zodiac, you've gone from the I of self-assertion in the first house to the final house, which symbolizes the dissolution that happens before rebirth. The twelfth house is where accumulated experiences are processed in the unconscious. Spiritually oriented astrologers look to this house for evidence of past lives and karma. Places where we go for solitude or to do spiritual or reparatory work belong here, such as retreats, religious institutions, or hospitals. Here is also where we withdraw from society voluntarily or involuntarily or are put in prison because of antisocial activity. Selfless giving through charitable acts is part of this house, as is dependence on charity.

In your daily life, the twelfth house reveals your deepest intimacies, your best-kept secrets, especially those you hide from yourself and keep repressed deep in the unconscious. It is where we surrender a sense of a separate self to a deep feeling of wholeness, such as selfless service in religion or any activity that involves merging with the greater whole. Many sports stars have important planets in the twelfth house that enable them to play in the zone, finding an inner, almost mystical, strength that transcends their limits.

Who's Home in Your Houses?

Houses are stronger or weaker depending on how many planets are inhabiting them. If there are many planets in a given house, it follows that the activities of that house will be especially important in your life. If the planet that rules the house is also located there, this too adds power to the house.

CHAPTER 6

Getting to Know All Your Planets

When you know a person's sun sign, you already know some very useful generic qualities about that person. But when you know the placement of all ten planets, that person becomes an astrological individual, with a unique horoscope. The horoscope chart lights up with colorations from many different signs and planets. Therefore, you'll have a much more accurate profile, and with the full planetary picture of the horoscope, you'll be more capable of predicting how that individual will act in a given situation.

The planets are the actors of the chart, each representing a basic force in life. The sign and house where the planet is located represent how and where this force will manifest. The importance of a planet in your horoscope depends on its position. A planet that's close to your rising sign will be highlighted in your chart. If two or more planets are grouped together in one sign, they usually operate like a team, playing off each other rather than expressing their energy singularly. A lone planet that stands far away from the others is usually outstanding and often calls the shots.

The sign of each planet also has a powerful influence. In some signs, the planetary energies are very much at home and can easily express themselves. In others, the planet has to work harder and is slightly out of sorts. The sign that most corresponds to the energies of a planet is said to be ruled by that planet and obviously is the best place for it to be. The next best place is in a sign where it is exalted, or especially harmonious. On the other hand, there are places in the horoscope where a planet has to work harder to play its role, such as the sign opposite a planet's rulership, which embodies the opposite area of life, and the sign opposite its exaltation. However, a planet that must work harder can actually be more complete, because it must stretch itself to meet the challenges of living in a more difficult sign. Like world leaders who've had to struggle for greatness, this planet may actually develop great strength and character.

Here's a list of the best places for each planet to be. Note that, as new planets were discovered, they replaced the traditional rulers of signs which best complemented their energies.

ARIES—Mars
TAURUS—Venus, in its most sensual form
GEMINI—Mercury, in its communicative role
CANCER—the moon
LEO—the sun
VIRGO—also Mercury, this time in its more critical capacity
LIBRA—also Venus, in its more aesthetic, judgmental form
SCORPIO—Pluto, replacing Mars, the sign's original ruler
SAGITTARIUS—Jupiter
CAPRICORN—Saturn
AQUARIUS—Uranus, replacing Saturn, its original ruler
PISCES—Neptune, replacing Jupiter, its original ruler

A person who has many planets in exalted signs is lucky indeed, for here is where the planet can accomplish the most and be its most influential and creative.

SUN—exalted in Aries, where its energy creates action
MOON—exalted in Taurus, where instincts and reactions operate on a highly creative level
MERCURY—exalted in Aquarius, where it can reach analytical heights
VENUS—exalted in Pisces, a sign whose sensitivity encourages love and creativity
MARS—exalted in Capricorn, a sign that puts energy to work productively
JUPITER—exalted in Cancer, where it encourages nurturing and growth

45

SATURN—at home in Libra, where it steadies the scales of justice and promotes balanced, responsible judgment

URANUS—powerful in Scorpio, where it promotes transformation

NEPTUNE—especially favored in Cancer, where it gains the security to transcend to a higher state

PLUTO—exalted in Pisces, where it dissolves the old cycle to make way for transition to the new

The Personal Planets: Mercury, Venus, and Mars

These planets work in your immediate personal life.

Mercury affects how you communicate and how your mental processes work. Are you a quick study who grasps information rapidly? Or do you learn more slowly and thoroughly? How is your concentration? Can you express yourself easily? Are you a good writer? All these questions can be answered by your Mercury placement.

Venus shows what you react to. What turns you on? What appeals to you aesthetically? Are you charming to others? Are you attractive to look at? Your taste, your refinement, your sense of balance and proportion are all Venus-ruled.

Mars is your outgoing energy, your drive and ambition. Do you reach out for new adventures? Are you assertive? Are you motivated? Self-confident? Hot-tempered? How you channel your energy and drive is revealed by your Mars placement.

Mercury Shows How Your Mind Works

Mercury shows how you think and speak, how logical you are. Since it stays close to the sun, read the description for Mercury in your sun sign, then the sign preceding and following it. Then decide which reflects the way you think.

Mercury in Aries

Your mind is very active and assertive. It approaches a plan aggressively. You never hesitate to say what you think, never shy away from a battle. In fact, you may relish a verbal confrontation. Tact is not your strong point, so you may have to learn not to trip over your tongue.

Mercury in Taurus

This is a cautious Mercury. Though you may be a slow learner, you have good concentration and mental stamina. You want to make your ideas really happen. You'll attack a problem methodically and consider every angle thoroughly, never jumping to conclusions. You'll stick with a subject until you master it.

Mercury in Gemini

You are a wonderful communicator with great facility for expressing yourself both verbally and in writing. You love gathering all kinds of information. You probably finish other people's sentences, and express yourself with eloquent hand gestures. You can talk to anybody anytime . . . and probably have phone and e-mail bills to prove it. You read anything from sci-fi to Shakespeare, and might need an extra room just for your book collection. Though you learn fast, you may lack focus and discipline. Watch a tendency to jump from subject to subject.

Mercury in Cancer

You rely on intuition more than logic. Your mental processes are usually colored by your emotions, so you may seem shy or hesitant to voice your opinions. However, this placement gives you the advantage of great imagination and empathy in the way you communicate with others.

Mercury in Leo

You are enthusiastic and very dramatic in the way you express yourself. You like to hold the attention of groups, and could be a great public speaker. Your mind thinks big, so you prefer to deal with the overall picture rather than with the details.

Mercury in Virgo

This is one of the best places for Mercury. It should give you critical ability, attention to details, and thorough analysis. Your mind focuses on the practical side of things. This type of thinking is very well suited to being a teacher or editor.

Mercury in Libra

You're either a born diplomat who smoothes over ruffled feathers or a talented debater. Many lawyers have this placement. However, since you're forever weighing the pros and cons of a situation, you may vacillate when making decisions.

Mercury in Scorpio

This is an investigative mind that stops at nothing to get the answers. You may have a sarcastic, stinging wit or a gift for the cutting remark. There's always a grain of truth to your verbal sallies, thanks to your penetrating insight.

Mercury in Sagittarius

You are a supersalesman with a tendency to expound. Though you are very broad-minded, you can be dogmatic when it comes to telling others what's good for them. You won't hesitate to tell the truth as you see it, so watch a tendency toward tactlessness. On the plus side, you have a great sense of humor. This position of Mercury is often considered by astrologers to be at a disadvantage because

Sagittarius opposes Gemini, the sign Mercury rules, and squares off with Virgo, another Mercury-ruled sign. What often happens is that Mercury in Sagittarius oversteps its bounds and loses sight of the facts in a situation. Do a reality check before making promises you may not be able to deliver.

Mercury in Capricorn

This placement endows good mental discipline. You have a love of learning and a very orderly approach to your subjects. You will patiently plod through the facts and figures until you have mastered the tasks. You grasp structured situations easily, but may be short on creativity.

Mercury in Aquarius

An independent, original thinker, you'll have more cutting-edge ideas than the average person. You will be quick to check out any unusual opportunities. Your opinions are so well-researched and grounded that once your mind is made up, it is difficult to change.

Mercury in Pisces

You have the psychic and intuitive mind of a natural poet. Learn to make use of your creative imagination. You may think in terms of helping others, but check a tendency to be vague and forgetful of details.

Venus Relates

Venus shows where you receive pleasure, what you love to do. Find your Venus placement from the charts at the end of this chapter by looking for the year of your birth in the left-hand column. Then follow the line of that year across the page until you reach the time period of your birthday. The sign heading that column will be your Venus. If you were born on a day when Venus was changing signs, check the signs preceding or following that day to determine if that sign feels more like your Venus nature.

Venus in Aries

You can't stand to be bored, confined, or ordered around. But a good challenge, maybe even a rousing row, turns you on. Confess—don't you pick a fight now and then just to get someone stirred up? You're attracted by the chase, not the catch, which could cause some problems in your love life if the object of your affection becomes too attainable. You like to wear red, and you can spot a trend before anyone else.

Venus in Taurus

All your senses work in high gear. You love to be surrounded by glorious tastes, smells, textures, sounds, and visuals. Austerity is not for you! Neither is being rushed. You like time to enjoy your pleasures. Soothing surroundings with plenty of creature comforts are your cup of tea. You like to feel secure in your nest, with no sudden jolts or surprises. You like familiar objects—in fact, you may hate to let anything or anyone go.

Venus in Gemini

You are a lively, sparkling personality who thrives in a situation that affords a constant variety and a frequent change of scenery. A varied social life is important to you, with plenty of stimulation and a chance to engage in some light flirtation. Commitment may be difficult, because playing the field is so much fun.

Venus in Cancer

An atmosphere where you feel protected, coddled, and mothered is best for you. You love to be surrounded by children in a cozy, homelike situation. You are attracted to those who are tender and nurturing, who make you feel secure and well provided for. You may be quite secretive about your emotional life, or attracted to clandestine relationships.

Venus in Leo

First-class attention in large doses turns you on, and so does the glitter of real gold and the flash of mirrors. You like to feel like a star at all times, surrounded by your admiring audience. The side effect is that you may be attracted to flatterers and tinsel, while the real gold requires some digging.

Venus in Virgo

Everything neatly in its place? On the surface, you are attracted to an atmosphere where everything is in perfect order, but underneath are some basic, earthy urges. You are attracted to those who appeal to your need to teach, to be of service, or to play out a Pygmalion fantasy. You are at your best when you are busy doing something useful.

Venus in Libra

Elegance and harmony are your key words. You can't abide an atmosphere of contention. Your taste tends toward the classic, with light harmonies of color—nothing clashing, trendy, or outrageous. You love doing things with a partner, and should be careful to pick one who is decisive but patient enough to let you weigh the pros and cons. And steer clear of argumentative types!

Venus in Scorpio

Hidden mysteries intrigue you. In fact, anything that is too open and aboveboard is a bit of a bore. You surely have a stack of whodunits by the bed, along with an erotic magazine or two. You like to solve puzzles, and may also be fascinated with the occult, crime, or scientific research. Intense, all-or-nothing situations add spice to your life, and you love to ferret out the secrets of others. But you could get burned by your flair for living dangerously. The color black, spicy food, dark wood furniture, and heady perfume all get you in the right mood.

Venus in Sagittarius

If you are not actually a world traveler, your surroundings are sure to reflect your love of faraway places. You like a casual outdoor atmosphere and a dog or two to pet. There should be plenty of room for athletic equipment and suitcases. You're attracted to kindred souls who love to travel and who share your freedom-loving philosophy of life. Athletics and spiritual or New Age pursuits could be other interests.

Venus in Capricorn

No fly-by-night relationships for you! You want substance in life, and you are attracted to whatever will help you get where you are going. Status objects turn you on. And so do those who have a serious, responsible, businesslike approach as well as those who remind you of a beloved parent. It is characteristic of this placement to be attracted to someone of a different generation. Antiques, traditional clothing, and dignified behavior are becoming to you.

Venus in Aquarius

This Venus wants to make friends, to be "cool." You like to be in a group, particularly one pushing a worthy cause. You feel quite at home surrounded by people, and could even court fame. Yet all the while you remain detached from any intense commitment. Original ideas and unpredictable people fascinate you. You don't like everything to be planned out in advance, preferring spontaneity and delightful surprises.

Venus in Pisces

This Venus loves to give of yourself, and you find plenty of takers. Stray animals and people appeal to your heart and your pocketbook, but be careful to look at their motives realistically once in a while. You are extremely vulnerable to sob stories of all kinds. Fantasy, the arts (especially film, dance, and theater), and psychic or spiritual activities also speak to you.

Mars Creates Action

Mars is the mover and shaker in your life. It shows how you pursue your goals, whether you have energy to burn or proceed at a slow, steady pace. It will also show how you get angry. Do you explode or do a slow burn or hold everything inside, then get revenge later?

To find your Mars, turn to the charts on pages 88–97. Then find your birth year in the left-hand column and trace the line across horizontally until you come to the column headed by the month of your birth. There you will find an abbreviation of your Mars sign. If the description of your Mars sign doesn't ring true, read the description of the signs preceding and following it. You may have been born on a day when Mars was changing signs, in which case your Mars might be in the adjacent sign.

Mars in Aries

In the sign it rules, Mars shows its brilliant fiery nature. You have an explosive temper and can be quite impatient. On the other hand, you have tremendous courage, energy, and drive. You'll let nothing stand in your way as you race to be first! Obstacles are met head-on and broken through by force. However, those that require patience and persistence can have you exploding in rage. You're a great starter, but not necessarily around for the finish.

Mars in Taurus

Slow, steady, concentrated energy gives you staying power to last until the finish line. You have great stamina, and you never give up. Your tactic is to wear away obstacles with your persistence. Often you come out a winner because you've had the patience to hang in there. When angered, you do a slow burn.

Mars in Gemini

You can't sit still for long. This Mars craves variety. You often have two or more things going on at once—it's all an amusing game to you. Your life can get very complicated, but that only adds spice and stimulation. What drives you into a nervous, hyper state? Boredom, sameness, routine, and confinement. You can do wonderful things with your hands, and you have a way with words.

Mars in Cancer

You rarely attack head-on. Instead, you'll keep things to yourself, make plans in secret, and always cover your actions. This might be interpreted by some as manipulative, but you are only being self-protective. You get furious when anyone knows too much about you. But you do like to know all about others. Your mothering and feeding instincts can be put to good use if you work in the food, hotel, or child-care business. You may have to overcome your fragile sense of security, which prompts you not to take risks and to get physically upset when criticized. Don't take things so personally!

Mars in Leo

You have a very dominant personality that takes center stage. Modesty is not one of your traits, nor is taking a backseat. You prefer giving the orders, and have been known to make a dramatic scene if they are not obeyed.

Properly used, this Mars confers leadership ability, endurance, and courage.

Mars in Virgo

You are the faultfinder of the zodiac. You notice every detail. Mistakes of any kind make you very nervous. You may worry, even if everything is going smoothly. You may not express your anger directly, but you sure can nag. You have definite likes and dislikes, and you are sure you can do the job better than anyone else. You are certainly more industrious and detail-oriented than other signs. Your Mars energy is often most positively expressed in some kind of teaching role.

Mars in Libra

This Mars will have a passion for beauty, justice, and art. Generally, you will avoid confrontations at all costs. You prefer to spend your energy finding diplomatic solutions or weighing pros and cons. Your other techniques are passive aggression or exercising your well-known charm to get people to do what you want.

Mars in Scorpio

This is a powerful placement, so intense that it demands careful channeling into worthwhile activities. Otherwise, you could become obsessed with your sexuality or might use your need for power and control to manipulate others. You are strong-willed, shrewd, and very private about your affairs, and you'll usually have a secret agenda behind your actions. Your great stamina, focus, and discipline would be excellent assets for careers in the military or medical fields, especially research or surgery. When angry, you don't get mad—you get even!

Mars in Sagittarius

This expansive Mars often propels people into sales, travel, athletics, or philosophy. Your energies function well when you are on the move. You have a hot temper, and are inclined to say what you think before you consider the consequences. You shoot for high goals—and talk endlessly about them—but you may be weak on groundwork. This Mars needs a solid foundation. Watch a tendency to take unnecessary risks.

Mars in Capricorn

This is an ambitious Mars with an excellent sense of timing. You have an eye for those who can be of use to you, and you may dismiss people ruthlessly when you're angry, but you drive yourself hard and deliver full value. This is a good placement for an executive. You'll aim for status and a high material position in life, and you'll keep climbing despite the odds. A great Mars to have!

Mars in Aquarius

This is the most rebellious Mars. You seem to have a drive to assert yourself against the status quo. You may enjoy provoking people, shocking them out of traditional views. Or this placement could express itself in an offbeat sex life. Somehow you often find yourself in unconventional situations. You enjoy being a leader of an active group, which pursues forward-looking studies, politics, or goals.

Mars in Pisces

This Mars is a good actor who knows just how to appeal to the sympathies of others. You create and project wonderful fantasies, or you use your sensitive antennae to crusade for those less fortunate. You get what you want through creating a veil of illusion and glamour. This is a good Mars for someone in the creative and imaginative fields—a dancer, performer, photographer, actor. Many famous film stars have this placement. Watch a tendency to manipulate by making others feel sorry for you.

Jupiter Expands Your Life

This big, bright, swirling mass of gases is associated with abundance, prosperity, and the kind of windfall you get without too much hard work. You're optimistic under Jupiter's influence, when anything seems possible. You'll travel, expand your mind with higher education, and publish to share your knowledge widely. On the other hand, Jupiter's influence is neither discriminating nor disciplined. It represents the principle of growth without judgment, and therefore could result in extravagance, weight gain, laziness, and carelessness, if not kept in check.

Be sure to look up your Jupiter in the tables in this book. When the current position of Jupiter is favorable, you may get that lucky break. This is a great time to try new things, take risks, travel, or get more education. Opportunities seem to open up easily, so take advantage of them.

Once a year, Jupiter changes signs. That means you are due for an expansive time every twelve years, when Jupiter travels through your sun sign. You'll also have up periods every four years, when Jupiter is in the same element as your sun sign.

Jupiter in Aries

You are the soul of enthusiasm and optimism. Your luckiest times are when you are getting started on an exciting project or selling an idea that you really believe in. You may have to watch a tendency to be arrogant with those who do not share your enthusiasm. You follow your impulses, often ignoring budget or other commonsense limitations. To produce real, solid benefits, you'll need patience and follow-through wherever this Jupiter falls in your horoscope.

Jupiter in Taurus

You'll spend on beautiful material things, especially those that come from nature—items made of rare woods, natural fabrics, or precious gems, for instance. You can't have too much comfort or too many sensual pleasures. Watch a tendency to overindulge in good food, or to overpamper yourself with nothing but the best. Spartan living is not for you! You may be especially lucky in matters of real estate.

Jupiter in Gemini

You are the great talker of the zodiac, and you may be a great writer, too. But restlessness could be your weak point. You jump around, talk too much, and could be a jack-of-all-trades. Keeping a secret is especially difficult, so you'll have to watch a tendency to spill the beans. Since you love to be at the center of a beehive of activity, you'll have a vibrant social life. Your best opportunities will come through your talent for language—speaking, writing, communicating, and selling.

Jupiter in Cancer

You are luckiest in situations where you can find emotional closeness or deal with basic security needs such as food, nurturing, or shelter. You may be a great collector. Or you may simply love to accumulate things—you are the one who stashes things away for a rainy day. You probably have a very good memory and love children. In fact, you may have many children to care for. The food, hotel, child-care, and shipping businesses hold good opportunities for you.

Jupiter in Leo

You are a natural showman who loves to live in a larger-than-life way. Yours is a personality full of color that always finds its way into the limelight. You can't have too much attention or applause. Showbiz is a natural place for you, and so is any area where you can play to a crowd.

Exercising your flair for drama, your natural playfulness, and your romantic nature brings you good fortune. But watch a tendency to be overly extravagant or to monopolize center stage.

Jupiter in Virgo

You actually love those minute details others find boring. To you, they make all the difference between the perfect and the ordinary. You are the fine craftsman who spots every flaw. You expand your awareness by finding the most efficient methods and by being of service to others. Many of you will be drawn to medical or teaching fields. You'll also have luck in publishing, crafts, nutrition, and service professions. Watch out for a tendency to overwork.

Jupiter in Libra

This is an other-directed Jupiter that develops best with a partner. The stimulation of others helps you grow. You are also most comfortable in harmonious, beautiful situations and you work well with artistic people. You have a great sense of fair play and an ability to evaluate the pros and cons of a situation. You usually prefer to play the role of diplomat rather than adversary.

Jupiter in Scorpio

You love the feeling of power and control, of taking things to their limit. You can't resist a mystery. Your shrewd, penetrating mind sees right through to the heart of most situations and people. You have luck in work that provides for solutions to matters of life and death. You may be drawn to undercover work, behind-the-scenes intrigue, psychotherapy, the occult, and sex-related ventures. Your challenge will be to develop a sense of moderation and tolerance for other beliefs. You may have luck in handling other people's money—insurance, taxes, and inheritance can bring you a windfall.

Jupiter in Sagittarius

Independent, outgoing, and idealistic, you'll shoot for the stars. This Jupiter compels you to travel far and wide, both physically and mentally, via higher education. You may have luck while traveling in an exotic place. You also have luck with outdoor ventures, exercise, and animals, particularly horses. Since you tend to be very open about your opinions, watch a tendency to be tactless and to exaggerate. Instead, use your wonderful sense of humor to make your point.

Jupiter in Capricorn

Jupiter is much more restrained in Capricorn, the sign of rules and authority. Here, Jupiter can make you overwork and heighten any ambition or sense of duty you may have. You'll expand in areas that advance your position, putting you farther up the social or corporate ladder. You are lucky working within the establishment in a very structured situation where you can show off your ability to organize and reap rewards for your hard work.

Jupiter in Aquarius

This is another freedom-loving Jupiter, with great tolerance and originality. You are at your best when you are working for a humanitarian cause and in the company of many supporters. This is a good Jupiter for a political career. You'll relate to all kinds of people on all social levels. You have an abundance of original ideas, but you are best off away from routine and any situation that imposes rigid rules. You need mental stimulation!

Jupiter in Pisces

You are a giver whose feelings and pocketbook are easily touched by others, so choose your companions with care. You could be the original sucker for a hard-luck story. Better find a worthy hospital or a charity that will appreciate your selfless support. You have a great creative imagination. You may attract good fortune in fields related to oil, perfume, pharmaceuticals, petroleum, dance, footwear, and alcohol. But beware of overindulgence in alcohol—focus on a creative outlet instead.

Saturn Puts on the Brakes

Jupiter speeds you up with *lucky breaks* and quick energy. Then along comes Saturn to slow you down with the *disciplinary brakes*. Saturn has unfairly been called a malefic planet, one of the bad guys of the zodiac. On the contrary, Saturn is one of our best friends, the kind who tells you what you need to hear even if it's not good news. Under a Saturn transit, we grow up, take responsibility for our lives, and emerge from whatever test this planet has in store as far wiser, more capable and mature human beings. It is when we are under pressure that we grow stronger.

When Saturn hits a critical point in your horoscope, you can count on an experience that will make you slow up, pull back, and reexamine your life. It is a call to eliminate what is not working and to shape up. By the end of its twenty-eight-year trip around the zodiac, Saturn will have tested you in all areas of your life. The major tests happen in seven-year cycles, when Saturn passes over the angles of your chart—your rising sign, the top of your chart or midheaven, your descendant, and the nadir, or bottom, of your chart. This is when the real life-changing experiences happen. But you are also in for a testing period whenever Saturn passes a planet in your chart or stresses that planet from a distance. Therefore, it is useful to check your planetary positions with the timetable of Saturn to prepare in advance, or at least to brace yourself.

When Saturn returns to its location at the time of your birth, at approximately age twenty-eight, you'll have your first Saturn return. At this time, a person usually takes stock or settles down to find his mission in life and assumes full adult duties and responsibilities.

Another way Saturn helps us is to reveal the karmic lessons from previous lives and give us the chance to over-come them. So look at Saturn's challenges as much-needed opportunities for self-improvement. Under a Jupiter influence, you'll have more fun, but Saturn gives you solid, long-lasting results.

Look up your natal Saturn in the tables in this book for clues on where you need work.

Saturn in Aries

Saturn here puts the brakes on Aries' natural drive and enthusiasm. There is often an angry side to this placement. You don't let anyone push you around, and you know what's best for yourself. Following orders is not your strong point, and neither is diplomacy. You tend to be quick to go on the offensive in relationships, attacking first, before anyone attacks you. Because no one quite lives up to your standards, you often wind up doing everything yourself. You'll have to learn to cooperate and tone down self-centeredness. Both Pat Buchanan and Saddam Hussein have this Saturn.

Saturn in Taurus

A big issue is getting control of the cash flow. There will be lean periods that can be frightening, but you have the patience and endurance to stick them out and the methodical drive to prosper in the end. Learn to take a philosophical attitude, like Ben Franklin, who also had this placement and who said, "A penny saved is a penny earned."

Saturn in Gemini

You are a serious student of life, but you may have difficulty communicating or sharing your knowledge. You may be shy, speak slowly, or have fears about communicating, like Eleanor Roosevelt. You dwell in the realms of science, theory, or abstract analysis—even when you are dealing with the emotions, like Sigmund Freud, who also had this placement.

Saturn in Cancer

Your tests come with establishing a secure emotional base. In doing so, you may have to deal with some very basic fears centering on your early home environment. Most of your Saturn tests will have emotional roots in those early childhood experiences. You may have difficulty remaining objective in terms of what you try to achieve. So it will be especially important for you to deal with negative feelings such as guilt, paranoia, jealousy, resentment, and suspicion. Galileo and Michelangelo also navigated these murky waters.

Saturn in Leo

This is an authoritarian Saturn—a strict, demanding parent who may deny the pleasure principle in your zeal to see that rules are followed. Though you may feel guilty about taking the spotlight, you are very ambitious and loyal. You have to watch a tendency toward rigidity, also toward overwork and holding back affection. Joseph Kennedy and Billy Graham share this placement.

Saturn in Virgo

This is a cautious, exacting Saturn. You are intensely hard on yourself. Most of all, you give yourself the roughest time with your constant worries about every little detail, often making yourself sick. You may have difficulties setting priorities and getting the job done. Your tests will come in learning tolerance and understanding of others. Charles de Gaulle, Mae West, and Nathaniel Hawthorne had this meticulous Saturn.

Saturn in Libra

Saturn is exalted here, which makes this planet an ally. You may choose very serious, older partners in life, perhaps stemming from a fear of dependency. You need to learn to stand solidly on your own before you commit to another.

You are extremely cautious as you deliberate every involvement—with good reason. It is best that you find an occupation that makes good use of your sense of duty and honor. Steer clear of fly-by-night situations. Both Khruschev and Mao Tse-tung had this placement.

Saturn in Scorpio

You have great staying power. This Saturn tests you in situations involving the control of others. You may feel drawn to some kind of intrigue or undercover work, like J. Edgar Hoover. Or there may be an air of mystery surrounding your life and death, like Marilyn Monroe and Robert Kennedy, who both had this placement. There are lessons to be learned from your sexual involvements. Often sex is used for manipulation or is somehow out of the ordinary. The Roman emperor Caligula and the transsexual Christine Jorgensen are extreme cases.

Saturn in Sagittarius

Your challenges and lessons will come from tests of your spiritual and philosophical values, as happened to Martin Luther King and Gandhi. You are high-minded and sincere with this reflective, moral placement. Uncompromising in your ethical standards, you could become a benevolent despot.

Saturn in Capricorn

With the help of Saturn at maximum strength, your judgment will improve with age. And like Spencer Tracy's screen image, you'll be the gray-haired hero with a strong sense of responsibility. You advance in life slowly but steadily, always with a strong hand at the helm and an eye for the advantageous situation. Like Pat Robertson, you're likely to stand for conservative values. Negatively, you may be a loner, prone to periods of melancholy.

Saturn in Aquarius

Your tests come from relationships with groups. Do you care too much about what others think? Do you feel like an outsider, like Greta Garbo? You may fear being different from others and therefore slight your own unique, forward-looking gifts. Or like Lord Byron and Howard Hughes, you may take the opposite tack and rebel in the extreme. You can apply discipline to accomplish great humanitarian goals, as Albert Schweitzer did.

Saturn in Pisces

Your fear of the unknown and the irrational may lead you to the safety and protection of an institution. You may go on the run like Jesse James, who had this placement, to avoid looking too deeply inside. Or you might go in the opposite, more positive direction and develop a disciplined psychoanalytic approach, which puts you more in control of your feelings. Some of you will take refuge in work with hospitals, charities, or religious institutions. Queen Victoria, who had this placement, symbolized an era when institutions of all kinds were sustained. Discipline applied to artistic work, especially poetry and dance, or to spiritual work, such as yoga or meditation, might be helpful.

How Uranus, Neptune, and Pluto Influence a Whole Generation

These three planets remain in signs such a long time that a whole generation bears the imprint of the sign. Mass movements, great sweeping changes, fads that characterize a generation, even the issues of the conflicts and wars of the time are influenced by these "outer three" planets. When one of those distant planets changes signs, there is a definite shift in the atmosphere, the feeling of the end of an era.

Since these planets are so far away from the sun—too distant to be seen by the naked eye—they pick up signals from the universe at large. These planetary receivers literally link the sun with distant energies, and then perform a similar function in your horoscope by linking your central character with intuitive, spiritual, transformative forces from the cosmos. Each planet has a special domain, and will reflect this in the area of your chart where it falls.

Uranus Is the Surprise Ingredient

Uranus is the unexpected ingredient that sets you and your generation apart. There is nothing ordinary about this quirky green planet that seems to be traveling on its side, surrounded by a swarm of moons. Is it any wonder that astrologers assigned it to Aquarius, the most eccentric and gregarious sign? Uranus seems to wend its way around the sun, marching to its own tune.

Significantly, Uranus follows Saturn, the planet of limitations and structures. Often we get caught up in the structures we have created to give ourselves a sense of security. However, if we lose contact with our spiritual roots, then Uranus is likely to jolt us out of our comfortable rut and wake us up.

Uranus energy is electrical, happening in sudden flashes. It is not influenced by karma or past events, nor does it regard tradition, sex, or sentiment. The Uranus key words are surprise and awakening. Suddenly, there's that flash of inspiration, that bright idea, that totally new approach to revolutionize whatever scheme you were undertaking. A Uranus event takes you by surprise; it happens from out of the blue, for better or for worse. The Uranus place in your life is where you awaken and become your own person, leaving the structures of Saturn behind. And it is probably the most unconventional place in your chart.

Look up the sign of Uranus at the time of your birth and see where you follow your own tune.

Uranus in Aries

Birth Dates:
  March 31, 1927–November 4, 1927

January 13, 1928–June 6, 1934
October 10, 1934–March 28, 1935

Your generation is original, creative, pioneering. It developed the computer, the airplane, and the cyclotron. You let nothing hold you back from exploring the unknown, and you have a powerful mixture of fire and electricity behind you. Women of your generation were among the first to be liberated. You were the unforgettable style setters. You have a surprise in store for everyone. Like Yoko Ono, Grace Kelly, and Jacqueline Onassis, your life may be jolted by sudden and violent changes.

Uranus in Taurus

Birth Dates:
June 6, 1934–October 10, 1934
March 28, 1935–August 7, 1941
October 5, 1941–May 15, 1942

The great territorial shake-ups of World War II began during your generation. You are independent, probably self-employed or would like to be. You have original ideas about making money, and you brace yourself for sudden changes of fortune. This Uranus can cause shake-ups, particularly in finances, but it can also make you a born entrepreneur, like Martha Stewart.

Uranus in Gemini

Birth Dates:
August 7, 1941–October 5, 1941
May 15, 1942–August 30, 1948
November 12, 1948–June 10, 1949

You were the first children to be influenced by television. Now, in your adult years, your generation stocks up on answering machines, cell phones, computers, and fax machines—any new way you can communicate. You have an inquiring mind, but your interests may be rather short-lived. This Uranus can be easily fragmented if there is no structure and focus.

Uranus in Cancer

Birth Dates:
   August 30, 1948–November 12, 1948
   June 10, 1949–August 24, 1955
   January 28, 1956–June 10, 1956
This generation came at a time when divorce was becoming commonplace, so your home image is unconventional. You may have an unusual relationship with your parents; you may have come from a broken home or an unconventional one. You'll have unorthodox ideas about parenting, intimacy, food, and shelter. You may also be interested in dreams, psychic phenomena, and memory work.

Uranus in Leo

Birth Dates:
   August 24, 1955–January 28, 1956
   June 10, 1956–November 1, 1961
   January 10, 1962–August 10, 1962
This generation understood how to use electronic media. Many of your group are now leaders in the high-tech industries, and you also understand how to use the new media to promote yourself. Like Isadora Duncan, you may have a very eccentric kind of charisma and a life that is sparked by unusual love affairs. Your children, too, may have traits that are out of the ordinary. Where this planet falls in your chart, you'll have a love of freedom, be a bit of an egomaniac, and show the full force of your personality in a unique way, like tennis great Martina Navratilova.

Uranus in Virgo

Birth Dates:
   November 1, 1961–January 10, 1962
   August 10, 1962–September 28, 1968
   May 20, 1969–June 24, 1969
You'll have highly individual work methods. Many of you will be finding newer, more practical ways to use computers. Like Einstein, who had this placement, you'll break the

rules brilliantly. Your generation came at a time of student rebellions, the civil rights movement, and the general acceptance of health foods. Chances are, you're concerned about pollution and cleaning up the environment. You may also be involved with nontraditional healing methods.

Uranus in Libra

Birth Dates:
September 28, 1968–May 20, 1969
June 24, 1969–November 21, 1974
May 1, 1975–September 8, 1975
Your generation will be always changing partners. Born during the era of women's liberation, you may have come from a broken home and may have no clear image of what a marriage entails. There will be many sudden splits and experiments before you settle down. Your generation will be much involved in legal and political reforms and in changing artistic and fashion looks.

Uranus in Scorpio

Birth Dates:
November 21, 1974–May 1, 1975
September 8, 1975–February 17, 1981
March 20, 1981–November 16, 1981
Interest in transformation, meditation, and life after death signaled the beginning of New Age consciousness. Your generation recognizes no boundaries, no limits, and no external controls. You'll have new attitudes toward death and dying, psychic phenomena, and the occult. Like Mae West and Casanova, you'll shock 'em sexually, too.

Uranus in Sagittarius

Birth Dates:
February 17, 1981–March 20, 1981
November 16, 1981–February 15, 1988
May 27, 1988–December 2, 1988
Could this generation be the first to travel in outer

space? An earlier generation with this placement included Charles Lindbergh and a time when the first zeppelins and the Wright Brothers were conquering the skies. Uranus here forecasts great discoveries, mind expansion, and long-distance travel. Like Galileo and Martin Luther, those born in these years will generate new theories about the cosmos and mankind's relation to it.

Uranus in Capricorn

Birth Dates:
    December 20, 1904–January 30, 1912
    September 4, 1912–November 12, 1912
    February 15, 1988–May 27, 1988
    December 2, 1988–April 1, 1995
    June 9, 1995–January 12, 1996

This generation, now growing up, will challenge traditions with the help of electronic gadgets. In these years, we got organized with the help of technology put to practical use. The Internet was born following the great economic boom of the 1990s. Great leaders who were movers and shakers of history, like Julius Caesar and Henry VIII, were born under this placement.

Uranus in Aquarius

Birth Dates:
    January 30, 1912–September 4, 1912
    November 12, 1912–April 1, 1919
    August 16, 1919–January 22, 1920
    April 1, 1995–June 9, 1995
    January 12, 1996–March 10, 2003
    September 15, 2003–December 30, 2003

Uranus in Aquarius is the strongest placement for this planet. Recently we've had the opportunity to witness the full force of its power of innovation, as well as its sudden wake-up calls and insistence on humanitarian values. This was a time of high-tech development, when home computers became as ubiquitous as television. It was a time of globalization, of surprise attacks (9/11), and underdeveloped countries demanding attention. The last generation with this placement produced great innovative minds such as Leonard Bernstein and Orson Welles. The next will become another radical breakthrough generation, much concerned with global issues that involve all humanity.

Uranus in Pisces

Birth Dates:
    April 1, 1919–August 16, 1919
    January 22, 1920–March 31, 1927
    November 4, 1927–January 12, 1928
    March 10, 2003–September 15, 2003
    December 20, 2003–May 28, 2010

Uranus is now in Pisces, ushering in a new generation. In the past century, Uranus in Pisces focused attention on the rise of electronic entertainment—radio and the cinema—and the secretiveness of Prohibition. This produced a generation of idealists exemplified by Judy Garland's theme "Somewhere over the Rainbow." Uranus in Pisces also hints at stealth activities, at hospital and prison reform, at high-tech drugs and medical experiments, at shake-ups and reforms in the Pisces-ruled petroleum industry, offshore drilling in new and unusual locations. Issues regarding the water and oil supply, water-related storm damage (Hurricane Katrina), sudden hurricanes, and floods demand our attention.

Neptune Is the Magic Solvent

Neptune is often maligned as the planet of illusions that dissolves reality, enabling you to escape the material world. Under Neptune's influence, you see what you want to see. But Neptune also encourages you to create. It embodies glamour, subtlety, mystery, and mysticism, and it governs anything that takes you beyond the mundane world, including out-of-body experiences.

Neptune acts to transcend your ordinary perceptions to take you to another level, where you experience either confusion or ecstasy. Its force can pull you off course only if you allow this to happen. Those who use Neptune wisely can translate their daydreams into poetry, theater, design, or inspired moves in the business world, avoiding the tricky "con artist" side of this planet.

Find your Neptune listed below.

Neptune in Cancer

Birth Dates:
    July 19, 1901–December 25, 1901
    May 21, 1902–September 23, 1914
    December 14, 1914–July 19, 1915
    March 19, 1916–May 2, 1916

Dreams of the homeland, idealistic patriotism, and glamorization of the nurturing assets of women characterized this time. You who were born here have unusual psychic ability and deep insights into basic needs of others.

Neptune in Leo

Birth Dates:
    September 23, 1914–December 14, 1914
    July 19, 1915–March 19, 1916
    May 2, 1916–September 21, 1928
    February 19, 1929–July 24, 1929

Neptune in Leo brought us the glamour and high living of the 1920s and the big spenders of that time. The Neptune temptations of gambling, seduction, theater, and lavish entertaining distracted from the realities of the age. Those born in that generation also made great advances in the arts.

Neptune in Virgo

Birth Dates:
    September 21, 1928–February 19, 1929
    July 24, 1929–October 3, 1942
    April 17, 1943–August 2, 1943

Neptune in Virgo encompassed the 1930s, the Great Depression, and the beginning of World War II, when a new order was born. There was a time of facing "what doesn't work." Many were unemployed and found solace at the movies, watching the great Virgo star Greta Garbo or the escapist dance films of Busby Berkeley. New public services were born. Those with Neptune in Virgo later spread the gospel of health and fitness. This generation's devotion to spending hours at the office inspired the term *workaholic*.

Neptune in Libra

Birth Dates:
    October 3, 1942–April 17, 1943
    August 2, 1943–December 24, 1955
    March 12, 1956–October 19, 1956
    June 15, 1957–August 6, 1957
This was the time of World War II and the postwar period, when the world regained balance and returned to relative stability. Neptune in Libra was the romantic generation who would later be concerned with relating. As this generation matured, there was a new trend toward marriage and commitment. Racial and sexual equality became important issues, as they redesigned traditional roles to suit modern times.

Neptune in Scorpio

Birth Dates:
    December 24, 1955–March 12, 1956
    October 19, 1956–June 15, 1957
    August 6, 1957–January 4, 1970
    May 3, 1970–November 6, 1970
Neptune in Scorpio brought in a generation that would become interested in transformative power. Born in an era that glamorized sex, drugs, rock and roll, and Eastern religion, they matured in a more sobering time of AIDS, cocaine abuse, and New Age spirituality. As they evolve, they will become active in healing the planet from the results of the abuse of power.

Neptune in Sagittarius

Birth Dates:
   January 4, 1970–May 3, 1970
   November 6, 1970–January 19, 1984
   June 23, 1984–November 21, 1984

Neptune in Sagittarius was the time when space and astronaut travel became a reality. The Neptune influence glamorized new approaches to mysticism, religion, and mind expansion. This generation will take a new approach to spiritual life, with emphasis on visions, mysticism, and clairvoyance.

Neptune in Capricorn

Birth Dates:
   January 19, 1984–June 23, 1984
   November 21, 1984–January 29, 1998

Neptune in Capricorn brought a time when delusions about material power were glamorized in the mid–1980s and 1990s. There was a boom in the stock market, and the Internet era spawned young tycoons who later lost it all. It was also a time when the psychic and occult worlds spawned a new category of business enterprise, and sold services on television.

Neptune in Aquarius

Birth Dates:
   January 29, 1998–April 4, 2011

This should continue to be a time of breakthroughs. Here the creative influence of Neptune reaches a universal audience. This is a time of dissolving barriers, of globalization—when we truly become one world. During this transit of high-tech Aquarius, new kinds of entertainment media reach across cultural differences. However, the transit of Neptune has also raised boundary issues between cultures, especially in Middle Eastern countries with Neptune-ruled oil fields. As Neptune raises issues of social and political structures not being as solid as they seem, this could continue to produce rebellion and chaos in the environment. However, by using imagination (Neptune) in partnership with a global view (Aquarius) we could reach creative solutions.

Those born with this placement should be true citizens of the world with a remarkable creative ability to transcend social and cultural barriers.

Pluto Can Transform You

Though Pluto is a tiny, mysterious body in space, its influence is great. When Pluto zaps a strategic point in your horoscope, your life changes dramatically.

Little Pluto is the power behind the scenes; it affects you at deep levels of consciousness, causing events to come to the surface that will transform you and your generation. Nothing escapes, or is sacred, with this probing planet. Its purpose is to wipe out the past so something new can happen.

The Pluto place in your horoscope is where you have invisible power (Mars governs the visible power), where you can transform, heal, and affect the unconscious needs of the masses. Pluto tells lots about how your generation projects power, what makes it seem cool to others. And when Pluto changes signs, there is a whole new concept of what's cool. Pluto's strange elliptical orbit occasionally runs inside the orbit of neighboring Neptune. Because of its eccentric path, the length of time Pluto stays in any given sign can vary from thirteen to thirty-two years. It covered only seven signs in the last century.

Pluto in Gemini

Birth Dates:
    Late 1800s–May 26, 1914

This was a time of mass suggestion and breakthroughs in communications, a time when many brilliant writers such as Ernest Hemingway and F. Scott Fitzgerald were born. Henry Miller, D. H. Lawrence, and James Joyce scandalized society by using explicit sexual images and language in their literature. "Muckraking" journalists exposed corruption. Pluto-ruled Scorpio President Theodore Roosevelt said, "Speak softly, but carry a big stick." This generation had an intense need to communicate and made major breakthroughs in knowledge. A compulsive restlessness and a thirst for a variety of experiences characterized many of this generation.

Pluto in Cancer

Birth Dates:
    May 26, 1914–June 14, 1939
    Dictators and mass media arose to wield emotional power over the masses. Women's rights was a popular issue. Deep sentimental feelings, acquisitiveness, and possessiveness characterized these times and people. Most of the great stars of the Hollywood era that embodied the American image were born during this period: Grace Kelly, Esther Williams, Frank Sinatra, Lana Turner, to name a few.

Pluto in Leo

Birth Dates:
    June 14, 1939–August, 19, 1957
    The performing arts played on the emotions of the masses. Mick Jagger, John Lennon, and rock and roll were born at this time. So were "baby boomers" like Bill and Hillary Clinton. Those born here tend to be self-centered, powerful, and boisterous. This generation does its own thing, for better or for worse.

Pluto in Virgo

Birth Dates:
    August 19, 1957–October 5, 1971
    April 17, 1972–July 30, 1972
    This is the "yuppie" generation that sparked a mass movement toward fitness, health, and career. It is a much more sober, serious, driven generation than the fun-loving Pluto in Leo. During this time, machines were invented to

process detail work efficiently. Inventions took a practical turn with answering machines, fax machines, car phones, and home office equipment—all making the workplace far more efficient.

Pluto in Libra

Birth Dates:
    October 5, 1971–April 17, 1972
    July 30, 1972–November 5, 1983
    May 18, 1984–August 27, 1984
A mellower generation, people born at this time are concerned with partnerships, working together, and finding diplomatic solutions to problems. Marriage is important to this generation, and they will define it by combining traditional values with equal partnership. This was a time of women's liberation, gay rights, ERA, and legal battles over abortion, all of which transformed our ideas about relationships.

Pluto in Scorpio

Birth Dates:
    November 5, 1983–May 18, 1984
    August 27, 1984–January 17, 1995
Pluto was in the sign it rules for a comparatively short period of time. However, this was a time of record achievements, destructive sexually transmitted diseases, nuclear power controversies, and explosive political issues. Pluto destroys in order to create new understanding—the phoenix rising from the ashes—which should be some consolation for those of you who felt Pluto's force before 1995. Sexual shockers were par for the course during these intense years when black clothing, transvestites, body piercing, tattoos, and sexually explicit advertising pushed the boundaries of good taste.

Pluto in Sagittarius

Birth Dates:
    January 17, 1995–April 20, 1995

November 10, 1995–January 26, 2008

During the most recent Pluto transit, we were pushed to expand our horizons, to find deeper spiritual meaning in life. Pluto's opposition with Saturn in 2001 brought an enormous conflict between traditional societies and the forces of change. It signals a time when religious convictions exerted more power in our political life as well.

Since Sagittarius is associated with travel, Pluto, the planet of extremes, made space travel a reality for some wealthy adventurers, who paid for the privilege of travel on space shuttles.

New dimensions in electronic publishing, concern with animal rights and the environment, and an increasing emphasis on extreme forms of religion are other signs of these times. Charismatic religious leaders asserted themselves and questions of the boundaries between church and state arose. There were also sexual scandals associated with the church. Because this period ends this year, hopefully we will have developed far-reaching philosphies to elevate our lives with a new sense of purpose.

Pluto in Capricorn

Birth Dates:
  January 25, 2008–June 13, 2008
  November 26, 2008–January 20, 2024

Since Pluto in Jupiter-ruled Sagittarius signaled a time of expansion and globalization, Pluto's entry into Saturn-ruled Capricorn this year will signal a time of adjustment, of facing reality and limitations, then finding pragmatic solutions. It will be a time when a new structure is imposed, when we become concerned with what actually works. Because Capricorn is associated with corporations and also with responsibility and duty, look for dramatic changes in business practices, hopefully with more attention paid to ethical and social responsibility as well as the bottom line. Big business will have enormous power during this transit, perhaps handling what governments have been unable to accomplish. There will be an emphasis on trimming down, perhaps a new belt-tightening regime. And since Capricorn is the sign of Father Time, there will be a new emphasis on the aging of the population. The generation born now is sure to be a more practical and realistic one than that of their older Pluto-in-Sagittarius siblings.

VENUS SIGNS 1901–2008

	Aries	Taurus	Gemini	Cancer	Leo	Virgo
1901	3/29–4/22	4/22–5/17	5/17–6/10	6/10–7/5	7/5–7/29	7/29–8/23
1902	5/7–6/3	6/3–6/30	6/30–7/25	7/25–8/19	8/19–9/13	9/13–10/7
1903	2/28–3/24	3/24–4/18	4/18–5/13	5/13–6/9	6/9–7/7	7/7–8/17 9/6–11/8
1904	3/13–5/7	5/7–6/1	6/1–6/25	6/25–7/19	7/19–8/13	8/13–9/6
1905	2/3–3/6 4/9–5/28	3/6–4/9 5/28–7/8	7/8–8/6	8/6–9/1	9/1–9/27	9/27–10/21
1906	3/1–4/7	4/7–5/2	5/2–5/26	5/26–6/20	6/20–7/16	7/16–8/11
1907	4/27–5/22	5/22–6/16	6/16–7/11	7/11–8/4	8/4–8/29	8/29–9/22
1908	2/14–3/10	3/10–4/5	4/5–5/5	5/5–9/8	9/8–10/8	10/8–11/3
1909	3/29–4/22	4/22–5/16	5/16–6/10	6/10–7/4	7/4–7/29	7/29–8/23
1910	5/7–6/3	6/4–6/29	6/30–7/24	7/25–8/18	8/19–9/12	9/13–10/6
1911	2/28–3/23	3/24–4/17	4/18–5/12	5/13–6/8	6/9–7/7	7/8–11/18
1912	4/13–5/6	5/7–5/31	6/1–6/24	6/24–7/18	7/19–8/12	8/13–9/5
1913	2/3–3/6 5/2–5/30	3/7–5/1 5/31–7/7	7/8–8/5	8/6–8/31	9/1–9/26	9/27–10/20
1914	3/14–4/6	4/7–5/1	5/2–5/25	5/26–6/19	6/20–7/15	7/16–8/10
1915	4/27–5/21	5/22–6/15	6/16–7/10	7/11–8/3	8/4–8/28	8/29–9/21
1916	2/14–3/9	3/10–4/5	4/6–5/5	5/6–9/8	9/9–10/7	10/8–11/2
1917	3/29–4/21	4/22–5/15	5/16–6/9	6/10–7/3	7/4–7/28	7/29–8/21
1918	5/7–6/2	6/3–6/28	6/29–7/24	7/25–8/18	8/19–9/11	9/12–10/5
1919	2/27–3/22	3/23–4/16	4/17–5/12	5/13–6/7	6/8–7/7	7/8–11/8
1920	4/12–5/6	5/7–5/30	5/31–6/23	6/24–7/18	7/19–8/11	8/12–9/4
1921	2/3–3/6 4/26–6/1	3/7–4/25 6/2–7/7	7/8–8/5	8/6–8/31	9/1–9/25	9/26–10/20
1922	3/13–4/6	4/7–4/30	5/1–5/25	5/26–6/19	6/20–7/14	7/15–8/9
1923	4/27–5/21	5/22–6/14	6/15–7/9	7/10–8/3	8/4–8/27	8/28–9/20
1924	2/13–3/8	3/9–4/4	4/5–5/5	5/6–9/8	9/9–10/7	10/8–11/12
1925	3/28–4/20	4/21–5/15	5/16–6/8	6/9–7/3	7/4–7/27	7/28–8/21

Libra	Scorpio	Sagittarius	Capricorn	Aquarius	Pisces
8/23–9/17	9/17–10/12	10/12–1/16	1/16–2/9	2/9–3/5	3/5–3/29
			11/7–12/5	12/5–1/11	
10/7–10/31	10/31–11/24	11/24–12/18	12/18–1/11	2/6–4/4	1/11–2/6
					4/4–5/7
8/17–9/6	12/9–1/5			1/11–2/4	2/4–2/28
11/8–12/9					
9/6–9/30	9/30–10/25	1/5–1/30	1/30–2/24	2/24–3/19	3/19–4/13
		10/25–11/18	11/18–12/13	12/13–1/7	
10/21–11/14	11/14–12/8	12/8–1/1/06			1/7–2/3
8/11–9/7	9/7–10/9	10/9–12/15	1/1–1/25	1/25–2/18	2/18–3/14
	12/15–12/25	12/25–2/6			
9/22–10/16	10/16–11/9	11/9–12/3	2/6–3/6	3/6–4/2	4/2–4/27
			12/3–12/27	12/27–1/20	
11/3–11/28	11/28–12/22	12/22–1/15			1/20–2/4
8/23–9/17	9/17–10/12	10/12–11/17	1/15–2/9	2/9–3/5	3/5–3/29
			11/17–12/5	12/5–1/15	
10/7–10/30	10/31–11/23	11/24–12/17	12/18–12/31	1/1–1/15	1/16–1/28
				1/29–4/4	4/5–5/6
11/19–12/8	12/9–12/31		1/1–1/10	1/11–2/2	2/3–2/27
9/6–9/30	1/1–1/4	1/5–1/29	1/30–2/23	2/24–3/18	3/19–4/12
	10/1–10/24	10/25–11/17	11/18–12/12	12/13–12/31	
10/21–11/13	11/14–12/7	12/8–12/31		1/1–1/6	1/7–2/2
8/11–9/6	9/7–10/9	10/10–12/5	1/1–1/24	1/25–2/17	2/18–3/13
	12/6–12/30	12/31			
9/22–10/15	10/16–11/8	1/1–2/6	2/7–3/6	3/7–4/1	4/2–4/26
		11/9–12/2	12/3–12/26	12/27–12/31	
11/3–11/27	11/28–12/21	12/22–12/31		1/1–1/19	1/20–2/13
8/22–9/16	9/17–10/11	1/1–1/14	1/15–2/7	2/8–3/4	3/5–3/28
		10/12–11/6	11/7–12/5	12/6–12/31	
10/6–10/29	10/30–11/22	11/23–12/16	12/17–12/31	1/1–4/5	4/6–5/6
11/9–12/8	12/9–12/31		1/1–1/9	1/10–2/2	2/3–2/26
9/5–9/30	1/1–1/3	1/4–1/28	1/29–2/22	2/23–3/18	3/19–4/11
	9/31–10/23	10/24–11/17	11/18–12/11	12/12–12/31	
10/21–11/13	11/14–12/7	12/8–12/31		1/1–1/6	1/7–2/2
8/10–9/6	9/7–10/10	10/11–11/28	1/1–1/24	1/25–2/16	2/17–3/12
	11/29–12/31				
9/21–10/14	1/1	1/2–2/6	2/7–3/5	3/6–3/31	4/1–4/26
	10/15–11/7	11/8–12/1	12/2–12/25	12/26–12/31	
11/13–11/26	11/27–12/21	12/22–12/31		1/1–1/19	1/20–2/12
8/22–9/15	9/16–10/11	1/1–1/14	1/15–2/7	2/8–3/3	3/4–3/27
		10/12–11/6	11/7–12/5	12/6–12/31	

VENUS SIGNS 1901–2008

	Aries	Taurus	Gemini	Cancer	Leo	Virgo
1926	5/7–6/2	6/3–6/28	6/29–7/23	7/24–8/17	8/18–9/11	9/12–10/5
1927	2/27–3/22	3/23–4/16	4/17–5/11	5/12–6/7	6/8–7/7	7/8–11/9
1928	4/12–5/5	5/6–5/29	5/30–6/23	6/24–7/17	7/18–8/11	8/12–9/4
1929	2/3–3/7	3/8–4/19	7/8–8/4	8/5–8/30	8/31–9/25	9/26–10/19
	4/20–6/2	6/3–7/7				
1930	3/13–4/5	4/6–4/30	5/1–5/24	5/25–6/18	6/19–7/14	7/15–8/9
1931	4/26–5/20	5/21–6/13	6/14–7/8	7/9–8/2	8/3–8/26	8/27–9/19
1932	2/12–3/8	3/9–4/3	4/4–5/5	5/6–7/12	9/9–10/6	10/7–11/1
			7/13–7/27	7/28–9/8		
1933	3/27–4/19	4/20–5/28	5/29–6/8	6/9–7/2	7/3–7/26	7/27–8/20
1934	5/6–6/1	6/2–6/27	6/28–7/22	7/23–8/16	8/17–9/10	9/11–10/4
1935	2/26–3/21	3/22–4/15	4/16–5/10	5/11–6/6	6/7–7/6	7/7–11/8
1936	4/11–5/4	5/5–5/28	5/29–6/22	6/23–7/16	7/17–8/10	8/11–9/4
1937	2/2–3/8	3/9–4/13	7/7–8/3	8/4–8/29	8/30–9/24	9/25–10/18
	4/14–6/3	6/4–7/6				
1938	3/12–4/4	4/5–4/28	4/29–5/23	5/24–6/18	6/19–7/13	7/14–8/8
1939	4/25–5/19	5/20–6/13	6/14–7/8	7/9–8/1	8/2–8/25	8/26–9/19
1940	2/12–3/7	3/8–4/3	4/4–5/5	5/6–7/4	9/9–10/5	10/6–10/31
			7/5–7/31	8/1–9/8		
1941	3/27–4/19	4/20–5/13	5/14–6/6	6/7–7/1	7/2–7/26	7/27–8/20
1942	5/6–6/1	6/2–6/26	6/27–7/22	7/23–8/16	8/17–9/9	9/10–10/3
1943	2/25–3/20	3/21–4/14	4/15–5/10	5/11–6/6	6/7–7/6	7/7–11/8
1944	4/10–5/3	5/4–5/28	5/29–6/21	6/22–7/16	7/17–8/9	8/10–9/2
1945	2/2–3/10	3/11–4/6	7/7–8/3	8/4–8/29	8/30–9/23	9/24–10/18
	4/7–6/3	6/4–7/6				
1946	3/11–4/4	4/5–4/28	4/29–5/23	5/24–6/17	6/18–7/12	7/13–8/8
1947	4/25–5/19	5/20–6/12	6/13–7/7	7/8–8/1	8/2–8/25	8/26–9/18
1948	2/11–3/7	3/8–4/3	4/4–5/6	5/7–6/28	9/8–10/5	10/6–10/31
			6/29–8/2	8/3–9/7		
1949	3/26–4/19	4/20–5/13	5/14–6/6	6/7–6/30	7/1–7/25	7/26–8/19
1950	5/5–5/31	6/1–6/26	6/27–7/21	7/22–8/15	8/16–9/9	9/10–10/3
1951	2/25–3/21	3/22–4/15	4/16–5/10	5/11–6/6	6/7–7/7	7/8–11/9

Libra	Scorpio	Sagittarius	Capricorn	Aquarius	Pisces
10/6–10/29	10/30–11/22	11/23–12/16	12/17–12/31	1/1–4/5	4/6–5/6
11/10–12/8	12/9–12/31	1/1–1/7	1/8	1/9–2/1	2/2–2/26
9/5–9/28	1/1–1/3	1/4–1/28	1/29–2/22	2/23–3/17	3/18–4/11
	9/29–10/23	10/24–11/16	11/17–12/11	12/12–12/31	
10/20–11/12	11/13–12/6	12/7–12/30	12/31	1/1–1/5	1/6–2/2
8/10–9/6	9/7–10/11	10/12–11/21	1/1–1/23	1/24–2/16	2/17–3/12
	11/22–12/31				
9/20–10/13	1/1–1/3	1/4–2/6	2/7–3/4	3/5–3/31	4/1–4/25
	10/14–11/6	11/7–11/30	12/1–12/24	12/25–12/31	
11/2–11/25	11/26–12/20	12/21–12/31		1/1–1/18	1/19–2/11
8/21–9/14	9/15–10/10	1/1–1/13	1/14–2/6	2/7–3/2	3/3–3/26
		10/11–11/5	11/6–12/4	12/5–12/31	
10/5–10/28	10/29–11/21	11/22–12/15	12/16–12/31	1/1–4/5	4/6–5/5
11/9–12/7	12/8–12/31		1/1–1/7	1/8–1/31	2/1–2/25
9/5–9/27	1/1–1/2	1/3–1/27	1/28–2/21	2/22–3/16	3/17–4/10
	9/28–10/22	10/23–11/15	11/16–12/10	12/11–12/31	
10/19–11/11	11/12–12/5	12/6–12/29	12/30–12/31	1/1–1/5	1/6–2/1
8/9–9/6	9/7–10/13	10/14–11/14	1/1–1/22	1/23–2/15	2/16–3/11
	11/15–12/31				
9/20–10/13	1/1–1/3	1/4–2/5	2/6–3/4	3/5–3/30	3/31–4/24
	10/14–11/6	11/7–11/30	12/1–12/24	12/25–12/31	
11/1–11/25	11/26–12/19	12/20–12/31		1/1–1/18	1/19–2/11
8/21–9/14	9/15–10/9	1/1–1/12	1/13–2/5	2/6–3/1	3/2–3/26
		10/10–11/5	11/6–12/4	12/5–12/31	
10/4–10/27	10/28–11/20	11/21–12/14	12/15–12/31	1/1–4/5	4/6–5/5
11/9–12/7	12/8–12/31		1/1–1/7	1/8–1/31	2/1–2/24
9/3–9/27	1/1–1/2	1/3–1/27	1/28–2/20	2/21–3/16	3/17–4/9
	9/28–10/21	10/22–11/15	11/16–12/10	12/11–12/31	
10/19–11/11	11/12–12/5	12/6–12/29	12/30–12/31	1/1–1/4	1/5–2/1
8/9–9/6	9/7–10/15	10/16–11/7	1/1–1/21	1/22–2/14	2/15–3/10
	11/8–12/31				
9/19–10/12	1/1–1/4	1/5–2/5	2/6–3/4	3/5–3/29	3/30–4/24
	10/13–11/5	11/6–11/29	11/30–12/23	12/24–12/31	
11/1–11/25	11/26–12/19	12/20–12/31		1/1–1/17	1/18–2/10
8/20–9/14	9/15–10/9	1/1–1/12	1/13–2/5	2/6–3/1	3/2–3/25
		10/10–11/5	11/6–12/5	12/6–12/31	
10/4–10/27	10/28–11/20	11/21–12/13	12/14–12/31	1/1–4/5	4/6–5/4
11/10–12/7	12/8–12/31		1/1–1/7	1/8–1/31	2/1–2/24

VENUS SIGNS 1901–2008

	Aries	Taurus	Gemini	Cancer	Leo	Virgo
1952	4/10–5/4	5/5–5/28	5/29–6/21	6/22–7/16	7/17–8/9	8/10–9/3
1953	2/2–3/3	3/4–3/31	7/8–8/3	8/4–8/29	8/30–9/24	9/25–10/18
	4/1–6/5	6/6–7/7				
1954	3/12–4/4	4/5–4/28	4/29–5/23	5/24–6/17	6/18–7/13	7/14–8/8
1955	4/25–5/19	5/20–6/13	6/14–7/7	7/8–8/1	8/2–8/25	8/26–9/18
1956	2/12–3/7	3/8–4/4	4/5–5/7	5/8–6/23	9/9–10/5	10/6–10/31
			6/24–8/4	8/5–9/8		
1957	3/26–4/19	4/20–5/13	5/14–6/6	6/7–7/1	7/2–7/26	7/27–8/19
1958	5/6–5/31	6/1–6/26	6/27–7/22	7/23–8/15	8/16–9/9	9/10–10/3
1959	2/25–3/20	3/21–4/14	4/15–5/10	5/11–6/6	6/7–7/8	7/9–9/20
					9/21–9/24	9/25–11/9
1960	4/10–5/3	5/4–5/28	5/29–6/21	6/22–7/15	7/16–8/9	8/10–9/2
1961	2/3–6/5	6/6–7/7	7/8–8/3	8/4–8/29	8/30–9/23	9/24–10/17
1962	3/11–4/3	4/4–4/28	4/29–5/22	5/23–6/17	6/18–7/12	7/13–8/8
1963	4/24–5/18	5/19–6/12	6/13–7/7	7/8–7/31	8/1–8/25	8/26–9/18
1964	2/11–3/7	3/8–4/4	4/5–5/9	5/10–6/17	9/9–10/5	10/6–10/31
			6/18–8/5	8/6–9/8		
1965	3/26–4/18	4/19–5/12	5/13–6/6	6/7–6/30	7/1–7/25	7/26–8/19
1966	5/6–5/31	6/1–6/26	6/27–7/21	7/22–8/15	8/16–9/8	9/9–10/2
1967	2/24–3/20	3/21–4/14	4/15–5/10	5/11–6/6	6/7–7/8	7/9–9/9
					9/10–10/1	10/2–11/9
1968	4/9–5/3	5/4–5/27	5/28–6/20	6/21–7/15	7/16–8/8	8/9–9/2
1969	2/3–6/6	6/7–7/6	7/7–8/3	8/4–8/28	8/29–9/22	9/23–10/17
1970	3/11–4/3	4/4–4/27	4/28–5/22	5/23–6/16	6/17–7/12	7/13–8/8
1971	4/24–5/18	5/19–6/12	6/13–7/6	7/7–7/31	8/1–8/24	8/25–9/17
1972	2/11–3/7	3/8–4/3	4/4–5/10	5/11–6/11		
			6/12–8/6	8/7–9/8	9/9–10/5	10/6–10/30
1973	3/25–4/18	4/18–5/12	5/13–6/5	6/6–6/29	7/1–7/25	7/26–8/19
1974	5/5–5/31	6/1–6/25	6/26–7/21	7/22–8/14	8/15–9/8	9/9–10/2
1975	2/24–3/20	3/21–4/13	4/14–5/9	5/10–6/6	6/7–7/9	7/10–9/2
					9/3–10/4	10/5–11/9

84

Libra	Scorpio	Sagittarius	Capricorn	Aquarius	Pisces
9/4–9/27	1/1–1/2	1/3–1/27	1/28–2/20	2/21–3/16	3/17–4/9
	9/28–10/21	10/22–11/15	11/16–12/10	12/11–12/31	
10/19–11/11	11/12–12/5	12/6–12/29	12/30–12/31	1/1–1/5	1/6–2/1
8/9–9/6	9/7–10/22	10/23–10/27	1/1–1/22	1/23–2/15	2/16–3/11
	10/28–12/31				
9/19–10/13	1/1–1/6	1/7–2/5	2/6–3/4	3/5–3/30	3/31–4/24
	10/14–11/5	11/6–11/30	12/1–12/24	12/25–12/31	
11/1–11/25	11/26–12/19	12/20–12/31		1/1–1/17	1/18–2/11
8/20–9/14	9/15–10/9	1/1–1/12	1/13–2/5	2/6–3/1	3/2–3/25
		10/10–11/5	11/6–12/6	12/7–12/31	
10/4–10/27	10/28–11/20	11/21–12/14	12/15–12/31	1/1–4/6	4/7–5/5
11/10–12/7	12/8–12/31		1/1–1/7	1/8–1/31	2/1–2/24
9/3–9/26	1/1–1/2	1/3–1/27	1/28–2/20	2/21–3/15	3/16–4/9
	9/27–10/21	10/22–11/15	11/16–12/10	12/11–12/31	
10/18–11/11	11/12–12/4	12/5–12/28	12/29–12/31	1/1–1/5	1/6–2/2
8/9–9/6	9/7–12/31		1/1–1/21	1/22–2/14	2/15–3/10
9/19–10/12	1/1–1/6	1/7–2/5	2/6–3/4	3/5–3/29	3/30–4/23
	10/13–11/5	11/6–11/29	11/30–12/23	12/24–12/31	
11/1–11/24	11/25–12/19	12/20–12/31		1/1–1/16	1/17–2/10
8/20–9/13	9/14–10/9	1/1–1/12	1/13–2/5	2/6–3/1	3/2–3/25
		10/10–11/5	11/6–12/7	12/8–12/31	
10/3–10/26	10/27–11/19	11/20–12/13	2/7–2/25	1/1–2/6	4/7–5/5
			12/14–12/31	2/26–4/6	
11/10–12/7	12/8–12/31		1/1–1/6	1/7–1/30	1/31–2/23
9/3–9/26	1/1	1/2–1/26	1/27–2/20	2/21–3/15	3/16–4/8
	9/27–10/21	10/22–11/14	11/15–12/9	12/10–12/31	
10/18–11/10	11/11–12/4	12/5–12/28	12/29–12/31	1/1–1/4	1/5–2/2
8/9–9/7	9/8–12/31		1/1–1/21	1/22–2/14	2/15–3/10
9/18–10/11	1/1–1/7	1/8–2/5	2/6–3/4	3/5–3/29	3/30–4/23
	10/12–11/5	11/6–11/29	11/30–12/23	12/24–12/31	
10/31–11/24	11/25–12/18	12/19–12/31		1/1–1/16	1/17–2/10
8/20–9/13	9/14–10/8	1/1–1/12	1/13–2/4	2/5–2/28	3/1–3/24
		10/9–11/5	11/6–12/7	12/8–12/31	
10/3–10/26	10/27–11/19	11/20–12/13	12/14–12/31	3/1–4/6	4/7–5/4
			1/30–2/28	1/1–1/29	
11/10–12/7	12/8–12/31		1/1–1/6	1/7–1/30	1/31–2/23

VENUS SIGNS 1901–2008

	Aries	Taurus	Gemini	Cancer	Leo	Virgo
1976	4/8–5/2	5/2–5/27	5/27–6/20	6/20–7/14	7/14–8/8	8/8–9/1
1977	2/2–6/6	6/6–7/6	7/6–8/2	8/2–8/28	8/28–9/22	9/22–10/17
1978	3/9–4/2	4/2–4/27	4/27–5/22	5/22–6/16	6/16–7/12	7/12–8/6
1979	4/23–5/18	5/18–6/11	6/11–7/6	7/6–7/30	7/30–8/24	8/24–9/17
1980	2/9–3/6	3/6–4/3	4/3–5/12	5/12–6/5	9/7–10/4	10/4–10/30
			6/5–8/6	8/6–9/7		
1981	3/24–4/17	4/17–5/11	5/11–6/5	6/5–6/29	6/29–7/24	7/24–8/18
1982	5/4–5/30	5/30–6/25	6/25–7/20	7/20–8/14	8/14–9/7	9/7–10/2
1983	2/22–3/19	3/19–4/13	4/13–5/9	5/9–6/6	6/6–7/10	7/10–8/27
					8/27–10/5	10/5–11/9
1984	4/7–5/2	5/2–5/26	5/26–6/20	6/20–7/14	7/14–8/7	8/7–9/1
1985	2/2–6/6	6/7–7/6	7/6–8/2	8/2–8/28	8/28–9/22	9/22–10/16
1986	3/9–4/2	4/2–4/26	4/26–5/21	5/21–6/15	6/15–7/11	7/11–8/7
1987	4/22–5/17	5/17–6/11	6/11–7/5	7/5–7/30	7/30–8/23	8/23–9/16
1988	2/9–3/6	3/6–4/3	4/3–5/17	5/17–5/27	9/7–10/4	10/4–10/29
			5/27–8/6	8/28–9/22	9/22–10/16	
1989	3/23–4/16	4/16–5/11	5/11–6/4	6/4–6/29	6/29–7/24	7/24–8/18
1990	5/4–5/30	5/30–6/25	6/25–7/20	7/20–8/13	8/13–9/7	9/7–10/1
1991	2/22–3/18	3/18–4/13	4/13–5/9	5/9–6/6	6/6–7/11	7/11–8/21
					8/21–10/6	10/6–11/9
1992	4/7–5/1	5/1–5/26	5/26–6/19	6/19–7/13	7/13–8/7	8/7–8/31
1993	2/2–6/6	6/6–7/6	7/6–8/1	8/1–8/27	8/27–9/21	9/21–10/16
1994	3/8–4/1	4/1–4/26	4/26–5/21	5/21–6/15	6/15–7/11	7/11–8/7
1995	4/22–5/16	5/16–6/10	6/10–7/5	7/5–7/29	7/29–8/23	8/23–9/16
1996	2/9–3/6	3/6–4/3	4/3–8/7	8/7–9/7	9/7–10/4	10/4–10/29
1997	3/23–4/16	4/16–5/10	5/10–6/4	6/4–6/28	6/28–7/23	7/23–8/17
1998	5/3–5/29	5/29–6/24	6/24–7/19	7/19–8/13	8/13–9/6	9/6–9/30
1999	2/21–3/18	3/18–4/12	4/12–5/8	5/8–6/5	6/5–7/12	7/12–8/15
					8/15–10/7	10/7–11/9
2000	4/6–5/1	5/1–5/25	5/25–6/13	6/13–7/13	7/13–8/6	8/6–8/31
2001	2/2–6/6	6/6–7/5	7/5–8/1	8/1–8/26	8/26–9/20	9/20–10/15
2002	3/7–4/1	4/1–4/25	4/25–5/20	5/20–6/14	6/14–7/10	7/10–8/7
2003	4/21–5/16	5/16–6/9	6/9–7/4	7/4–7/29	7/29–8/22	8/22–9/15
2004	2/8–3/5	3/5–4/3	4/3–8/7	8/7–9/6	9/6–10/3	10/3–10/28
2005	3/22–4/15	4/15–5/10	5/10–6/3	6/3–6/28	6/28–7/23	7/23–8/17
2006	5/3–5/29	5/29–6/24	6/24–7/19	7/19–8/12	8/12–9/6	9/6–9/30
2007	2/21–3/16	3/17–4/10	4/11–5/7	5/8–6/4	6/5–7/13	7/14–8/7
					8/10–10/6	10/7–11/7
2008	4/6–4/30	5/1–5/24	5/25–6/17	6/18–7/11	7/12–8/4	8/5–8/29

Libra	Scorpio	Sagittarius	Capricorn	Aquarius	Pisces
9/1–9/26	9/26–10/20	1/1–1/26	1/26–2/19	2/19–3/15	3/15–4/8
10/17–11/10	11/10–12/4	12/4–12/27	12/27–1/20/78		1/4–2/2
8/6–9/7	9/7–1/7			1/20–2/13	2/13–3/9
9/17–10/11	10/11–11/4	1/7–2/5	2/5–3/3	3/3–3/29	3/29–4/23
		11/4–11/28	11/28–12/22	12/22–1/16/80	
10/30–11/24	11/24–12/18	12/18–1/11/81			1/16–2/9
8/18–9/12	9/12–10/9	10/9–11/5	1/11–2/4	2/4–2/28	2/28–3/24
			11/5–12/8	12/8–1/23/82	
10/2–10/26	10/26–11/18	11/18–12/12	1/23–3/2	3/2–4/6	4/6–5/4
			12/12–1/5/83		
11/9–12/6	12/6–1/1/84			1/5–1/29	1/29–2/22
9/1–9/25	9/25–10/20	1/1–1/25	1/25–2/19	2/19–3/14	3/14–4/7
		10/20–11/13	11/13–12/9	12/10–1/4	
10/16–11/9	11/9–12/3	12/3–12/27	12/28–1/19		1/4–2/2
8/7–9/7	9/7–1/7			1/20–2/13	2/13–3/9
9/16–10/10	10/10–11/3	1/7–2/5	2/5–3/3	3/3–3/28	3/28–4/22
		11/3–11/28	11/28–12/22	12/22–1/15	
10/29–11/23	11/23–12/17	12/17–1/10			1/15–2/9
8/18–9/12	9/12–10/8	10/8–11/5	1/10–2/3	2/3–2/27	2/27–3/23
			11/5–12/10	12/10–1/16/90	
10/1–10/25	10/25–11/18	11/18–12/12	1/16–3/3	3/3–4/6	4/6–5/4
			12/12–1/5		
11/9–12/6	12/6–12/31	12/31–1/25/92		1/5–1/29	1/29–2/22
8/31–9/25	9/25–10/19	10/19–11/13	1/25–2/18	2/18–3/13	3/13–4/7
			11/13–12/8	12/8–1/3/93	
10/16–11/9	11/9–12/2	12/2–12/26	12/26–1/19		1/3–2/2
8/7–9/7	9/7–1/7			1/19–2/12	2/12–3/8
9/16–10/10	10/10–11/13	1/7–2/4	2/4–3/2	3/2–3/28	3/28–4/22
		11/3–11/27	11/27–12/21	12/21–1/15	
10/29–11/23	11/23–12/17	12/17–1/10/97			1/15–2/9
8/17–9/12	9/12–10/8	10/8–11/5	1/10–2/3	2/3–2/27	2/27–3/23
			11/5–12/12	12/12–1/9	
9/30–10/24	10/24–11/17	11/17–12/11	1/9–3/4	3/4–4/6	4/6–5/3
11/9–12/5	12/5–12/31	12/31–1/24		1/4–1/28	1/28–2/21
8/31–9/24	9/24–10/19	10/19–11/13	1/24–2/18	2/18–3/12	3/13–4/6
			11/13–12/8	12/8	
10/15–11/8	11/8–12/2	12/2–12/26	12/26/01–1/18/02	12/8/00–1/3/01	1/3–2/2
8/7–9/7	9/7–1/7/03		12/26/01–1/18	1/18–2/11	2/11–3/7
9/15–10/9	10/9–11/2	1/7–2/4	2/4–3/2	3/2–3/27	3/27–4/21
		11/2–11/26	11/26–12/21	12/21–1/14/04	
10/28–11/22	11/22–12/16	12/16–1/9/05		1/1–1/14	1/14–2/8
8/17–9/11	9/11–10/8	10/8–11/15	1/9–2/2	2/2–2/26	2/26–3/23
			11/5–12/15	12/15–1/1/06	
9/30–10/24	10/24–11/17	11/17–12/11	1/1–3/5	3/5–4/6	4/6–5/3
11/8–12/4	12/5–12/29	12/30–1/24/08		1/3–1/26	1/27–2/20
8/30–9/22	9/23–10/17	10/18–11/11	1/24–2/16	2/17–3/11	3/12–4/5
			11/12–12/6	12/7–1/2/09	

How to Use the Mars, Jupiter, and Saturn Tables

Find the year of your birth on the left side of each column. The dates when the planet entered each sign are listed on the right side of each column. (Signs are abbreviated to three letters.) Your birthday should fall on or between each date listed, and your planetary placement should correspond to the earlier sign of that period.

All planet changes are calculated for the Greenwich Mean Time zone.

MARS SIGNS 1901–2008

1901	MAR	1	Leo		OCT	1	Vir
	MAY	11	Vir		NOV	20	Lib
	JUL	13	Lib	1905	JAN	13	Scp
	AUG	31	Scp		AUG	21	Sag
	OCT	14	Sag		OCT	8	Cap
	NOV	24	Cap		NOV	18	Aqu
1902	JAN	1	Aqu		DEC	27	Pic
	FEB	8	Pic	1906	FEB	4	Ari
	MAR	19	Ari		MAR	17	Tau
	APR	27	Tau		APR	28	Gem
	JUN	7	Gem		JUN	11	Can
	JUL	20	Can		JUL	27	Leo
	SEP	4	Leo		SEP	12	Vir
	OCT	23	Vir		OCT	30	Lib
	DEC	20	Lib		DEC	17	Scp
1903	APR	19	Vir	1907	FEB	5	Sag
	MAY	30	Lib		APR	1	Cap
	AUG	6	Scp		OCT	13	Aqu
	SEP	22	Sag		NOV	29	Pic
	NOV	3	Cap	1908	JAN	11	Ari
	DEC	12	Aqu		FEB	23	Tau
1904	JAN	19	Pic		APR	7	Gem
	FEB	27	Ari		MAY	22	Can
	APR	6	Tau		JUL	8	Leo
	MAY	18	Gem		AUG	24	Vir
	JUN	30	Can		OCT	10	Lib
	AUG	15	Leo		NOV	25	Scp

1909	JAN	10	Sag		MAR	9	Pic
	FEB	24	Cap		APR	16	Ari
	APR	9	Aqu		MAY	26	Tau
	MAY	25	Pic		JUL	6	Gem
	JUL	21	Ari		AUG	19	Can
	SEP	26	Pic		OCT	7	Leo
	NOV	20	Ari	1916	MAY	28	Vir
1910	JAN	23	Tau		JUL	23	Lib
	MAR	14	Gem		SEP	8	Scp
	MAY	1	Can		OCT	22	Sag
	JUN	19	Leo		DEC	1	Cap
	AUG	6	Vir	1917	JAN	9	Aqu
	SEP	22	Lib		FEB	16	Pic
	NOV	6	Scp		MAR	26	Ari
	DEC	20	Sag		MAY	4	Tau
1911	JAN	31	Cap		JUN	14	Gem
	MAR	14	Aqu		JUL	28	Can
	APR	23	Pic		SEP	12	Leo
	JUN	2	Ari		NOV	2	Vir
	JUL	15	Tau	1918	JAN	11	Lib
	SEP	5	Gem		FEB	25	Vir
	NOV	30	Tau		JUN	23	Lib
1912	JAN	30	Gem		AUG	17	Scp
	APR	5	Can		OCT	1	Sag
	MAY	28	Leo		NOV	11	Cap
	JUL	17	Vir		DEC	20	Aqu
	SEP	2	Lib	1919	JAN	27	Pic
	OCT	18	Scp		MAR	6	Ari
	NOV	30	Sag		APR	15	Tau
1913	JAN	10	Cap		MAY	26	Gem
	FEB	19	Aqu		JUL	8	Can
	MAR	30	Pic		AUG	23	Leo
	MAY	8	Ari		OCT	10	Vir
	JUN	17	Tau		NOV	30	Lib
	JUL	29	Gem	1920	JAN	31	Scp
	SEP	15	Can		APR	23	Lib
1914	MAY	1	Leo		JUL	10	Scp
	JUN	26	Vir		SEP	4	Sag
	AUG	14	Lib		OCT	18	Cap
	SEP	29	Scp		NOV	27	Aqu
	NOV	11	Sag	1921	JAN	5	Pic
	DEC	22	Cap		FEB	13	Ari
1915	JAN	30	Aqu		MAR	25	Tau

	MAY	6	Gem		OCT	26	Scp
	JUN	18	Can		DEC	8	Sag
	AUG	3	Leo	1928	JAN	19	Cap
	SEP	19	Vir		FEB	28	Aqu
	NOV	6	Lib		APR	7	Pic
	DEC	26	Scp		MAY	16	Ari
1922	FEB	18	Sag		JUN	26	Tau
	SEP	13	Cap		AUG	9	Gem
	OCT	30	Aqu		OCT	3	Can
	DEC	11	Pic		DEC	20	Gem
1923	JAN	21	Ari	1929	MAR	10	Can
	MAR	4	Tau		MAY	13	Leo
	APR	16	Gem		JUL	4	Vir
	MAY	30	Can		AUG	21	Lib
	JUL	16	Leo		OCT	6	Scp
	SEP	1	Vir		NOV	18	Sag
	OCT	18	Lib		DEC	29	Cap
	DEC	4	Scp	1930	FEB	6	Aqu
1924	JAN	19	Sag		MAR	17	Pic
	MAR	6	Cap		APR	24	Ari
	APR	24	Aqu		JUN	3	Tau
	JUN	24	Pic		JUL	14	Gem
	AUG	24	Aqu		AUG	28	Can
	OCT	19	Pic		OCT	20	Leo
	DEC	19	Ari	1931	FEB	16	Can
1925	FEB	5	Tau		MAR	30	Leo
	MAR	24	Gem		JUN	10	Vir
	MAY	9	Can		AUG	1	Lib
	JUN	26	Leo		SEP	17	Scp
	AUG	12	Vir		OCT	30	Sag
	SEP	28	Lib		DEC	10	Cap
	NOV	13	Scp	1932	JAN	18	Aqu
	DEC	28	Sag		FEB	25	Pic
1926	FEB	9	Cap		APR	3	Ari
	MAR	23	Aqu		MAY	12	Tau
	MAY	3	Pic		JUN	22	Gem
	JUN	15	Ari		AUG	4	Can
	AUG	1	Tau		SEP	20	Leo
1927	FEB	22	Gem		NOV	13	Vir
	APR	17	Can	1933	JUL	6	Lib
	JUN	6	Leo		AUG	26	Scp
	JUL	25	Vir		OCT	9	Sag
	SEP	10	Lib		NOV	19	Cap

Year	Mon	Day	Sign		Year	Mon	Day	Sign
	DEC	28	Aqu			FEB	17	Tau
1934	FEB	4	Pic			APR	1	Gem
	MAR	14	Ari			MAY	17	Can
	APR	22	Tau			JUL	3	Leo
	JUN	2	Gem			AUG	19	Vir
	JUL	15	Can			OCT	5	Lib
	AUG	30	Leo			NOV	20	Scp
	OCT	18	Vir		1941	JAN	4	Sag
	DEC	11	Lib			FEB	17	Cap
1935	JUL	29	Scp			APR	2	Aqu
	SEP	16	Sag			MAY	16	Pic
	OCT	28	Cap			JUL	2	Ari
	DEC	7	Aqu		1942	JAN	11	Tau
1936	JAN	14	Pic			MAR	7	Gem
	FEB	22	Ari			APR	26	Can
	APR	1	Tau			JUN	14	Leo
	MAY	13	Gem			AUG	1	Vir
	JUN	25	Can			SEP	17	Lib
	AUG	10	Leo			NOV	1	Scp
	SEP	26	Vir			DEC	15	Sag
	NOV	14	Lib		1943	JAN	26	Cap
1937	JAN	5	Scp			MAR	8	Aqu
	MAR	13	Sag			APR	17	Pic
	MAY	14	Scp			MAY	27	Ari
	AUG	8	Sag			JUL	7	Tau
	SEP	30	Cap			AUG	23	Gem
	NOV	11	Aqu		1944	MAR	28	Can
	DEC	21	Pic			MAY	22	Leo
1938	JAN	30	Ari			JUL	12	Vir
	MAR	12	Tau			AUG	29	Lib
	APR	23	Gem			OCT	13	Scp
	JUN	7	Can			NOV	25	Sag
	JUL	22	Leo		1945	JAN	5	Cap
	SEP	7	Vir			FEB	14	Aqu
	OCT	25	Lib			MAR	25	Pic
	DEC	11	Scp			MAY	2	Ari
1939	JAN	29	Sag			JUN	11	Tau
	MAR	21	Cap			JUL	23	Gem
	MAY	25	Aqu			SEP	7	Can
	JUL	21	Cap			NOV	11	Leo
	SEP	24	Aqu			DEC	26	Can
	NOV	19	Pic		1946	APR	22	Leo
1940	JAN	4	Ari			JUN	20	Vir

	AUG	9	Lib		OCT	12	Cap
	SEP	24	Scp		NOV	21	Aqu
	NOV	6	Sag		DEC	30	Pic
	DEC	17	Cap	1953	FEB	8	Ari
1947	JAN	25	Aqu		MAR	20	Tau
	MAR	4	Pic		MAY	1	Gem
	APR	11	Ari		JUN	14	Can
	MAY	21	Tau		JUL	29	Leo
	JUL	1	Gem		SEP	14	Vir
	AUG	13	Can		NOV	1	Lib
	OCT	1	Leo		DEC	20	Scp
	DEC	1	Vir	1954	FEB	9	Sag
1948	FEB	12	Leo		APR	12	Cap
	MAY	18	Vir		JUL	3	Sag
	JUL	17	Lib		AUG	24	Cap
	SEP	3	Scp		OCT	21	Aqu
	OCT	17	Sag		DEC	4	Pic
	NOV	26	Cap	1955	JAN	15	Ari
1949	JAN	4	Aqu		FEB	26	Tau
	FEB	11	Pic		APR	10	Gem
	MAR	21	Ari		MAY	26	Can
	APR	30	Tau		JUL	11	Leo
	JUN	10	Gem		AUG	27	Vir
	JUL	23	Can		OCT	13	Lib
	SEP	7	Leo		NOV	29	Scp
	OCT	27	Vir	1956	JAN	14	Sag
	DEC	26	Lib		FEB	28	Cap
1950	MAR	28	Vir		APR	14	Aqu
	JUN	11	Lib		JUN	3	Pic
	AUG	10	Scp		DEC	6	Ari
	SEP	25	Sag	1957	JAN	28	Tau
	NOV	6	Cap		MAR	17	Gem
	DEC	15	Aqu		MAY	4	Can
1951	JAN	22	Pic		JUN	21	Leo
	MAR	1	Ari		AUG	8	Vir
	APR	10	Tau		SEP	24	Lib
	MAY	21	Gem		NOV	8	Scp
	JUL	3	Can		DEC	23	Sag
	AUG	18	Leo	1958	FEB	3	Cap
	OCT	5	Vir		MAR	17	Aqu
	NOV	24	Lib		APR	27	Pic
1952	JAN	20	Scp		JUN	7	Ari
	AUG	27	Sag		JUL	21	Tau

	SEP	21	Gem		NOV	6	Vir
	OCT	29	Tau	1965	JUN	29	Lib
1959	FEB	10	Gem		AUG	20	Scp
	APR	10	Can		OCT	4	Sag
	JUN	1	Leo		NOV	14	Cap
	JUL	20	Vir		DEC	23	Aqu
	SEP	5	Lib	1966	JAN	30	Pic
	OCT	21	Scp		MAR	9	Ari
	DEC	3	Sag		APR	17	Tau
1960	JAN	14	Cap		MAY	28	Gem
	FEB	23	Aqu		JUL	11	Can
	APR	2	Pic		AUG	25	Leo
	MAY	11	Ari		OCT	12	Vir
	JUN	20	Tau		DEC	4	Lib
	AUG	2	Gem	1967	FEB	12	Scp
	SEP	21	Can		MAR	31	Lib
1961	FEB	5	Gem		JUL	19	Scp
	FEB	7	Can		SEP	10	Sag
	MAY	6	Leo		OCT	23	Cap
	JUN	28	Vir		DEC	1	Aqu
	AUG	17	Lib	1968	JAN	9	Pic
	OCT	1	Scp		FEB	17	Ari
	NOV	13	Sag		MAR	27	Tau
	DEC	24	Cap		MAY	8	Gem
1962	FEB	1	Aqu		JUN	21	Can
	MAR	12	Pic		AUG	5	Leo
	APR	19	Ari		SEP	21	Vir
	MAY	28	Tau		NOV	9	Lib
	JUL	9	Gem		DEC	29	Scp
	AUG	22	Can	1969	FEB	25	Sag
	OCT	11	Leo		SEP	21	Cap
1963	JUN	3	Vir		NOV	4	Aqu
	JUL	27	Lib		DEC	15	Pic
	SEP	12	Scp	1970	JAN	24	Ari
	OCT	25	Sag		MAR	7	Tau
	DEC	5	Cap		APR	18	Gem
1964	JAN	13	Aqu		JUN	2	Can
	FEB	20	Pic		JUL	18	Leo
	MAR	29	Ari		SEP	3	Vir
	MAY	7	Tau		OCT	20	Lib
	JUN	17	Gem		DEC	6	Scp
	JUL	30	Can	1971	JAN	23	Sag
	SEP	15	Leo		MAR	12	Cap

	MAY	3	Aqu		JUN	6	Tau
	NOV	6	Pic		JUL	17	Gem
	DEC	26	Ari		SEP	1	Can
1972	FEB	10	Tau		OCT	26	Leo
	MAR	27	Gem	1978	JAN	26	Can
	MAY	12	Can		APR	10	Leo
	JUN	28	Leo		JUN	14	Vir
	AUG	15	Vir		AUG	4	Lib
	SEP	30	Lib		SEP	19	Scp
	NOV	15	Scp		NOV	2	Sag
	DEC	30	Sag		DEC	12	Cap
1973	FEB	12	Cap	1979	JAN	20	Aqu
	MAR	26	Aqu		FEB	27	Pic
	MAY	8	Pic		APR	7	Ari
	JUN	20	Ari		MAY	16	Tau
	AUG	12	Tau		JUN	26	Gem
	OCT	29	Ari		AUG	8	Can
	DEC	24	Tau		SEP	24	Leo
1974	FEB	27	Gem		NOV	19	Vir
	APR	20	Can	1980	MAR	11	Leo
	JUN	9	Leo		MAY	4	Vir
	JUL	27	Vir		JUL	10	Lib
	SEP	12	Lib		AUG	29	Scp
	OCT	28	Scp		OCT	12	Sag
	DEC	10	Sag		NOV	22	Cap
1975	JAN	21	Cap		DEC	30	Aqu
	MAR	3	Aqu	1981	FEB	6	Pic
	APR	11	Pic		MAR	17	Ari
	MAY	21	Ari		APR	25	Tau
	JUL	1	Tau		JUN	5	Gem
	AUG	14	Gem		JUL	18	Can
	OCT	17	Can		SEP	2	Leo
	NOV	25	Gem		OCT	21	Vir
1976	MAR	18	Can		DEC	16	Lib
	MAY	16	Leo	1982	AUG	3	Scp
	JUL	6	Vir		SEP	20	Sag
	AUG	24	Lib		OCT	31	Cap
	OCT	8	Scp		DEC	10	Aqu
	NOV	20	Sag	1983	JAN	17	Pic
1977	JAN	1	Cap		FEB	25	Ari
	FEB	9	Aqu		APR	5	Tau
	MAR	20	Pic		MAY	16	Gem
	APR	27	Ari		JUN	29	Can

	AUG	13	Leo	1990	JAN	29	Cap
	SEP	30	Vir		MAR	11	Aqu
	NOV	18	Lib		APR	20	Pic
1984	JAN	11	Scp		MAY	31	Ari
	AUG	17	Sag		JUL	12	Tau
	OCT	5	Cap		AUG	31	Gem
	NOV	15	Aqu		DEC	14	Tau
	DEC	25	Pic	1991	JAN	21	Gem
1985	FEB	2	Ari		APR	3	Can
	MAR	15	Tau		MAY	26	Leo
	APR	26	Gem		JUL	15	Vir
	JUN	9	Can		SEP	1	Lib
	JUL	25	Leo		OCT	16	Scp
	SEP	10	Vir		NOV	29	Sag
	OCT	27	Lib	1992	JAN	9	Cap
	DEC	14	Scp		FEB	18	Aqu
1986	FEB	2	Sag		MAR	28	Pic
	MAR	28	Cap		MAY	5	Ari
	OCT	9	Aqu		JUN	14	Tau
	NOV	26	Pic		JUL	26	Gem
1987	JAN	8	Ari		SEP	12	Can
	FEB	20	Tau	1993	APR	27	Leo
	APR	5	Gem		JUN	23	Vir
	MAY	21	Can		AUG	12	Lib
	JUL	6	Leo		SEP	27	Scp
	AUG	22	Vir		NOV	9	Sag
	OCT	8	Lib		DEC	20	Cap
	NOV	24	Scp	1994	JAN	28	Aqu
1988	JAN	8	Sag		MAR	7	Pic
	FEB	22	Cap		APR	14	Ari
	APR	6	Aqu		MAY	23	Tau
	MAY	22	Pic		JUL	3	Gem
	JUL	13	Ari		AUG	16	Can
	OCT	23	Pic		OCT	4	Leo
	NOV	1	Ari		DEC	12	Vir
1989	JAN	19	Tau	1995	JAN	22	Leo
	MAR	11	Gem		MAY	25	Vir
	APR	29	Can		JUL	21	Lib
	JUN	16	Leo		SEP	7	Scp
	AUG	3	Vir		OCT	20	Sag
	SEP	19	Lib		NOV	30	Cap
	NOV	4	Scp	1996	JAN	8	Aqu
	DEC	18	Sag		FEB	15	Pic

Year	Mon	Day	Sign	Year	Mon	Day	Sign
	MAR	24	Ari		MAR	1	Tau
	MAY	2	Tau		APR	13	Gem
	JUN	12	Gem		MAY	28	Can
	JUL	25	Can		JUL	13	Leo
	SEP	9	Leo		AUG	29	Vir
	OCT	30	Vir		OCT	15	Lib
1997	JAN	3	Lib		DEC	1	Scp
	MAR	8	Vir	2003	JAN	17	Sag
	JUN	19	Lib		MAR	4	Cap
	AUG	14	Scp		APR	21	Aqu
	SEP	28	Sag		JUN	17	Pic
	NOV	9	Cap		DEC	16	Ari
	DEC	18	Aqu	2004	FEB	3	Tau
1998	JAN	25	Pic		MAR	21	Gem
	MAR	4	Ari		MAY	7	Can
	APR	13	Tau		JUN	23	Leo
	MAY	24	Gem		AUG	10	Vir
	JUL	6	Can		SEP	26	Lib
	AUG	20	Leo		NOV	11	Sep
	OCT	7	Vir		DEC	25	Sag
	NOV	27	Lib	2005	FEB	6	Cap
1999	JAN	26	Scp		MAR	20	Aqu
	MAY	5	Lib		MAY	1	Pic
	JUL	5	Scp		JUN	12	Ari
	SEP	2	Sag		JUL	28	Tau
	OCT	17	Cap	2006	FEB	17	Gem
	NOV	26	Aqu		APR	14	Can
2000	JAN	4	Pic		JUN	3	Leo
	FEB	12	Ari		JUL	22	Vir
	MAR	23	Tau		SEP	8	Lib
	MAY	3	Gem		OCT	23	Scp
	JUN	16	Can		DEC	6	Sag
	AUG	1	Leo	2007	JAN	16	Cap
	SEP	17	Vir		FEB	25	Aqu
	NOV	4	Lib		APR	6	Pic
	DEC	23	Scp		MAY	15	Ari
2001	FEB	14	Sag		JUNE	24	Tau
	SEP	8	Cap		AUG	7	Gem
	OCT	27	Aqu		SEP	28	Can
	DEC	8	Pic		DEC	31	Gem*
2002	JAN	18	Ari				

*Repeat means planet is retrograde.

2008	MAR	4	Can		OCT	3	Scp
	MAY	9	Leo		NOV	16	Sag
	JUL	1	Vir		DEC	27	Cap
	AUG	19	Lib				

JUPITER SIGNS 1901–2008

1901	JAN	19	Cap			SEP	11	Pic
1902	FEB	6	Aqu		1928	JAN	23	Ari
1903	FEB	20	Pic			JUN	4	Tau
1904	MAR	1	Ari		1929	JUN	12	Gem
	AUG	8	Tau		1930	JUN	26	Can
	AUG	31	Ari		1931	JUL	17	Leo
1905	MAR	7	Tau		1932	AUG	11	Vir
	JUL	21	Gem		1933	SEP	10	Lib
	DEC	4	Tau		1934	OCT	11	Scp
1906	MAR	9	Gem		1935	NOV	9	Sag
	JUL	30	Can		1936	DEC	2	Cap
1907	AUG	18	Leo		1937	DEC	20	Aqu
1908	SEP	12	Vir		1938	MAY	14	Pic
1909	OCT	11	Lib			JUL	30	Aqu
1910	NOV	11	Scp			DEC	29	Pic
1911	DEC	10	Sag		1939	MAY	11	Ari
1913	JAN	2	Cap			OCT	30	Pic
1914	JAN	21	Aqu			DEC	20	Ari
1915	FEB	4	Pic		1940	MAY	16	Tau
1916	FEB	12	Ari		1941	MAY	26	Gem
	JUN	26	Tau		1942	JUN	10	Can
	OCT	26	Ari		1943	JUN	30	Leo
1917	FEB	12	Tau		1944	JUL	26	Vir
	JUN	29	Gem		1945	AUG	25	Lib
1918	JUL	13	Can		1946	SEP	25	Scp
1919	AUG	2	Leo		1947	OCT	24	Sag
1920	AUG	27	Vir		1948	NOV	15	Cap
1921	SEP	25	Lib		1949	APR	12	Aqu
1922	OCT	26	Scp			JUN	27	Cap
1923	NOV	24	Sag			NOV	30	Aqu
1924	DEC	18	Cap		1950	APR	15	Pic
1926	JAN	6	Aqu			SEP	15	Aqu
1927	JAN	18	Pic			DEC	1	Pic
	JUN	6	Ari		1951	APR	21	Ari

1952	APR	28	Tau
1953	MAY	9	Gem
1954	MAY	24	Can
1955	JUN	13	Leo
	NOV	17	Vir
1956	JAN	18	Leo
	JUL	7	Vir
	DEC	13	Lib
1957	FEB	19	Vir
	AUG	7	Lib
1958	JAN	13	Scp
	MAR	20	Lib
	SEP	7	Scp
1959	FEB	10	Sag
	APR	24	Scp
	OCT	5	Sag
1960	MAR	1	Cap
	JUN	10	Sag
	OCT	26	Cap
1961	MAR	15	Aqu
	AUG	12	Cap
	NOV	4	Aqu
1962	MAR	25	Pic
1963	APR	4	Ari
1964	APR	12	Tau
1965	APR	22	Gem
	SEP	21	Can
	NOV	17	Gem
1966	MAY	5	Can
	SEP	27	Leo
1967	JAN	16	Can
	MAY	23	Leo
	OCT	19	Vir
1968	FEB	27	Leo
	JUN	15	Vir
	NOV	15	Lib
1969	MAR	30	Vir
	JUL	15	Lib
	DEC	16	Scp
1970	APR	30	Lib

	AUG	15	Scp
1971	JAN	14	Sag
	JUN	5	Scp
	SEP	11	Sag
1972	FEB	6	Cap
	JUL	24	Sag
	SEP	25	Cap
1973	FEB	23	Aqu
1974	MAR	8	Pic
1975	MAR	18	Ari
1976	MAR	26	Tau
	AUG	23	Gem
	OCT	16	Tau
1977	APR	3	Gem
	AUG	20	Can
	DEC	30	Gem
1978	APR	12	Can
	SEP	5	Leo
1979	FEB	28	Can
	APR	20	Leo
	SEP	29	Vir
1980	OCT	27	Lib
1981	NOV	27	Scp
1982	DEC	26	Sag
1984	JAN	19	Cap
1985	FEB	6	Aqu
1986	FEB	20	Pic
1987	MAR	2	Ari
1988	MAR	8	Tau
	JUL	22	Gem
	NOV	30	Tau
1989	MAR	11	Gem
	JUL	30	Can
1990	AUG	18	Leo
1991	SEP	12	Vir
1992	OCT	10	Lib
1993	NOV	10	Scp
1994	DEC	9	Sag
1996	JAN	3	Cap
1997	JAN	21	Aqu
1998	FEB	4	Pic

1999	FEB	13	Ari	2003	AUG	27	Vir
	JUN	28	Tau	2004	SEP	24	Lib
	OCT	23	Ari	2005	OCT	26	Scp
2000	FEB	14	Tau	2006	NOV	24	Sag
	JUN	30	Gem	2007	DEC	17	Cap
2001	JUL	14	Can	2008			Cap
2002	AUG	1	Leo				

SATURN SIGNS 1903–2008

1903	JAN	19	Aqu		OCT	18	Pic
1905	APR	13	Pic	1938	JAN	14	Ari
	AUG	17	Aqu	1939	JUL	6	Tau
1906	JAN	8	Pic		SEP	22	Ari
1908	MAR	19	Ari	1940	MAR	20	Tau
1910	MAY	17	Tau	1942	MAY	8	Gem
	DEC	14	Ari	1944	JUN	20	Can
1911	JAN	20	Tau	1946	AUG	2	Leo
1912	JUL	7	Gem	1948	SEP	19	Vir
	NOV	30	Tau	1949	APR	3	Leo
1913	MAR	26	Gem		MAY	29	Vir
1914	AUG	24	Can	1950	NOV	20	Lib
	DEC	7	Gem	1951	MAR	7	Vir
1915	MAY	11	Can		AUG	13	Lib
1916	OCT	17	Leo	1953	OCT	22	Scp
	DEC	7	Can	1956	JAN	12	Sag
1917	JUN	24	Leo		MAY	14	Scp
1919	AUG	12	Vir		OCT	10	Sag
1921	OCT	7	Lib	1959	JAN	5	Cap
1923	DEC	20	Scp	1962	JAN	3	Aqu
1924	APR	6	Lib	1964	MAR	24	Pic
	SEP	13	Scp		SEP	16	Aqu
1926	DEC	2	Sag		DEC	16	Pic
1929	MAR	15	Cap	1967	MAR	3	Ari
	MAY	5	Sag	1969	APR	29	Tau
	NOV	30	Cap	1971	JUN	18	Gem
1932	FEB	24	Aqu	1972	JAN	10	Tau
	AUG	13	Cap		FEB	21	Gem
	NOV	20	Aqu	1973	AUG	1	Can
1935	FEB	14	Pic	1974	JAN	7	Gem
1937	APR	25	Ari		APR	18	Can

1975	SEP	17	Leo	1993	MAY	21	Pic
1976	JAN	14	Can		JUN	30	Aqu
	JUN	5	Leo	1994	JAN	28	Pic
1977	NOV	17	Vir	1996	APR	7	Ari
1978	JAN	5	Leo	1998	JUN	9	Tau
	JUL	26	Vir		OCT	25	Ari
1980	SEP	21	Lib	1999	MAR	1	Tau
1982	NOV	29	Scp	2000	AUG	10	Gem
1983	MAY	6	Lib		OCT	16	Tau
	AUG	24	Scp	2001	APR	21	Gem
1985	NOV	17	Sag	2003	JUN	3	Can
1988	FEB	13	Cap	2005	JUL	16	Leo
	JUN	10	Sag	2007	SEP	2	Vir
	NOV	12	Cap	2008			Vir
1991	FEB	6	Aqu				

CHAPTER 7

The Leader of the Parade: Your Rising Sign

Your rising sign is the degree of the zodiac ascending over the eastern horizon at the time you were born. (That's why it's often called the ascendant.) It is important to know the rising sign, because it determines *where* things happen in the horoscope chart. It marks the first point in the horoscope, the beginning of the first house, one of twelve divisions of the horoscope, each of which represents a different area of life. After the rising sign, the other houses parade around the chart in sequence, with the following sign on the house cusp.

You can learn much about a person by the signs and interactions of the sun, moon, and planets in the horoscope, but you need to know the rising sign to determine where in that person's life an activity will take place. For example, you might know that a person has Mars in Aries, which will describe that person's dynamic, fiery energy. But if you also know that the person has a Capricorn rising sign, this Mars will fall in the fourth house of home and family, so you know where that energy will operate. Without a valid rising sign, the collection of planets have no homes. One would have no idea which area of life would be influenced by a particular planet.

Due to the earth's rotation, the rising sign changes every two hours, which means that even though other babies born later or earlier on the same day in the same hospital as you were will have most planets in the same signs as you, they may not have the same rising sign and their planets may fall in different houses in the chart. For instance, if Mars is in Gemini and your rising sign is Taurus, Mars will most likely be active in the second or financial house of your chart. Someone born later in the day, when the rising sign is Virgo, would have Mars positioned at the top of the chart, energizing the tenth house of career.

Most astrologers insist on knowing the exact time of a client's birth before analyzing a chart. The more accurate your birth time, the more accurately an astrologer can position the planets in your chart by determining the correct rising sign.

How Your Rising Sign Can Influence Your Sun Sign

Your rising sign has an important relationship with your sun sign. Some will complement the sun sign; others hide it under a totally different mask, as if playing an entirely different role, making it difficult to guess the person's sun sign from outer appearances. This may be the reason why you might not look or act like your sun sign's archetype. For example, a Leo with a conservative Capricorn ascendant would come across as much more serious than a Leo with a fiery Aries or Sagittarius ascendant.

Though the rising sign usually creates the first impression you make, there are exceptions. When the sun sign is reinforced by other planets in the same sign, this might overpower the impression of the rising sign. For instance, a Leo sun plus a Leo Venus and Leo Jupiter would counteract the more conservative image that would otherwise be conveyed by the person's Capricorn ascendant.

Those born early in the morning when the sun was on the horizon will be most likely to project the image of their sun sign. These people are often called a "double Aries" or a "double Virgo" because the same sun sign and ascendant reinforce each other.

Find Your Rising Sign

Look up your rising sign from the chart at the end of this chapter. Since rising signs change every two hours, it is important to know your birth time as close to the minute as possible. Even a few minutes' difference could change the rising sign and therefore the setup of your chart. If you are unsure about the exact time, but know within a few hours, check the following descriptions to see which is most like the personality you project.

Aries Rising: Alpha Energy

You are the most aggressive version of your sun sign, with boundless energy that can be used productively if it's channeled in the right direction. Watch a tendency to overreact emotionally and blow your top. You come across as openly competitive, a positive asset in business or sports. Be on guard against impatience, which could lead to head injuries. Your walk and bearing could have the telltale head-forward Aries posture. You may wear more bright colors, especially red, than others of your sign. You may also have a tendency to drive your car faster.

Can you see the alpha Aries tendency in Barbra Streisand (a sun-sign Taurus) and Bette Midler (a sun-sign Sagittarius)?

Taurus Rising: Down to Earth

You're slow-moving, with a beautiful (or distinctive) speaking or singing voice that can be especially soothing or melodious. You probably surround yourself with comfort, good food, luxurious environments, and other sensual pleasures. You prefer welcoming others into your home to gadding about. You may have a talent for business, especially in trading, appraising, and real estate. A Taurus ascendant gives a well-padded physique that gains weight easily, like Liza Minnelli. This ascendant can also endow females with a curvaceous beauty.

Gemini Rising: A Way with Words

You're naturally sociable, with lighter, more ethereal mannerisms than others of your sign, especially if you're female.

You love to communicate with people, and express your ideas and feelings easily, like British prime minister Tony Blair. You may have a talent for writing or public speaking. You thrive on variety, a constantly changing scene, and a lively social life. However, you may relate to others at a deeper level than might be suspected. And you will be far more sympathetic and caring than you project. You will probably travel widely, changing partners and jobs several times (or juggle two at once). Physically, your nerves are quite sensitive. Occasionally, you would benefit from a calm, tranquil atmosphere away from your usual social scene.

Cancer Rising: Nurturing Instincts

You are naturally acquisitive, possessive, private, a moneymaker, like Bill Gates or Michael Bloomberg. You easily pick up on others' needs and feelings—a great gift in business, the arts, and personal relationships. But you must guard against overreacting or taking things too personally, especially during full moon periods. Find creative outlets for your natural nurturing gifts, such as helping the less fortunate, particularly children. Your insights would be helpful in psychology. Your desire to feed and care for others would be useful in the restaurant, hotel, or child-care industries. You may be especially fond of wearing romantic old clothes, collecting antiques, and, of course, dining on exquisite food. Since your body may retain fluids, pay attention to your diet. To relax, escape to places near water.

Leo Rising: Diva Dazzle

You may come across as more poised than you really feel. However, you play it to the hilt, projecting a proud royal presence. A Leo ascendant gives you a natural flair for drama, like Marilyn Monroe, and you might be accused of stealing the spotlight. You'll also project a much more outgoing, optimistic, sunny personality than others of your sign. You take care to please your public by always projecting your best star quality, probably tossing a luxuriant mane of hair, sporting a striking hairstyle, or dressing to impress. Females often dazzle with spectacular jewelry. Since you may have a strong parental nature, you could well be the regal family matriarch or patriarch, like George W. Bush.

Virgo Rising: High Standards

Virgo rising masks your inner nature with a practical, analytical outer image. You seem neat, orderly, more particular than others of your sign. Others in your life may feel they must live up to your high standards. Though at times you may be openly critical, this masks a well-meaning desire to have only the best for loved ones. Your sharp eye for details could be used in the financial world, or your literary skills could draw you to teaching or publishing. The healing arts, health care, and service-oriented professions attract many with a Virgo ascendant. You're likely to take good care of yourself, with great attention to health, diet, and exercise, like Madonna. You might even show some hypochondriac tendencies, like Woody Allen. Physically, you may have a very sensitive digestive system.

Libra Rising: The Charmer

Libra rising gives you a charming, social public persona, like Bill Clinton. You tend to avoid confrontations in relationships, preferring to smooth the way or negotiate diplomatically rather than give in to an emotional reaction. Because you are interested in all aspects of a situation, you may be slow to reach decisions. Physically, you'll have good proportions and symmetry. You will move with natural grace and balance. You're likely to have pleasing, if not beautiful, facial features, with a winning smile, like Cary Grant. You'll show natural good taste and harmony in your clothes and home decor. Legal, diplomatic, or public relations professions could draw your interest.

Scorpio Rising: An Air of Mystery

You project an intriguing air of mystery with this ascendant, as the Scorpio secretiveness and sense of underlying power combines with your sun sign. As with Jackie O, there's more to you than meets the eye. You seem like someone who is always in control and who can move comfortably in the world of power. Your physical look comes across as intense. Many of you have remarkable eyes, with a direct, penetrating gaze. But you'll never reveal your private agenda, and you tend to keep your true feelings under wraps (watch a tendency toward paranoia). You may have an interesting romantic history with secret love affairs, like Grace Kelly. Many of you heighten your air of mystery by wearing black. You're happiest near water and should provide yourself with a seaside retreat.

Sagittarius Rising: The Explorer

You travel with this ascendant. You may also be a more outdoor, sportive type, with an athletic, casual, outgoing air. Your moods are camouflaged with cheerful optimism or a philosophical attitude. Though you don't hesitate to speak your mind, like Ted Turner, who was called the Mouth of the South, you can also laugh at your troubles or crack a joke more easily than others of your sign. A Sagittarius ascendant can also draw you to the field of higher education or to spiritual life. You'll seem to have less attachment to things and people, and may explore the globe. Your strong, fast legs are a physical bonus.

Capricorn Rising: Serious Business

This rising sign makes you come across as serious, goal-oriented, disciplined, and careful with cash. You are not one of the zodiac's big spenders, though you might splurge occasionally on items with good investment value. You're the traditional, conservative type in dress and environment, and you might come across as quite normal and business-like, like Rupert Murdoch. You'll function well in a structured or corporate environment where you can climb to the top. (You are always aware of who's the boss.) In your personal life, you could be a loner or a single parent who is "father and mother" to your children.

Aquarius Rising: One of a Kind

You come across as less concerned about what others think and could even be a bit eccentric. You're more at ease with groups of people than others in your sign, and you may be attracted to public life, like Jay Leno. Your appearance may be unique, either unconventional or unimportant to you. Those of you whose sun is in a water sign (Cancer, Scorpio, Pisces) may exercise your nurturing qualities with a large group, an extended family, or a day-care or community center.

Pisces Rising: Romantic Roles

Your creative, nurturing talents are heightened and so is your ability to project emotional drama. And, like Antonio Banderas, your dreamy eyes and poetic air bring out the protective instinct in others. You could be attracted to the arts, especially theater, dance, film, and photography, or to psychology, spiritual practice, and charity work. You are happiest when you are using your creative ability to help others. Since you are vulnerable to mood swings, it is especially important for you to find interesting, creative work where you can express your talents and heighten your self-esteem. Accentuate the positive. Be wary of escapist tendencies, particularly involving alcohol or drugs to which you are supersensitive, like Whitney Houston.

RISING SIGNS—A.M. BIRTHS

	1 AM	2 AM	3 AM	4 AM	5 AM	6 AM	7 AM	8 AM	9 AM	10 AM	11 AM	12 NOON
Jan 1	Lib	Sc	Sc	Sc	Sag	Sag	Cap	Cap	Aq	Aq	Pis	Ar
Jan 9	Lib	Sc	Sc	Sag	Sag	Sag	Cap	Cap	Aq	Aq	Pis	Ar
Jan 17	Sc	Sc	Sc	Sag	Sag	Cap	Cap	Aq	Aq	Pis	Ar	Tau
Jan 25	Sc	Sc	Sag	Sag	Sag	Cap	Cap	Aq	Pis	Ar	Tau	Tau
Feb 2	Sc	Sc	Sag	Sag	Cap	Cap	Aq	Pis	Pis	Ar	Tau	Gem
Feb 10	Sc	Sag	Sag	Sag	Cap	Cap	Aq	Pis	Ar	Tau	Tau	Gem
Feb 18	Sc	Sag	Sag	Cap	Cap	Aq	Pis	Pis	Ar	Tau	Gem	Gem
Feb 26	Sag	Sag	Sag	Cap	Aq	Aq	Pis	Ar	Tau	Tau	Gem	Gem
Mar 6	Sag	Sag	Cap	Cap	Aq	Aq	Pis	Pis	Ar	Tau	Gem	Can
Mar 14	Sag	Cap	Cap	Aq	Aq	Pis	Ar	Tau	Tau	Gem	Gem	Can
Mar 22	Sag	Cap	Cap	Aq	Pis	Ar	Ar	Tau	Gem	Gem	Can	Can
Mar 30	Cap	Cap	Aq	Pis	Pis	Ar	Tau	Tau	Gem	Can	Can	Can
Apr 7	Cap	Cap	Aq	Pis	Ar	Ar	Tau	Gem	Gem	Can	Can	Leo
Apr 14	Cap	Aq	Aq	Pis	Ar	Tau	Tau	Gem	Gem	Can	Can	Leo
Apr 22	Cap	Aq	Pis	Ar	Ar	Tau	Gem	Gem	Gem	Can	Leo	Leo
Apr 30	Aq	Aq	Pis	Ar	Tau	Tau	Gem	Can	Can	Can	Leo	Leo
May 8	Aq	Pis	Ar	Ar	Tau	Gem	Gem	Can	Can	Leo	Leo	Leo
May 16	Aq	Pis	Ar	Tau	Gem	Gem	Can	Can	Can	Leo	Leo	Vir
May 24	Pis	Ar	Ar	Tau	Gem	Gem	Can	Can	Leo	Leo	Leo	Vir
June 1	Pis	Ar	Tau	Gem	Gem	Can	Can	Can	Leo	Leo	Vir	Vir
June 9	Ar	Ar	Tau	Gem	Gem	Can	Can	Leo	Leo	Leo	Vir	Vir
June 17	Ar	Tau	Gem	Gem	Can	Can	Can	Leo	Leo	Vir	Vir	Vir
June 25	Tau	Tau	Gem	Gem	Can	Can	Leo	Leo	Leo	Vir	Vir	Lib
July 3	Tau	Gem	Gem	Can	Can	Can	Leo	Leo	Vir	Vir	Vir	Lib
July 11	Tau	Gem	Gem	Can	Can	Leo	Leo	Leo	Vir	Vir	Lib	Lib
July 18	Gem	Gem	Can	Can	Can	Leo	Leo	Vir	Vir	Vir	Lib	Lib
July 26	Gem	Gem	Can	Can	Leo	Leo	Vir	Vir	Vir	Lib	Lib	Lib
Aug 3	Gem	Can	Can	Can	Leo	Leo	Vir	Vir	Vir	Lib	Lib	Sc
Aug 11	Gem	Can	Can	Leo	Leo	Leo	Vir	Vir	Lib	Lib	Lib	Sc
Aug 18	Can	Can	Can	Leo	Leo	Vir	Vir	Vir	Lib	Lib	Sc	Sc
Aug 27	Can	Can	Leo	Leo	Leo	Vir	Vir	Lib	Lib	Lib	Sc	Sc
Sept 4	Can	Can	Leo	Leo	Leo	Vir	Vir	Vir	Lib	Lib	Sc	Sc
Sept 12	Can	Leo	Leo	Leo	Vir	Vir	Lib	Lib	Lib	Sc	Sc	Sag
Sept 20	Leo	Leo	Leo	Vir	Vir	Vir	Lib	Lib	Sc	Sc	Sc	Sag
Sept 28	Leo	Leo	Leo	Vir	Vir	Lib	Lib	Lib	Sc	Sc	Sag	Sag
Oct 6	Leo	Leo	Vir	Vir	Vir	Lib	Lib	Sc	Sc	Sc	Sag	Sag
Oct 14	Leo	Vir	Vir	Vir	Lib	Lib	Lib	Sc	Sc	Sag	Sag	Cap
Oct 22	Leo	Vir	Vir	Lib	Lib	Lib	Sc	Sc	Sc	Sag	Sag	Cap
Oct 30	Vir	Vir	Vir	Lib	Lib	Sc	Sc	Sc	Sag	Sag	Cap	Cap
Nov 7	Vir	Vir	Lib	Lib	Lib	Sc	Sc	Sc	Sag	Sag	Cap	Cap
Nov 15	Vir	Vir	Lib	Lib	Sc	Sc	Sc	Sag	Sag	Cap	Cap	Aq
Nov 23	Vir	Lib	Lib	Lib	Sc	Sc	Sag	Sag	Sag	Cap	Cap	Aq
Dec 1	Vir	Lib	Lib	Sc	Sc	Sc	Sag	Sag	Cap	Cap	Aq	Aq
Dec 9	Lib	Lib	Lib	Sc	Sc	Sag	Sag	Sag	Cap	Cap	Aq	Pis
Dec 18	Lib	Lib	Sc	Sc	Sc	Sag	Sag	Cap	Cap	Aq	Aq	Pis
Dec 28	Lib	Lib	Sc	Sc	Sag	Sag	Sag	Cap	Aq	Aq	Pis	Ar

RISING SIGNS—P.M. BIRTHS

	1 PM	2 PM	3 PM	4 PM	5 PM	6 PM	7 PM	8 PM	9 PM	10 PM	11 PM	12 MID-NIGHT
Jan 1	Tau	Gem	Gem	Can	Can	Can	Leo	Leo	Vir	Vir	Vir	Lib
Jan 9	Tau	Gem	Gem	Can	Can	Leo	Leo	Leo	Vir	Vir	Vir	Lib
Jan 17	Gem	Gem	Can	Can	Can	Leo	Leo	Vir	Vir	Vir	Lib	Lib
Jan 25	Gem	Gem	Can	Can	Leo	Leo	Leo	Vir	Vir	Lib	Lib	Lib
Feb 2	Gem	Can	Can	Can	Leo	Leo	Vir	Vir	Vir	Lib	Lib	Sc
Feb 10	Gem	Can	Can	Leo	Leo	Leo	Vir	Vir	Lib	Lib	Lib	Sc
Feb 18	Can	Can	Can	Leo	Leo	Vir	Vir	Vir	Lib	Lib	Sc	Sc
Feb 26	Can	Can	Leo	Leo	Leo	Vir	Vir	Lib	Lib	Lib	Sc	Sc
Mar 6	Can	Leo	Leo	Leo	Vir	Vir	Vir	Lib	Lib	Sc	Sc	Sc
Mar 14	Can	Leo	Leo	Vir	Vir	Vir	Lib	Lib	Lib	Sc	Sc	Sag
Mar 22	Leo	Leo	Leo	Vir	Vir	Lib	Lib	Lib	Sc	Sc	Sc	Sag
Mar 30	Leo	Leo	Vir	Vir	Vir	Lib	Lib	Sc	Sc	Sc	Sag	Sag
Apr 7	Leo	Leo	Vir	Vir	Lib	Lib	Lib	Sc	Sc	Sc	Sag	Sag
Apr 14	Leo	Vir	Vir	Vir	Lib	Lib	Sc	Sc	Sc	Sag	Sag	Cap
Apr 22	Leo	Vir	Vir	Lib	Lib	Lib	Sc	Sc	Sc	Sag	Sag	Cap
Apr 30	Vir	Vir	Vir	Lib	Lib	Sc	Sc	Sc	Sag	Sag	Cap	Cap
May 8	Vir	Vir	Lib	Lib	Lib	Sc	Sc	Sag	Sag	Sag	Cap	Cap
May 16	Vir	Vir	Lib	Lib	Sc	Sc	Sc	Sag	Sag	Cap	Cap	Aq
May 24	Vir	Lib	Lib	Lib	Sc	Sc	Sag	Sag	Sag	Cap	Cap	Aq
June 1	Vir	Lib	Lib	Sc	Sc	Sc	Sag	Sag	Cap	Cap	Aq	Aq
June 9	Lib	Lib	Lib	Sc	Sc	Sag	Sag	Sag	Cap	Cap	Aq	Pis
June 17	Lib	Lib	Sc	Sc	Sc	Sag	Sag	Cap	Cap	Aq	Aq	Pis
June 25	Lib	Lib	Sc	Sc	Sag	Sag	Sag	Cap	Cap	Aq	Pis	Ar
July 3	Lib	Sc	Sc	Sc	Sag	Sag	Cap	Cap	Aq	Aq	Pis	Ar
July 11	Lib	Sc	Sc	Sag	Sag	Sag	Cap	Cap	Aq	Pis	Ar	Tau
July 18	Sc	Sc	Sc	Sag	Sag	Cap	Cap	Aq	Aq	Pis	Ar	Tau
July 26	Sc	Sc	Sag	Sag	Sag	Cap	Cap	Aq	Pis	Ar	Tau	Tau
Aug 3	Sc	Sc	Sag	Sag	Cap	Cap	Aq	Aq	Pis	Ar	Tau	Gem
Aug 11	Sc	Sag	Sag	Sag	Cap	Cap	Aq	Pis	Ar	Tau	Tau	Gem
Aug 18	Sc	Sag	Sag	Cap	Cap	Aq	Pis	Pis	Ar	Tau	Gem	Gem
Aug 27	Sag	Sag	Sag	Cap	Cap	Aq	Pis	Ar	Tau	Tau	Gem	Gem
Sept 4	Sag	Sag	Cap	Cap	Aq	Pis	Pis	Ar	Tau	Gem	Gem	Can
Sept 12	Sag	Sag	Cap	Aq	Aq	Pis	Ar	Tau	Tau	Gem	Gem	Can
Sept 20	Sag	Cap	Cap	Aq	Pis	Pis	Ar	Tau	Gem	Gem	Can	Can
Sept 28	Cap	Cap	Aq	Aq	Pis	Ar	Tau	Tau	Gem	Gem	Can	Can
Oct 6	Cap	Cap	Aq	Pis	Ar	Ar	Tau	Gem	Gem	Can	Can	Leo
Oct 14	Cap	Aq	Aq	Pis	Ar	Tau	Tau	Gem	Gem	Can	Can	Leo
Oct 22	Cap	Aq	Pis	Ar	Ar	Tau	Gem	Gem	Can	Can	Leo	Leo
Oct 30	Aq	Aq	Pis	Ar	Tau	Tau	Gem	Can	Can	Can	Leo	Leo
Nov 7	Aq	Aq	Pis	Ar	Tau	Tau	Gem	Can	Can	Can	Leo	Leo
Nov 15	Aq	Pis	Ar	Tau	Gem	Gem	Can	Can	Can	Leo	Leo	Vir
Nov 23	Pis	Ar	Ar	Tau	Gem	Gem	Can	Can	Leo	Leo	Leo	Vir
Dec 1	Pis	Ar	Tau	Gem	Gem	Can	Can	Can	Leo	Leo	Vir	Vir
Dec 9	Ar	Tau	Tau	Gem	Gem	Can	Can	Leo	Leo	Leo	Vir	Vir
Dec 18	Ar	Tau	Gem	Gem	Can	Can	Can	Leo	Leo	Vir	Vir	Vir
Dec 28	Tau	Tau	Gem	Gem	Can	Can	Leo	Leo	Vir	Vir	Vir	Lib

CHAPTER 8

Astrology's Magic Symbols: The Glyphs

One of the first things an astrology student learns is how to read the symbols on a horoscope chart. These symbols or *glyphs* represent a kind of code, a pictorial language understood by astrologers around the globe and used by all astrology software programs. You'll miss out if you don't learn the glyphs. Once you learn them, you can begin to find your way around the chart, beginning your journey to deeper understanding. You can also make use of free charts available on any number of Internet sites and perhaps purchase one of the many astrology software programs.

The glyphs are fascinating little pictures in themselves, with built-in clues to help you not only decipher which sign or planet each represents, but what the symbol means in a deeper, more esoteric sense. Actually the physical act of writing the symbol is a mystical experience in itself, a way to invoke the deeper meaning of the sign or planet through age-old visual elements that have been with us since time began.

Since there are only twelve signs and ten planets (not counting a few asteroids and other space objects some astrologers use), it's a lot easier than learning to read a foreign language. Here's a code cracker for the glyphs, beginning with the glyphs for the planets. To those who already know their glyphs, don't just skim over the chapter. These familiar graphics have hidden meanings you will discover!

The Glyphs for the Planets

The glyphs for the planets are easy to learn. They're simple combinations of the most basic visual elements: the circle, the semicircle or arc, and the cross. However, each component of a glyph has a special meaning in relation to the other parts of the symbol.

The circle, which has no beginning or end, is one of the oldest symbols of spirit or spiritual forces. Early diagrams of the heavens—spiritual territory—are shown in circular form. The never-ending line of the circle is the perfect symbol for eternity. The semicircle or arc is an incomplete circle, symbolizing the receptive, finite soul, which contains spiritual potential in the curving line.

The vertical line of the cross symbolizes movement from heaven to earth. The horizontal line describes temporal movement, here and now, in time and space. Combined in a cross, the vertical and horizontal planes symbolize manifestation in the material world.

The Sun Glyph ☉

The sun is always shown by this powerful solar symbol, a circle with a point in the center. The center point is you, your spiritual center, and the symbol represents your infinite personality incarnating (the point) into the finite cycles of birth and death.

The sun has been represented by a circle or disk since ancient Egyptian times when the solar disk represented the sun god, Ra. Some archaeologists believe the great stone circles found in England were centers of sun worship. This particular version of the symbol was brought into common use in the sixteenth century after German occultist and scholar Cornelius Agrippa (1486–1535) wrote a book called *Die Occulta Philosophia,* which became accepted as the authority in the field. Agrippa collected many medieval astrological and magical symbols in this book, which have been used by astrologers since then.

The Moon Glyph ☽

The moon glyph is the most recognizable symbol on a chart, a left-facing arc stylized into the crescent moon. As part of a circle, the arc symbolizes the potential fulfillment of the entire circle, the life force that is still incomplete. Therefore, it is the ideal representation of the reactive, receptive, emotional nature of the moon.

The Mercury Glyph ☿

Mercury contains all three elemental symbols: the crescent, the circle, and the cross in vertical order. This is the "Venus with a hat" glyph (compare with the symbol of Venus). With another stretch of the imagination, can't you see the winged cap of Mercury the messenger? Think of the upturned crescent as antennae that tune in and transmit messages from the sun, reminding you that Mercury is the way you communicate, the way your mind works. The upturned arc is receiving energy into the spirit or solar circle, which will later be translated into action on the material plane, symbolized by the cross. All the elements are equally sized because Mercury is neutral; it doesn't play favorites! This planet symbolizes objective, detached, unemotional thinking.

The Venus Glyph ♀

Here the relationship is between two components: the circle of spirit and the cross of matter. Spirit is elevated over matter, pulling it upward. Venus asks, "What is beautiful? What do you like best? What do you love to have done to you?" Consequently, Venus determines both your ideal of beauty and what feels good sensually. It governs your own allure and power to attract, as well as what attracts and pleases you.

The Mars Glyph ♂

In this glyph, the cross of matter is stylized into an arrow-head pointed up and outward, propelled by the circle of spirit. With a little imagination, you can visualize it as the shield and spear of Mars, the ancient god of war. You can deduce that Mars embodies your spiritual energy projected into the outer world. It's your assertiveness, your initiative, your aggressive drive, what you like to do to others, your temper. If you know someone's Mars, you know whether they'll blow up when angry or do a slow burn. Your task is to use your outgoing Mars energy wisely and well.

The Jupiter Glyph ♃

Jupiter is the basic cross of matter, with a large stylized crescent perched on the left side of the horizontal, temporal plane. You might think of the crescent as an open hand, because one meaning of Jupiter is "luck," what's handed to you. You don't have to work for what you get from Jupiter; it comes to you, if you're open to it.

The Jupiter glyph might also remind you of a jumbo jet plane, with a huge tail fin, about to take off. This is the planet of travel, mental and spiritual, of expanding your horizons via new ideas, new spiritual dimensions, and new places. Jupiter embodies the optimism and enthusiasm of the traveler about to embark on an exciting adventure.

The Saturn Glyph ♄

Flip Jupiter over, and you've got Saturn. This might not be immediately apparent because Saturn is usually stylized into an "h" form like the one shown here. The principle it expresses is the opposite of Jupiter's expansive tendencies. Saturn pulls you back to earth: the receptive arc is pushed down underneath the cross of matter. Before there are any rewards or expansion, the duties and obligations of the material world must be considered. Saturn says, "Stop, wait, finish your chores before you take off!"

Saturn's glyph also resembles the sickle of old "Father Time." Saturn was first known as Chronos, the Greek god of time, for time brings all matter to an end. When it was the most distant planet (before the discovery of Uranus), Saturn was believed to be the place where time stopped.

After the soul departed from earth, it journeyed back to the outer reaches of the universe and finally stopped at Saturn, or at "the end of time."

The Uranus Glyph ♅

The glyph for Uranus is often stylized to form a capital *H* after Sir William Herschel, who discovered the planet. But the more esoteric version curves the two pillars of the H into crescent antennae, or "ears," like satellite disks receiving signals from space. These are perched on the horizontal material line of the cross of matter and pushed from below by the circle of the spirit. To many sci-fi fans, Uranus looks like an orbiting satellite.

Uranus channels the highest energy of all, the white electrical light of the universal spiritual force that holds the cosmos together. This pure electrical energy is gathered from all over the universe. Because Uranus energy doesn't follow any ordinary celestial drumbeat, it can't be controlled or predicted (which is also true of those who are strongly influenced by this eccentric planet). In the symbol, this energy is manifested through the balance of polarities (the two opposite arms of the glyph) like the two polarized wires of a lightbulb.

The Neptune Glyph ♆

Neptune's glyph is usually stylized to look like a trident, the weapon of the Roman god Neptune. However, on a more esoteric level, it shows the large upturned crescent of the soul pierced through by the cross of matter. Neptune nails down, or materializes, soul energy, bringing impulses from the soul level into manifestation. That is why Neptune is associated with imagination or "imagining in," making an image of the soul. Neptune works through feelings, sensitivity, and the mystical capacity to bring the divine into the earthly realm.

The Pluto Glyph ♀

Pluto is written two ways. One is a composite of the letters *PL,* the first two letters of the word Pluto and coincidentally the initials of Percival Lowell, one of the planet's discoverers. The other, more esoteric symbol is a small circle above a large open crescent that surmounts the cross of matter. This depicts Pluto's power to regenerate. Imagine a new little spirit emerging from the sheltering cup of the soul. Pluto rules the forces of life and death. After this planet has passed a sensitive point in your chart, you are transformed, reborn in some way.

Sci-fi fans might visualize this glyph as a small satellite (the circle) being launched. It was shortly after Pluto's discovery that we learned how to harness the nuclear forces that made space exploration possible. Pluto rules the transformative power of atomic energy, which totally changed our lives and from which there is no turning back.

The Glyphs for the Signs

On an astrology chart, the glyph for the sign will appear after that of the planet. For example, when you see the moon glyph followed first by a number and then by another glyph representing the sign, this means that the moon was passing over a certain degree of that astrological sign at the time of the chart. On the dividing lines between the houses on your chart, you'll find the symbol for the sign that rules the house.

Because sun sign symbols do not contain the same basic geometric components of the planetary glyphs, we must look elsewhere for clues to their meanings. Many have been passed down from ancient Egyptian and Chaldean civilizations with few modifications. Others have been adapted over the centuries.

In deciphering many of the glyphs, you'll often find that the symbols reveal a dual nature of the sign, which is not always apparent in the usual sun sign descriptions. For instance, the Gemini glyph is similar to the Roman numeral for two, and reveals this sign's longing to discover a twin soul. The Cancer glyph may be interpreted as resembling either the nurturing breasts or the self-protective claws of a crab, both symbols associated with the contrasting qualities of this sign. Libra's glyph embodies the duality of the spirit balanced with material reality. The Sagittarius glyph shows that the aspirant must also carry along the earthly animal nature in his quest. The Capricorn sea goat is another symbol with dual emphasis. The goat climbs high, yet is always pulled back by the deep waters of the unconscious. Aquarius embodies the double waves of mental detachment, balanced by the desire for connection with others, in a friendly way. Finally, the two fishes of Pisces, which are forever tied together, show the duality of the soul and the spirit that must be reconciled.

The Aries Glyph ♈

Since the symbol for Aries is the Ram, this glyph is obviously associated with a ram's horns, which characterize one aspect of the Aries personality—an aggressive, me-first, leaping-headfirst attitude. But the symbol can be interpreted in other ways as well. Some astrologers liken it to a fountain of energy, which Aries people also embody. The first sign of the zodiac bursts on the scene eagerly, ready to go. Another analogy is to the eyebrows and nose of the human head, which Aries rules, and the thinking power that is initiated by the brain.

One theory of this symbol links it to the Egyptian god Amun, represented by a ram in ancient times. As Amun-Ra, this god was believed to embody the creator of the universe, the leader of all the other gods. This relates easily to the position of Aries as the leader (or first sign) of the zodiac, which begins at the spring equinox, a time of the year when nature is renewed.

The Taurus Glyph ♉

This is another easy glyph to draw and identify. It takes little imagination to decipher the bull's head with long curving horns. Like its symbol the Bull, the archetypal Taurus is slow to anger but ferocious when provoked, as well as stubborn, steady, and sensual. Another association is the larynx (and thyroid) of the throat area (ruled by Taurus) and the eustachian tubes running up to the ears, which coincides with the relationship of Taurus to the voice, song, and music. Many famous singers, musicians, and composers have prominent Taurus influences.

Many ancient religions involved a bull as the central figure in fertility rites or initiations, usually symbolizing the victory of man over his animal nature. Another possible origin is in the sacred bull of Egypt, who embodied the incarnate form of Osiris, god of death and resurrection. In early Christian imagery, the Taurus Bull represented St. Luke.

The Gemini Glyph ♊

The standard glyph immediately calls to mind the Roman numeral for two (II) and the Twins symbol, as it is called, for Gemini. In almost all drawings and images used for this sign, the relationship between two persons is emphasized. Usually one twin will be touching the other, which signifies communication, human contact, the desire to share.

The top line of the Gemini glyph indicates mental communication, while the bottom line indicates shared physical space.

The most famous Gemini legend is that of the twin sons, Castor and Pollux, one of whom had a mortal father while the other was the son of Zeus, king of the gods. When it came time for the mortal twin to die, his grief-stricken brother pleaded with Zeus, who agreed to let them spend half the year on earth in mortal form and half in immortal life, with the gods on Mount Olympus. This reflects a basic duality of humankind, which possesses an immortal soul yet is also subject to the limits of mortality.

The Cancer Glyph ♋

Two convenient images relate to the Cancer glyph. It is easiest to decode the curving claws of the Cancer symbol, the Crab. Like the crab's, Cancer's element is water. This sensitive sign also has a hard protective shell to protect its tender interior. The crab must be wily to escape predators, scampering sideways and hiding under rocks. The crab also responds to the cycles of the moon, as do all shellfish. The other image is that of two female breasts, which Cancer rules, showing that this is a sign that nurtures and protects others as well as itself.

In ancient Egypt, Cancer was also represented by the scarab beetle, a symbol of regeneration and eternal life.

The Leo Glyph ♌

Notice that the Leo glyph seems to be an extension of Cancer's glyph, with a significant difference. In the Cancer glyph, the lines curve inward protectively. The Leo glyph expresses energy outwardly. And there is no duality in the symbol, the Lion, or in Leo, the sign.

Lions have belonged to the sign of Leo since earliest times. It is not difficult to imagine the king of beasts with his sweeping mane and curling tail from this glyph. The upward sweep of the glyph easily describes the positive energy of Leo: the flourishing tail, the flamboyant qualities. Anther analogy, perhaps a stretch of the imagination, is that of a heart leaping up with joy and enthusiasm, also very typical of Leo, which also rules the heart. In early Christian imagery, the Leo Lion represented St. Mark.

The Virgo Glyph ♍

You can read much into this mysterious glyph. For instance, it could represent the initials of "Mary Virgin," or a young woman holding a staff of wheat, or stylized female genitalia, all common interpretations. The M shape might also remind you that Virgo is ruled by Mercury. The cross beneath the symbol reveals the grounded, practical nature of this earth sign.

The earliest zodiacs link Virgo with the Egyptian goddess Isis, who gave birth to the god Horus after her husband

Osiris had been killed, in the archetype of a miraculous conception. There are many ancient statues of Isis nursing her baby son, which are reminiscent of medieval Virgin and Child motifs. This sign has also been associated with the image of the Holy Grail, when the Virgo symbol was substituted with a chalice.

The Libra Glyph ♎︎

It is not difficult to read the standard image for Libra, the Scales, into this glyph. There is another meaning, however, that is equally relevant: the setting sun as it descends over the horizon. Libra's natural position on the zodiac wheel is the descendant, or sunset position (as the Aries natural position is the ascendant, or rising sign). Both images relate to Libra's personality. Libra is always weighing pros and cons for a balanced decision. In the sunset image, the sun (male) hovers over the horizontal earth (female) before setting. Libra is the space between these lines, harmonizing yin and yang, spiritual and material, male and female, ideal and real worlds. The glyph has also been linked to the kidneys, which are associated with Libra.

The Scorpio Glyph ♏︎

With its barbed tail, this glyph is easy to identify as the Scorpion for the sign of Scorpio. It also represents the male sexual parts, over which the sign rules. From the arrowhead, you can draw the conclusion that Mars was once its ruler. Some earlier Egyptian glyphs for Scorpio represent it as an erect serpent, so the Serpent is an alternate symbol.

Another symbol for Scorpio, which is not identifiable in this glyph, is the Eagle. Scorpios can go to extremes, either in soaring like the eagle or self-destructing like the scorpion. In early Christian imagery, which often used zodiacal symbols, the Scorpio Eagle was chosen to symbolize the intense apostle St. John the Evangelist.

The Sagittarius Glyph ♐

This is one of the easiest to spot and draw: an upward pointing arrow lifting up a cross. The arrow is pointing skyward, while the cross represents the four elements of the material world, which the arrow must convey. Elevating materiality into spirituality is an important Sagittarius quality, which explains why this sign is associated with higher learning, religion, philosophy, travel—the aspiring professions. Sagittarius can also send barbed arrows of frankness in the pursuit of truth, so the Archer symbol for Sagittarius is apt. (Sagittarius is also the sign of the supersalesman.)

Sagittarius is symbolically represented by the centaur, a mythological creature who is half man, half horse, aiming his arrow toward the skies. Though Sagittarius is motivated by spiritual aspiration, it also must balance the powerful appetites of the animal nature. The centaur Chiron, a figure in Greek mythology, became a wise teacher who, after many adventures and world travels, was killed by a poisoned arrow.

The Capricorn Glyph ♑

One of the most difficult symbols to draw, this glyph may take some practice. It is a representation of the sea goat: a mythical animal that is a goat with a curving fish's tail. The goat part of Capricorn wants to leave the waters of the emotions and climb to the elevated areas of life. But the fish tail is the unconscious, the deep chaotic psychic level that draws the goat back. Capricorn is often trying to escape the deep, feeling part of life by submerging himself in work, steadily ascending to the top. To some people, the glyph represents a seated figure with a bent knee, a reminder that Capricorn governs the knee area of the body.

An interesting aspect of this glyph is the contrast of the sharp pointed horns—which represent the penetrating, shrewd, conscious side of Capricorn—with the swishing tail—which represents its serpentine, unconscious, emotional force. One Capricorn legend, which dates from Roman times, tells of the earthy fertility god, Pan, who tried to save himself from uncontrollable sexual desires by jumping into the Nile. His upper body then turned into a goat, while the lower part became a fish. Later, Jupiter gave him a safe haven as a constellation in the skies.

The Aquarius Glyph ≈

This ancient water symbol can be traced back to an Egyptian hieroglyph representing streams of life force. Symbolized by the Water Bearer, Aquarius is distributor of the waters of life—the magic liquid of regeneration. The two waves can also be linked to the positive and negative charges of the electrical energy that Aquarius rules, a sort of universal wavelength. Aquarius is tuned in intuitively to higher forces via this electrical force. The duality of the glyph could also refer to the dual nature of Aquarius, a sign that runs hot and cold and that is friendly but also detached in the mental world of air signs.

In Greek legends, Aquarius is represented by Ganymede, who was carried to heaven by an eagle in order to become the cupbearer of Zeus and to supervise the annual flooding of the Nile. The sign later became associated with aviation and notions of flight.

The Pisces Glyph)(

Here is an abstraction of the familiar image of Pisces, two Fishes swimming in opposite directions yet bound together by a cord. The Fishes represent the spirit—which yearns for the freedom of heaven—and the soul—which remains attached to the desires of the temporal world. During life on earth, the spirit and the soul are bound together. When they complement each other, instead of pulling in opposite directions, they facilitate the Pisces creativity. The ancient version of this glyph, taken from the Egyptians, had no connecting line, which was added in the fourteenth century.

In another interpretation, it is said that the left fish indicates the direction of involution or the beginning of a cycle, while the right fish signifies the direction of evolution, the way to completion of a cycle. It's an appropriate grand finale for Pisces, the last sign of the zodiac.

CHAPTER 9

High-Tech Astrology: The Best Software for Your Budget and Ability

After you've acquired some basic knowledge—the signs, houses, planets, and glyphs—you have the tools to take astrology to the next level by reading charts and relating the planets to the lives of friends, relatives, and daily events.

If you have a computer, the easiest way to do this is to use astrology software that can put a chart on the screen in seconds and even help you interpret it.

When it comes to astrology software, there are endless options. How do you make the right choice? First, define your goals. Do you want to do charts of friends and family, study celebrity charts, or check the aspects every day on your Palm Pilot? Do you want to invest in a more comprehensive program that adapts to your changing needs as you learn astrology?

The good news is that there's a program for every level of interest in all price points—starting with free. For the dabbler, there are the affordable Winstar Express and Time Passages. For the serious student, there are Astrolog (free), Solar Fire, Kepler, Winstar Plus—software that does every technique on planets and gives you beautiful chart printouts. You can do a chart of someone you've just met on your PDA with Astracadabra. If you're a Mac user, you'll be satisfied with the wonderful IO and Time Passages software.

However, since all the programs use the astrology symbols, or glyphs, for planets and signs, rather than written words, you should learn the glyphs before you purchase your software. Our chapter on the glyphs in this book will help you do just that. Here are some software options for you to explore.

Easy for Beginners

Time Passages

Designed for either a Macintosh or Windows computer, Time Passages is straightforward and easy to use. It allows you to generate charts and interpretation reports for yourself or friends and loved ones at the touch of a button. If you haven't yet learned the astrology symbols, this might be the program for you; just roll your mouse over any symbol of the planets, signs, or house cusps, and you'll be shown a description in plain English below the chart. Then click on the planet, sign, or house cusp and up pops a detailed interpretation. It couldn't be easier. A new basic edition, under fifty dollars at this writing, is bargain priced and ideal for beginners.

Time Passages
(866) 772-7876 (866-77-ASTRO)
Web site: www.astrograph.com

Growth Opportunities

Astrolabe

Astrolabe is one of the top astrology software resources. Check out the latest version of their powerful Solar Fire software for Windows. A breeze to use, it will grow with your increasing knowledge of astrology to the most sophisticated levels. This company also markets a variety of programs for all levels of expertise and a wide selection of computer-generated astrology readings. This is a good resource for innovative software as well as applications for older computers.

The Astrolabe Web site is a great place to start your astrology tour of the Internet. Visitors to the site are greeted with a chart of the time you log on. And you can get your chart calculated, also free, with an interpretation e-mailed to you.

Astrolabe
Box 1750-R
Brewster, MA 02631
Phone: (800) 843-6682
Web site: www.alabe.com

Matrix Software

You'll find a wide variety of software at student and advanced levels in all price ranges, demo disks, and lots of interesting readings. Check out Winstar Express, a powerful but reasonably priced program suitable for all skill levels. The Matrix Web site offers lots of fun activities for Web surfers, such as free readings from the *I Ching,* the runes, and the tarot. There are many free desktop backgrounds with astrology themes. Go here to connect with news groups and online discussions. Their online almanac helps you schedule the best day to sign on the dotted line, ask for a raise, or plant your tomatoes.

Matrix Software
126 South Michigan Avenue
Big Rapids, MI 49307
Phone: (800) 416-3924
Web site: www.astrologysoftware.com

Astro Communications Services (ACS)

Books, software for Mac and IBM compatibles, individual charts, and telephone readings are offered by this California company. Their freebies include astrology greeting cards and new moon reports. Find technical astrology materials here, such as *The American Ephemeris* and PC atlases. ACS will calculate and send charts to you, a valuable service if you do not have a computer.

ACS Publications
P.O. Box 1646
El Cajon, CA 92022-1646
Phone: (800) 514-5070
Fax: (619) 631-0180
Web site: www.astrocom.com

Air Software

Here you'll find powerful, creative astrology software, and current stock market analysis. Financial astrology programs for stock market traders are a specialty. There are some interesting freebies at this site; check out the maps of eclipse paths for any year and a free astrology clock program.

Air Software
115 Caya Avenue
West Hartford, CT 06110
Phone: (800) 659-1247
Web site: www.alphee.com

Kepler: State of the Art

Here's a program that has everything. Gorgeous graphic images, audio-visual effects, and myriad sophisticated chart options are built into this fascinating software. It's even got an astrological encyclopedia, plus diagrams and images to help you understand advanced concepts. This program is expensive, but if you're serious about learning astrology, it's an investment that will grow with you! Check out its features at www.astrologysoftwareshop.com.

Time Cycles Research: For Mac Users

Here's where Mac users can find astrology software that's as sophisticated as it gets. If you have a Mac, you'll love their beautiful graphic IO Series programs.

Time Cycles Research
P.O. Box 797
Waterford, CT 06385
Web site: www.timecycles.com
(800) 827-2240

Shareware and Freeware: The Price Is Right!

Halloran Software: A Super Shareware Program

Check out Halloran Software's Web site (www.halloran.com), which offers several levels of Windows astrology software. Beginners should consider their Astrology for Windows shareware program, which is available in unregistered demo form as a free download and in registered form for a very reasonable price.

Halloran Software
P.O. Box 75713
Los Angeles, CA 90075
(800) 732-4628

Astrolog

If you're computer-savvy, you can't go wrong with Walter Pullen's amazingly complete Astrolog program, which is offered absolutely free at the site. The Web address is www.astrolog.org/astrolog.htm.

Astrolog is an ultrasophisticated program with all the features of much more expensive programs. It comes in versions for all formats—DOS, Windows, Mac, UNIX—and has some cool features, such as a revolving globe and a constellation map. If you are looking for astrology software with bells and whistles that doesn't cost big bucks, this program has it all!

Programs for the Pocket PDA and Palm Pilot

Would you like to have astrology at your fingertips everywhere you go? No need to drag along your laptop. You can check the chart of the moment or of someone you've just met on your pocket PDA or Palm Pilot. As with most other programs, you'll need to know the astrological symbols in order to read the charts.

For the pocket PC that has the Microsoft Pocket PC 2002 or the Microsoft Windows Mobile 2003 operating system, there is the versatile Astracadabra, which can interchange charts with the popular Solar Fire software. It can be ordered at www.leelehman.com or www.astrologysoftwareshop.com.

For the Palm OS5 and compatible handheld devices, there is Astropocket from www.yves.robert.org/features.html. This is a shareware program, which allows you to use all the features free. However, you cannot store more than one chart at a time until you pay a mere twenty-eight-dollar registration fee for the complete version.

CHAPTER 10

Travel the World of Astrology

There's a world of astrology waiting to welcome you, and thanks to the Internet, it's now possible to connect instantly with astrology fans and events around the globe. There are so many ways out there to expand your knowledge and share with others. Consider studying with a famous astrologer or attending a local astrology club or regional workshop. You could even combine your vacation with an astrological workshop in an exotic locale such as Bali or Mexico.

You need only type the word *astrology* into any Internet search engine and watch hundreds of listings of astrology-related sites pop up. There are local meetings and international conferences where you can connect with other astrologers, and books and tapes to help you study at home.

To help you sort out the variety of options available, here are our top picks of the Internet and the astrological community at large.

Nationwide Astrology Organizations and Conferences

Meet the World's Best Astrologers at UAC!

From May 14 to 21, 2008, the best astrologers from around the world will gather in Denver, Colorado, site of the United

Astrology Conference. UAC is jointly sponsored by three nonprofit educational organizations: AFAN (Association for Astrological Networking), ISAR (International Society for Astrological Research), and NCGR (National Council for Geocosmic Research). This conference attracts astrology fans from North and South America, Europe, Russia, India, Japan, South Africa, Australia, and New Zealand.

Here's your chance to meet and socialize with the world's top astrologers, who'll be participating in a global forum on modern astrology. There will be an all-star lineup of lectures on a variety of financial, metaphysical, psychological, and scientific topics for astrology professionals, students, and beginners. Whatever your level of expertise, there's a track for you at UAC.

Preview the conference at the convention site Web site, www.uacastrology.com.

National Council for Geocosmic Research (NCGR)

Whether you'd like to know more about such specialties as financial astrology or techniques for timing events, or if you'd prefer the psychological or mythological approach, you'll meet the top astrologers at conferences sponsored by the National Council for Geocosmic Research. NCGR is dedicated to providing quality education, bringing astrologers and astrology fans together at conferences, and promoting fellowship. Their course structure provides a systematized study of the many facets of astrology. The organization sponsors educational workshops, taped lectures, conferences, and a directory of professional astrologers. For an annual membership fee, you get their excellent publications and newsletters, plus the opportunity to network with other astrology buffs at local chapter events. (At this writing there are chapters in twenty-six states and four countries.)

To join NCGR for the latest information on upcoming events and chapters in your city, consult their Web site: www.geocosmic.org.

American Federation of Astrologers (AFA)

Established in 1938, this is one of the oldest astrological organizations in the United States. AFA offers conferences, conventions, and a thorough correspondence course. If you are looking for a reading, their interesting Web site will refer you to an accredited AFA astrologer.

AFA
6535 S. Rural Road
Tempe, AZ 85283
Phone: (888) 301-7630 or (480) 838-1751
Fax: (480) 838-8293
Web site: www.astrologers.com

Association for Astrological Networking (AFAN)

Did you know that astrologers are still being harassed for practicing astrology? AFAN provides support and legal information and works toward improving the public image of astrology. AFAN's network of local astrologers links with the international astrological community. Here are the people who will go to bat for astrology when it is attacked in the media. Everyone who cares about astrology should join!

AFAN
8306 Wilshire Boulevard
PMB 537
Beverly Hills, CA 90211
Phone: (800) 578-2326
E-mail: info@afan.org
Web site: www.afan.org

International Society for Astrology Research (ISAR)

An international organization of professional astrologers dedicated to encouraging the highest standards of quality in the field of astrology with an emphasis on research. Among ISAR's benefits are a quarterly journal, a weekly e-mail newsletter, frequent conferences, and a free membership directory.

ISAR
P.O. Box 38613
Los Angeles, CA 90038
Fax: (805) 933-0301
Web site: www.isarastrology.com

Astrology Magazines

In addition to articles by top astrologers, most of these have listings of astrology conferences, events, and local happenings.

Horoscope Guide
Kappa Publishing Group
6198 Butler Pike
Suite 200
Blue Bell, PA 19422-2600
Web site: www.kappapublishing.com/astrology

Dell Horoscope
Their Web site (www.dellhoroscope.com) features a listing of local astrological meetings.

Customer Service
6 Prowitt Street
Norwalk, CT 06855
(800) 220-7443

The Mountain Astrologer

A favorite magazine of astrology fans! *The Mountain Astrologer* also has an interesting Web site featuring the latest news from an astrological point of view, plus feature articles from the magazine.

The Mountain Astrologer
P.O. Box 970
Cedar Ridge, CA 95924
Phone: (800) 247-4828
Web site: www.mountainastrologer.com

Astrology College

Kepler College of Astrological Arts and Sciences

A degree-granting college, which is also a center of astrology, has long been the dream of the astrological community and is a giant step forward in providing credibility to the profession. Therefore, the opening of Kepler College in 2000 was a historical event for astrology. It is the only college in the western hemisphere authorized to issue B.A. and M.A. degrees in Astrological Studies. Here is where to study with the best scholars, teachers, and communicators in the field. A long-distance study program is available for those interested.

For more information, contact:

Kepler College of Astrological Arts and Sciences
4630 200th Street SW
Suite A-1
Lynnwood, WA 98036
Phone: (425) 673-4292
Fax: (425) 673-4983
Web site: www.kepler.edu

Our Favorite Web Sites

Of the thousands of astrological Web sites that come and go on the Internet, these have stood the test of time and are likely to still be operating when this book is published.

Astrodienst (www.astro.com)

Don't miss this fabulous international site that has long been one of the best astrology resources on the Internet. It's also a great place to view and download your own astrology chart. The world atlas on this site will give you the accurate longitude and latitude of your birthplace for setting up your horoscope. Then you can print out your free chart in a range of easy-to-read formats. Other attractions: a list of famous people born on your birth date, a feature that helps you choose the best vacation spot, plus articles by world-famous astrologers.

AstroDatabank (www.astrodatabank.com)

When the news is breaking, you can bet this site will be the first to get accurate birthdays of the headliners. The late astrologer Lois Rodden was a stickler for factual information and her meticulous research is being continued, much to the benefit of the astrological community. The Web site specializes in charts of current newsmakers, political figures, and international celebrities. You can also participate in discussions and analysis of the charts and see what some of the world's best astrologers have to say about them. Their AstroDatabank program, which you can purchase at the site, provides thousands of verified birthdays sorted into categories. It's an excellent research tool.

StarIQ (www.stariq.com)

Find out how top astrologers view the latest headlines at the must-see StarIQ site. Many of the best minds in astrology comment on the latest news, stock market ups and downs, political contenders. You can sign up to receive e-mail forecasts at the most important times keyed to your individual chart. (This is one of the best of the many on-line forecasts.)

Astro-Noetics (www.astro-noetics.com)

For those who are ready to explore astrology's interface with politics, popular culture, and current events, here is a sophisticated site with in-depth articles and personality profiles. Lots of depth and content here for the astrology-savvy surfer.

Astrology Books (www.astroamerica.com)

The Astrology Center of America sells a wide selection of books on all aspects of astrology, from the basics to the most advanced, at this online bookstore. Also available are many hard-to-find and recycled books.

Astrology Scholars' Sites

See what one of astrology's great teachers, Robert Hand, has to offer on his site: www.robhand.com. A leading expert on the history of astrology, he's on the cutting edge of the latest research.

The Project Hindsight group of astrologers is devoted to restoring the astrology of the Hellenistic period, the primary source for all later Western astrology. There are fascinating articles for astrology fans on this site, www.project-hindsight.com.

Financial Astrology Sites

Financial astrology is a hot specialty, with many tipsters, players, and theorists. There are online columns, newsletters, specialized financial astrology software, and mutual funds run by astrology seers. One of the more respected financial astrologers is Ray Merriman, whose stock market comments on www.mmacycles.com are a must read for those following the bulls and bears. Other top financial astrologers offer tips and forecasts at the www.afund.com and www.alphee.com sites.

CHAPTER 11

Is It Time for a Personal Reading?

Looking for answers to a burning personal question? A reading with a professional astrologer might help. A reading can be an empowering experience if you want to reach your full potential. You could use it for sizing up a lover or business situation to find out what the future has in store. If you're in a quandary about a problem, some astrological perspective could be an eye-opener. It might help you make over your life by choosing a more satisfying career or moving to a more favorable location. You could use it to find the optimum time for an important event such as a wedding or get the competitive edge in a meeting.

Another good reason for a reading is to refine your knowledge of astrology by consulting with someone who has years of experience analyzing charts. You might choose someone with a special technique that intrigues you. Armed with the knowledge of your chart that you have acquired so far, you can then learn to interpret subtle nuances or gain insight on your talents and abilities.

How do you choose when there are so many different kinds of readings available, especially since the Internet has brought astrology into the mainstream? Besides individual one-on-one readings with a professional astrologer, there are personal readings by mail, telephone, Internet, and tape. Well-advertised computer-generated reports and celebrity-sponsored readings are sure to attract your attention on commercial Web sites and in magazines. Then there are astrologers who specialize in certain areas such as finance or medical astrology. And unfortunately, there are many questionable practitioners who range from streetwise gypsy fortune-tellers to unscrupulous scam artists.

The following basic guidelines can help you sort out your options to find the reading that's right for you.

One-on-One Consultations with a Professional Astrologer

Nothing compares to a one-on-one consultation with a professional astrologer who has analyzed thousands of charts and can pinpoint the potential in yours. During your reading, you can get your specific questions answered. For instance, how to get along better with your mate or coworker. There are many astrologers who now combine their skills with training in psychology and are well-suited to help you examine your alternatives.

To give you an accurate reading, an astrologer needs certain information from you: the date, time, and place where you were born. (A horoscope can be cast about anyone or anything that has a specific time and place.) Most astrologers will then enter this information into a computer, which will calculate a chart in seconds. From the resulting chart, the astrologer will do an interpretation.

If you don't know your exact birth time, you can usually locate it at the Bureau of Vital Statistics at the city hall or county seat of the state where you were born. If you still have no success in getting your time of birth, some astrologers can estimate an approximate birth time by using past events in your life to determine the chart. This technique is called *rectification*.

How to Find an Astrologer

Choose your astrologer with the same care as you would any trusted adviser such as a doctor, lawyer, or banker. Unfortunately, anyone can claim to be an astrologer—to date, there is no licensing of astrologers or universally established professional criteria. However, there are nation-wide organizations of serious, committed astrologers that can help you in your search.

Good places to start your investigation are organizations such as the American Federation of Astrologers (AFA) or the National Council for Geocosmic Research (NCGR), which offer a program of study and certification. If you live near a major city, there is sure to be an active NCGR chapter or astrology club in your area; many are listed in astrology magazines available at your local newsstand. In response to many requests for referrals, both the AFA and the NCGR have directories of professional astrologers listed on their Web sites; these directories include a glossary of terms and an explanation of specialties within the astrological field. Contact the NCGR and AFA headquarters for information (see chapter 10 in this book).

Warning Signals

As a potentially lucrative freelance business, astrology has always attracted self-styled experts who may not have the knowledge or the counseling experience to give a helpful reading. These astrologers can range from the well-meaning amateur to the charlatan or street-corner gypsy who has for many years given astrology a bad name. Be very wary of astrologers who claim to have occult powers or who make pretentious claims of celebrated clients or miraculous achievements. You can often tell from the initial phone conversation if the astrologer is legitimate. He or she should ask for your birthday time and place, then conduct the conversation in a professional manner. Any astrologer who gives a reading based only on your sun sign is highly suspect.

When you arrive at the reading, the astrologer should be prepared. The consultation should be conducted in a private, quiet place. The astrologer should be interested in your problems of the moment. A good reading involves feedback on your part. So if the reading is not relating to your concerns, you should let the astrologer know. You should feel free to ask questions and get clarifications of technical terms. The more you actively participate, rather than expecting the astrologer to carry the reading or come forth with oracular predictions, the more meaningful your experience will be. An astrologer should help you validate your current experience and be frank about possible negative happenings, but also suggest a positive course of action.

In their approach to a reading, some astrologers may be more literal, others more intuitive. Those who have had counseling training may take a more psychological approach. Though some astrologers may seem to have an almost psychic ability, extrasensory perception or any other parapsychological talent is not essential. A very accurate picture can be drawn from the data in your horoscope chart.

An astrologer may do several charts for each client, including one for the time of birth and a *progressed chart,* showing the evolution from birth to the present time. According to your individual needs, there are many other possibilities, such as a chart for a different location if you are contemplating a change of place. Relationships between any two people, things, or events can be interpreted with a chart that compares one partner's horoscope with the other's. A composite chart, which uses the midpoint between planets in two individual charts to describe the relationship, is another commonly used device.

An astrologer will be particularly interested in transits, those times when cycling planets activate the planets or sensitive points in your birth chart. These indicate important events in your life.

Many astrologers offer tape-recorded readings, another option to consider, especially if the astrologer you choose lives at a distance. In this case, you'll be mailed a taped reading based on your birth chart. This type of reading is more personal than a computer printout and can give you valuable insights, though it is not equivalent to a live dialogue with the astrologer when you can discuss your specific interests and issues of the moment.

The Telephone Reading

Telephone readings come in two varieties: a dial-in taped reading, usually recorded in advance by an astrologer, or a live consultation with an "astrologer" on the other end of the line. The taped readings are general daily or weekly forecasts, applied to all members of your sign and charged by the minute. The quality depends on the astrologer. One caution: Be aware that these readings can run up quite a telephone bill, especially if you get into the habit of calling every day. Be sure that you are aware of the per-minute cost of each call beforehand.

Live telephone readings also vary with the expertise of the astrologer. Ideally, the astrologer at the other end of the line enters your birth date into a computer, which then quickly calculates your chart. This chart will be referred to during the consultation. The advantage of a live telephone reading is that your individual chart is used and you can ask about a specific problem. However, before you invest in any reading, be sure that your astrologer is qualified and that you fully understand in advance how much you will be charged. There should be no unpleasant financial surprises later.

Computer-Generated Reports

Companies that offer computer programs (such as ACS, Matrix, Astrolabe) also offer a variety of computer-generated horoscope readings. These can be quite comprehensive, offering a beautiful printout of the chart plus many pages of detailed information about each planet and aspect of the chart. You can then study it at your convenience. Of course, the interpretations will be general, since there is no personal input from you, and may not cover your immediate concerns. Since computer-generated horoscopes are much lower in cost than live consultations, you might consider one as either a supplement or a preparation for an eventual live reading. You'll then be more familiar with your chart and able to plan specific questions in advance. They also make terrific gifts for astrology fans. There are several companies, listed in chapter 9, that offer computerized readings prepared by reputable astrologers.

Whichever option you decide to pursue, may your reading be an empowering one!

CHAPTER 12

Your Baby-scope: Children Born in 2008

Parents of several children may see a marked difference between children born in 2008 and their older siblings, as the cosmic atmosphere is changing, which should imprint the personalities of this year's children.

Astrologers look to the slow-moving outer planets—Uranus, Neptune, and Pluto—to describe a generation. This year, Uranus and Neptune are still passing through Pisces and Aquarius, both visionary and spiritual signs. However, there is also much more earth-sign emphasis than in previous years due to the earthly pull of Pluto in Capricorn, plus the closer planets, Jupiter and Saturn, also in earth signs, which will counterbalance this spirituality with extreme practicality and pragmatism. This generation will be focused on getting the job done, on fixing up the planet, and on making things work.

Astrology can be an especially helpful tool that can be used to design an environment that will enhance and encourage each child's positive qualities. Some parents start before conception, planning the birth of their child as far as possible to harmonize with the signs of other family members. However, each baby has its own schedule, so if yours arrives a week early or late, or elects a different sign than you'd planned, recognize that the new sign may be more in line with the mission your child is here to accomplish. In other words, if you were hoping for a Libra child and he arrives during Virgo, that Virgo energy may be just what is needed to stimulate or complement your family. Remember that there are many astrological elements besides the sun sign that indicate strong family ties. Usually each child will share a particular planetary placement, an emphasis on a particular sign or house, or a certain chart configuration with his parents and other family members. Often there is a significant planetary angle that will define the parent-child relationship, such as family sun signs that form a T-square or a triangle.

One important thing you can do is to be sure the exact moment of birth is recorded. This will be essential in calculating an accurate astrological chart. The following descriptions can be applied to the sun or moon sign (if known) of a child—the sun sign will describe basic personality and the moon sign indicates the child's emotional needs.

The Aries Child

Baby Aries is quite a handful! This energetic child will walk—and run—as soon as possible and perform daring feats of exploration. Caregivers should be vigilant. Little Aries seems to know no fear (and is especially vulnerable to head injuries). Many Aries children, in their rush to get on with life, seem hyperactive and are easily frustrated when they can't get their own way. Violent temper tantrums and dramatic physical displays are par for the course with these children, necessitating a time-out chair.

The very young Aries should be monitored carefully, since he is prone to take risks and may injure himself. An Aries loves to take things apart and may break toys easily, but with encouragement, the child will develop formidable coordination. Aries's bossy tendencies should be molded into leadership qualities, rather than bullying. Otherwise, the me-first Aries will have many clashes with other strong-willed youngsters. Encourage these children to take out aggressions and frustrations in active, competitive sports, where they usually excel. When a young Aries learns to focus his energies long enough to master a subject and learns consideration for others, the indomitable Aries spirit will rise to the head of the class.

Aries born in 2008 will be a more subdued version of

this sign, but still loaded with energy. The Capricorn effect should make little Aries easier to discipline and more focused on achievement. A natural leader!

The Taurus Child

This is a cuddly, affectionate child who eagerly explores the world of the senses, especially the senses of taste and touch. The Taurus child can be a big eater and will put on weight easily if not encouraged to exercise. Since this child likes comfort and gravitates to beauty, try coaxing little Taurus to exercise to music or take him outdoors for hikes or long walks. Though Taurus may be a slow learner, this sign has an excellent retentive memory and generally masters a subject thoroughly. Taurus is interested in results and will see each project patiently through to completion, continuing long after others have given up. This year's earth-sign planet will give him a wonderful sense of support and accomplishment.

Choose Taurus toys carefully to help develop innate talents. Construction toys, such as blocks or erector sets, appeal to their love of building. Paints or crayons develop their sense of color. Many Taurus have musical talents and love to sing, which is apparent at a young age.

This year's Taurus will want a pet or two and a few plants of his own. Give little Taurus a minigarden and watch the natural green thumb develop. This child has a strong sense of acquisition and an early grasp of material value. After filling a piggy bank, Taurus graduates to a savings account, before other children have started to learn the value of money.

This year's Taurus gets a bonanza of good luck and support from Jupiter, Pluto, and Saturn—all in compatible earth signs. These should give little Taurus an especially easygoing disposition and provide many opportunities to live up to his sign's potential.

The Gemini Child

Little Gemini will talk as soon as possible, filing the air with questions and chatter. This is a friendly child who enjoys social contact, seems to require company, and adapts quickly to different surroundings. Geminis have quick minds that easily grasp the use of words, books, and telephones and will probably learn to talk and read at an earlier age than most. Though they are fast learners, Gemini may have a short attention span, darting from subject to subject. Projects and games that help focus the mind could be used to help them concentrate. Musical instruments, typewriters, and computers help older Gemini children combine mental with manual dexterity. Geminis should be encouraged to finish what they start before they go on to another project. Otherwise, they can become jack-of-all-trade types who have trouble completing anything they do. Their dispositions are usually cheerful and witty, making these children popular with their peers and delightful company at home.

This year's Gemini baby should go to the head of the class. Uranus in Pisces could inspire Gemini to make an unusual career choice, perhaps in a financial field. When he grows up, this year's Gemini may change jobs several times before he finds a position that satisfies his need for stimulation and variety.

The Cancer Child

This emotional, sensitive child is especially influenced by patterns set early in life. Young Cancers cling to their first memories as well as their childhood possessions. They thrive in calm emotional waters, with a loving, protective mother, and usually remain close to her (even if their relationship with her was difficult) throughout their lives. Divorce, death—anything that disturbs the safe family unit—

are devastating to Cancers, who may need extra support and reassurance during a family crisis.

They sometimes need a firm hand to push the positive, creative side of their personality and discourage them from getting swept away by emotional moods or resorting to emotional manipulation to get their way. Praised and encouraged to find creative expression, Cancer will be able to express his positive side consistently on a firm, secure foundation.

This year's Cancer baby should be a social, cooperative child, oriented toward others, thanks to Jupiter and Pluto blessing relationships.

The Leo Child

Leo children love the limelight and will plot to get the lion's share of attention. These children assert themselves with flair and drama and can behave like tiny tyrants to get their way. But in general, they have sunny, positive dispositions and are rarely subject to blue moods. At school, they're the ones who are voted most popular, head cheerleader, or homecoming queen. Leo is sure to be noticed for personality, if not for stunning looks or academic work; the homely Leo will be a class clown and the unhappy Leo may be the class bully.

Above all, a Leo child cannot tolerate being ignored for long. Drama or performing-arts classes, sports, and school politics are healthy ways for Leo to be a star. But Leos must learn to take lesser roles occasionally, or they will have some painful put-downs in store. Usually, the popularity of Leos is well earned; they are hard workers who try to measure up to their own high standards—and usually succeed.

This year's Leo should be a less flamboyant, more down-to-earth version of his sign, as the earthy planets exert their influence. This should add more financial and practical talents to the expressive Leo personality.

The Virgo Child

The young Virgo can be a quiet, rather serious child, with a quick, intelligent mind. Early on, little Virgo shows far more attention to detail and concern with small things than other children do. Little Virgo has a built-in sense of order and a fascination with how things work. It is important for these children to have a place of their own, which they can order as they wish and where they can read or busy themselves with crafts and hobbies.

This child's personality can be very sensitive. Little Virgo may get hyper and overreact to seemingly small irritations, which can take the form of stomach upsets or delicate digestive systems. But this child will flourish where there is mental stimulation and a sense of order. Virgos thrive in school, especially in writing or language skills, and seem truly happy when buried in books. Chances are, young Virgo will learn to read ahead of classmates. Hobbies that involve detail work or that develop fine craftsmanship are especially suited to young Virgos.

Baby Virgo of 2008 is likely to be an especially high achiever with Saturn also in Virgo, adding focus and discipline, while Jupiter transiting the house of self-expression endows extra creativity.

The Libra Child

The Libra child learns early about the power of charm and appearance. This is often a very physically appealing child with an enchanting dimpled smile, who is naturally sociable and enjoys the company of both children and adults. It is a rare Libra child who is a discipline problem, but when their behavior is unacceptable, they respond better to calm discussion than displays of emotion, especially if the discussion revolves around fairness. Because young Libras without a strong direction tend to drift with the mood of the group, these children should be encouraged to develop their unique talents and powers of discrimination so they can later stand on their own.

In school, this child is usually popular and will often have to choose between social invitations and studies. In the teen years, social pressures mount as the young Libra begins to look for a partner. This is the sign of best friends, so Libra's choice of companions can have a strong effect on his future direction. Beautiful Libra girls may be tempted to go steady or have an unwise early marriage. Chances are, both sexes will fall in and out of love several times in their search for the ideal partner.

Little Libra of 2008 is an especially social, talkative child who gets along well with siblings because Jupiter in Capricorn enhances family life. This child is endowed with much imagination and creativity, as well as communication skills.

The Scorpio Child

The Scorpio child may seem quiet and shy, but will surprise others with intense feelings and formidable willpower. Scorpio children are single-minded when they want something and intensely passionate about whatever they do. One of a caregiver's tasks is to teach this child to balance activities and emotions, yet at the same time to make the most of his or her great concentration and intense commitment.

Since young Scorpios do not show their depth of feelings easily, parents will have to learn to read almost imperceptible signs that troubles are brewing beneath the surface. Both Scorpio boys and girls enjoy games of power and control on or off the playground. Scorpio girls may take an early interest in the opposite sex, masquerading as tomboys, while Scorpio boys may be intensely competitive and loners. When their powerful energies are directed into work, sports, or challenging studies, Scorpio is a superachiever, focused on a goal. With trusted friends, young Scorpio is devoted and caring—the proverbial friend through thick and thin, loyal for life.

Scorpio 2008 has a strong financial emphasis, which could make these children big money earners in adulthood. Uranus in Pisces in their house of creativity should put them on the cutting edge of whichever field they choose.

The Sagittarius Child

This restless, athletic child will be out of the playpen and off on adventures as soon as possible. Little Sagittarius is remarkably well-coordinated, attempting daredevil feats on any wheeled vehicle from scooters to skateboards. These natural athletes need little encouragement to channel their energies into sports. Their cheerful, friendly dispositions earn them popularity in school, and once they have found a subject where their talent and imagination can soar, they will do well academically. They love animals, especially horses, and will be sure to have a pet or two, if not a home zoo. When they are old enough to take care of themselves, they'll clamor to be off on adventures of their own, away from home, if possible.

This child loves to travel, will not get homesick at summer camp, and may sign up to be a foreign-exchange student or spend summers abroad. Outdoor adventure appeals to little Sagittarius, especially if it involves an active sport, such as skiing, cycling, or mountain climbing. Give them enough space and encouragement, and their fiery spirit will propel them to achieve high goals.

Baby Sagittarius of 2008 has a natural generosity of spirit and an optimistic, expansive nature. He will also demand a great deal of freedom. He may need reality checks from time to time, since he may be a risk taker, especially in the financial area. He should learn early in life how to handle money.

The Capricorn Child

These purposeful, goal-oriented children will work to capacity if they feel this will bring results. They're not ones who enjoy work for its own sake—there must be an end in sight. Authority figures can do much to motivate these children, but once set on an upward path, young Capricorns will mobilize energy and talent and work harder, and with more perseverance, than any other sign. Capricorn has built-in self-discipline that can achieve remarkable results, even if lacking the flashy personality, quick brain power, or penetrating insight of others. Once involved, young Capricorn will stick to a task until it is mastered. These children also know how to use others to their advantage and may well become team captains or class presidents.

A wise parent will set realistic goals for the Capricorn child, paving the way for the early thrill of achievement. Youngsters should be encouraged to express their caring, feeling side to others, as well as their natural aptitude for leadership. Capricorn children may be especially fond of grandparents and older relatives and will enjoy spending time with them and learning from them. It is not uncommon for young Capricorns to have an older mentor or teacher who guides them. With their great respect for authority, Capricorn children will take this influence very much to heart.

The Capricorn born in 2008 will have an upbeat, cheerful personality, thanks to the presence of lucky Jupiter in Capricorn. This child should have a generous, expansive nature and be more outgoing than the usual member of this sign.

The Aquarius Child

The Aquarius child has an innovative, well-focused mind that often streaks so far ahead of those of peers that this child seems like an oddball. Routine studies never hold the restless youngster for long; he will look for another, more experimental place to try out his ideas and develop his inventions. Life is a laboratory to the inquiring Aquarius mind. School politics, sports, science, and the arts offer scope for such talents. But if there is no room for expression within approved social limits, Aquarius is sure to rebel. Questioning institutions and religions comes naturally, so these children may find an outlet elsewhere, becoming rebels with a cause. It is better not to force this child to conform, but rather to channel forward-thinking young minds into constructive group activities.

This year's Aquarius will have far-out glamour as well as charisma, thanks to his ruler, Uranus, in a friendly bond with Neptune. This could be a rock star, a statesman, or a scientist.

The Pisces Child

Give young Pisces praise, applause, and a gentle, but firm, push in the right direction. Lovable Pisces children may be abundantly talented, but may be hesitant to express themselves, because they are quite sensitive and easily hurt. It is a parent's challenge to help them gain self-esteem and self-confidence. However, this same sensitivity makes them trusted friends who'll have many confidants as they develop socially. It also endows many Pisces with spectacular creative talent.

Pisces adores drama and theatrics of all sorts; therefore, encourage them to channel their creativity into art forms rather than indulging in emotional dramas. Understand that they may need more solitude than other children, as they develop their creative ideas. But though daydreaming can be creative, it is important that these natural dreamers not dwell too long in the world of fantasy. Teach them practical coping skills for the real world. Since Pisces are physically sensitive, parents should help them build strong bodies with proper diet and regular exercise. Young Pisces may gravitate to more individual sports, such as swimming, sailing, and skiing, rather than to team sports. Or they may prefer more artistic physical activities like dance or ice skating.

Born givers, these children are often drawn to the underdog (they fall quickly for sob stories) and attract those who might take advantage of their empathic nature. Teach them to choose friends wisely and to set boundaries in relationships, to protect their emotional vulnerability—invaluable lessons in later life.

With the planet Uranus now in Pisces, the 2008 baby

belongs to a generation of Pisces movers and shakers. This child may have a rebellious streak that rattles the status quo. But this generation also has a visionary nature, which will be much concerned with the welfare of the world at large.

CHAPTER 13

Your Leap Year Guide to Love

The year 2008 is a leap year, when ladies traditionally make the first romantic moves. However, it's no longer unusual for women to pursue the object of their desire aggressively, no matter what the year. So if you want to charm a Capricorn, hook a Pisces, or corral a Taurus, here are sun-sign seduction tips guaranteed to keep your lover begging for more.

How to Love Every Sign

Aries: Daredevil Lover

This highly physical sign is walking dynamite with a brief attention span. Don't be too easy to get, ladies. A little challenge, a lively debate, and a merry chase only heat up your admirers. They want to see what you're made of. Once you've lured them into your lair, be a challenge, a bit of a daredevil, and pull out your X-rated tricks. Don't give your all—let them know there's more where that came from. Make it exciting, show you're up for adventure. Wear bright red somewhere interesting. Since Aries rules the head and face, be sure to focus on these areas in your lovemaking. Use your lips, tongue, breath, and even your eyelashes to the max. Practice scalp massages and deep-kissing techniques. Aries won't wait, so when you make your move, be sure you're ready to follow through. No head games or teasing!

To keep you happy, you've got to voice your own needs, because this lover will be focused on his. Teach him how to please, or this could be a one-sided adventure.

Taurus: Sweet Treats

Taurus wins as the most sensual sign, with the most sexual stamina. This man is earthy and lusty in bed; he can go on all night. This is not a sign to tease. Like the Bull, he'll see red, not bed. So make him comfortable, then bombard all his senses. Good food gets Taurus in the mood. So do the right music and fragrance, revealing clothes, and luxurious bed linens. Give him a massage with delicious-smelling and -tasting oils; focus on the neck area.

Don't forget to turn off the phone! Taurus hates interruptions. Since they can be very vocal lovers, choose a setting where you won't be disturbed. And don't ever rush; enjoy a long, slow, delicious encounter.

Gemini: Playtime

Playful Gemini loves games, so make your seduction fun. Be their lost twin soul, their confidant. Good communication is essential, so share deep secrets, live out fantasies. This sign adores variety. Nothing bores Gemini more than making love the same way all the time, or bringing on the heavy emotions. So trot out all the roles you've been longing to play. Here's the perfect partner. But remember to keep it light and fun. Gemini's turn-on zone is the hands, and this sign gives the best massages. Gadgets that can be activated with a touch amuse Gemini. This sign is great at doing two things at once, like making love while watching an erotic film. Turn the cell phone off unless you want company. On the other hand, Gemini is your sign for superhot phone sex.

Gemini loves a change of scene. So experiment on the floor, in the shower, or on the kitchen table. Borrow a friend's apartment or rent a room in a hotel for variety.

Cancer: In the Mood

The key to Cancer is to get this moon child in the mood. Consult the moon—a full moon is best. Wining, dining, old-fashioned courtship, and breakfast in bed are turn-ons. Whatever makes your Cancer feel secure will promote shedding inhibitions in the sack. (Don't try any of your Aries daredevil techniques here!) Cancer prefers familiar, comfortable, homey surroundings. Cancer's turn-on zone is the breasts. Cancer women often have naturally inflated chests. Cancer men may fantasize about a well-endowed playmate. If your breasts are enhanced, show them off. Cancer will want to know all your deepest secrets, so invent a few good ones. But lots of luck delving into their innermost thoughts!

A sure thing: Take your Cancer near water. The sight and sound of the sea can be their aphrodisiac. A moonlit beach, a deserted swimming pool, a Jacuzzi, and a bubble bath are good seduction spots. Listen to the rain patter on the roof in a mountain cabin.

Leo: The Royal Treatment

Leo must be the best and hear it from you often. In return, they'll perform for you, telling you just what you want to hear (true or not). They like a lover with style and endurance, to be swept off their feet and into bed. Leos like to go first-class all the way, so build them up with lots of attention, wining and dining, special gifts.

Never mention other lovers or make them feel like second best. A sure signal for Leo to look elsewhere is a competitive spouse. Leos take great pride in their body, so you should pour on the admiration. A few well-placed mirrors could inspire them. So would a striptease of beautiful lingerie, expensive fragrance on the sheets, and, if female, an occasional luxury hotel room, with champagne and caviar delivered by room service. Leo's erogenous zone is the lower back, so a massage with expensive oils would make your lion purr with pleasure.

Virgo: Pedestal Perfect

Virgo's standards are so sky-high that you may feel intimidated at first. The key to pleasing fussy Virgo lovers is to look for the hot fantasy beneath their cool surface. Secret tip: They're really looking for someone to make over. So let Virgo play teacher and you play willing student; the doctor-patient routine works as well.

Let Virgo help you improve your life, quit smoking, learn French, or diet. Read an erotic book together, then practice the techniques. Or study the esoteric, erotic exercises from Asia.

The Virgo erogenous zone is the tummy area, which should be your base of operations. Virgo likes things pristine and clean. Fall into crisp, immaculate white sheets. Wear a sheer white nightie. Smell shower-fresh with no heavy perfume. Be sure your surroundings pass the hospital test. A shower together afterward (with great-smelling soap) could get the ball rolling again.

Libra: The Beauty Lover

Libra must be turned on aesthetically. Make sure you look as beautiful as possible and wear something stylishly seductive but never vulgar. Have a mental affair first, as you flirt and flatter this sign. Then proceed to the physical. Approach Libra like a dance partner, ready to waltz or tango.

Libra must be in the mood for love; otherwise, forget it. Any kind of ugliness is a turnoff. Provide the right atmosphere, elegant and harmonious. No loud noise, clashing colors, or uncomfortable beds. Libra is not an especially spontaneous lover, so it is best to spend time warming them up. Libra's back is his erogenous zone, your cue to provide back rubs with scented potions. Once in bed, you can be a bit aggressive sexually. Libra loves strong, decisive moves. Set the scene, know what you want, and let Libra be happy to provide it.

Scorpio: The Legendary Lover

Scorpio is legendary in bed, often called the sex sign of the zodiac. But seducing them is often a power game. Scorpio likes to be in control, even the quiet, unassuming ones. Scorpio loves a mystery, so don't tell all. Keep them guessing about you, offering tantalizing hints along the way. The hint of danger often turns Scorpio on, so you'll find members of this sign experimenting with the exotic and highly erotic forms of sex. Sadomasochism and bondage, anything that tests the limits of power could be a turn-on for Scorpio.

Invest in some sexy black leather and some powerful music (depending on your tastes). Clothes that lace, buckle, or zip tempt Scorpio to untie you. Present yourself as a mysterious package just waiting to be unwrapped.

Once in bed, there are no holds barred with Scorpio. They'll find your most pleasurable pressure points and touch you as you've never been touched before. They are quickly aroused (the genital area belongs to this sign) and willing to try anything. But they can be possessive. Don't expect your Scorpio to share you with anyone. It's all or nothing for them.

Sagittarius: The Sexual Athletes

Sagittarius men are the Don Juans of the zodiac, love-'em-and-leave-'em types who are difficult to pin down. Your seduction strategy is to join them in their many pursuits, then hook them with love on the road. Sagittarius enjoys sex in venues that suggest movement: planes, SUVs, or boats. But a favorite turn-on place is outdoors, in nature. A deserted hiking path, a field of tall grass, a remote woodland glade all give the Centaur sexy ideas. Athletic Sagittarius might go for some personal training in an empty gym. Join your Sagittarius for amorous aerobics, meditate together, or explore the tantric forms of sex. Lovemaking after hiking and skiing would be healthy fun.

Sagittarius enjoys lovers from exotic ethnic backgrounds or lovers met in spiritual pursuits or on college campuses. Sagittarius are great cheerleaders and motivators, and will enjoy feeling that they have inspired you to be all that you can be.

There may be a canine or feline companion sharing your Sagittarius lover's bed with you, so check your allergies. And bring Fido or Felix a toy to keep him occupied.

Capricorn: Animal Instincts

The great news about Capricorn lovers is that they improve with age. They are probably the sexiest seniors. So stick around, if you have a young one. They're lusty in bed (it's not the sign of the Goat for nothing), and can be quite raunchy and turned on by X-rated words and deeds. If this is not your thing, let them know. The Capricorn erogenous zone is the knees. Some discreet fondling in public places could be your opener. Capricorn tends to think of sex as part of a game plan for the future. They are well-organized, and might regard lovemaking as relaxation after a long day's work. This sign often combines business with pleasure. So look for a Capricorn where there's a convention, trade show, or work-related conference.

Getting Capricorn's mind off his agenda and onto yours could take some doing. Separate him from his buddies by whispering sexy secrets in his ear. Then convince him you're an asset to his image and a boon to his health. Though he may seem uptight at first, you'll soon discover he's a love animal who makes a wonderful and permanent pet.

Aquarius: Far-Out Lover

This sign really does not want an all-consuming passion or an all-or-nothing relationship. Aquarius need space. But once they feel free to experiment with a spontaneous and exciting partner, Aquarius can give you a far-out sexual adventure.

Passion begins in the mind, so a good mental buildup is key. Aquarius is an inventive sign who believes love is a playground without rules. Plan surprise, unpredictable encounters in unusual places. Find ways to make love transcendental, an extraordinary and unique experience. Be ready to try anything Aquarius suggests, if only once. Calves and ankles are the special Aquarius erogenous zones, so perfect your legwork.

Be careful not to be too possessive. Your Aquarius needs lots of space, tolerance for friends (including old lovers), and their many outside interests.

Pisces: Fantasy Time

Pisces is the sign of fantasy and imagination. This sign has great theatrical talent. Pisces looks for lovers who will take care of them. Pisces will return the favor! Here is someone who can psych out your deepest desires without mentioning them. Pisces falls for sob stories and is always ready to empathize. It wouldn't hurt to have a small problem for Pisces to help you overcome. It might help if you cry on his shoulder, for this sign needs to be needed. Use your imagination when setting the scene for love. A dramatic setting brings out Pisces theatrical talents. Or creatively use the element of water. Rain on the roof, waterfalls, showers, beach houses, waterbeds, and Jacuzzis could turn up the heat. Experiment with pulsating jets of water. Skinny-dip at midnight in deserted pools.

The Pisces erogenous zone is the feet. This is your cue to give a sensuous foot massage using scented lotions. Let him paint your toes. Beautiful toenails in sexy sandals are a special turn-on.

Your Hot Planets: Mars and Venus Tango Together

Here's a tip for finding your hottest love match. If your lover's Mars sign makes favorable aspects to your Venus, is in the same element (earth, air, fire, water), or is in the same sign, your lover will do what you want done! Mars influences how we act when we make love, while Venus shows what we like done to us. Sometimes fighting and making up is the sexiest fun of all. If you're the type who needs a spark to keep lust alive (you know who you are!), then look for Mars and Venus in different signs of the same quality (fixed or cardinal or mutable). For instance, a fixed sign (Taurus, Leo, Scorpio, Aquarius) paired with another fixed sign can have a sexy standoff, a hot tug of war before you finally surrender. Two cardinal signs (Aries, Cancer, Libra, Capricorn) set off passionate fireworks when they clash. Mutable signs (Gemini, Virgo, Sagittarius, Pisces) play a fascinating game of cat and mouse, never quite catching each other.

The Best Time for Love

The best time for love is when Venus is in your sign, making you the most desirable sign in the zodiac. This only lasts about three weeks (unless Venus is retrograde), so don't waste time! And find out the time this year when Venus is in your sign by consulting the Venus chart at the end of chapter 6.

Who's the Sexiest Sign of the Zodiac?

It depends on what sign you are. Astrology has traditionally given this honor to Scorpio, the sign associated with the sex organs. However, we are all a combination of different signs (and turn-ons). Gemini's communicating ability and manual dexterity could deliver the magic touch. Cancer's tenderness and understanding could bring out your passion more than regal Leo.

Who'll Be Faithful?

The earth signs of Capricorn, Taurus, and Virgo are usually the most faithful. They tend to be more home-oriented and family-oriented, and they are usually choosy about their mates. It's impractical, inconvenient, and probably expensive to play around, so they think.

Who's Most Likely to Cheat?

The mutable signs of Gemini, Pisces, and Sagittarius win the playboy or playgirl sweepstakes. These signs tend to be changeable, fickle, and easily bored. But they're so much fun!

CHAPTER 14

Signs of Success: Wealth-Building Advice from the Stars

Are you a serial spender or a savvy saver? Here's where to find out your sign's bottom line when it comes to managing money. Though no sign wins the financial sweepstakes—all have their share of billionaires and paupers—the signs of success are those who make the most of their particular financial talents. This year's financial winners are the earth signs (Taurus, Virgo, and especially Capricorn), who should profit from the lucky rays of Jupiter in Capricorn. Yet all of us could benefit from some of Capricorn's self-discipline when it comes to spending wisely and budgeting carefully.

Aries

You've got a taste for fast money, quick turnover, and edgy investments, with no patience for gradual long-term gains. You're an impulse buyer with the nerve for risky tactics that could backfire. On the other hand, you're a pioneer who can see into the future, who dares to take a gamble on a new idea or product that could change the world . . . like Sam Walton of the Wal-mart stores who changed the way we shop. You need a backup plan in case one of your big ideas burns out. To protect your money, get a backup plan you can follow without thinking about it. Have an automatic percentage of your income put into a savings or retirement plan. Then give yourself some extra funds to play with. Your weak point is your impatience; you're not one to wait out a slow market or watch savings slowly accumulate.

Taurus

You're a saver who loves to see your cash accumulate, as well as your possessions. You have no qualms about steadily increasing your fortune. You're a savvy trader and a shrewd investor, in there for long-term gains. You have low toleration for risk, hate to lose anything. But you do enjoy luxuries, may need to reward yourself frequently. You might pass up an opportunity because it seems too risky. Take a chance once in a while. You're especially lucky in real estate.

Gemini

With Gemini, the cash can flow in and then out just as quickly. You naturally multitask and are sure to have several projects going at once, as well as several credit cards, which can easily get out of hand. Saving is not one of your strong points . . . too boring. You fall in and out of love with different ideas, have probably tried a round of savings techniques. Diversification is your best strategy. Have several different kinds of investments—at least one should be a long-term plan. Set savings goals and then regularly deposit small amounts into your accounts.

Cancer

You can be a natural moneymaker with your peerless intuition. You can spot a winner that everyone else misses. Consider Cancer success stories like those of cosmetics queen Estée Lauder and Roxanne Quimby, of Burt's Bees, who turned her friend's stash of beeswax into a thriving cosmetics business. Who knew? So trust your intuition. You are a saver who always has a backup plan just in case. Remember to treat and nurture yourself as well as others. Investments in the food industry, restaurants, hotels, shipping, and water-related industries are Cancer territory.

Leo

You love the first-class lifestyle, but may not always have the resources to support it. Finding a way to fund your extravagant tastes is the Leo challenge. Some courses in money management or an expert financial coach could set you on the right track. However, you're also a terrific salesperson, fabulous in high-profile jobs that pay a lot. You're the community tastemaker. Satisfy your appetite for "the best" by working for a quality company that sells luxury goods, splendid real estate, dream vacations, first-class travel—that way you'll have access to the lifestyle without having to pay for it.

Virgo

Your sign is a stickler for details and that includes your money management. You like to follow your spending and saving closely and enjoy planning and budgeting and price comparison. Your sign usually has no problem sticking to a savings or investment plan. You have a critical eye for quality and like to bargain—shop to get the best value. In fact, Virgo billionaire Warren Buffet is known for value investing. You buy cheap and sell at a profit. Investing in health care and organic products and food could be profitable for you.

Libra

Oh, do you ever love to shop! And you often have an irresistible urge to acquire an exquisite object, like a designer dress you can't really afford, or splurge on the perfect antique armoire once you've found it. You don't like to settle for second-rate or bargain buys. Learning to prioritize your spending is especially difficult for your sign, so try to find a good money manager to do it for you. Following a strictly balanced budget is your key to financial success. With Libra's keen eye for quality and good taste, you are a savvy picker at auctions and antiques fairs, so you might be able to turn around your purchase for a profit.

Scorpio

Scorpios prefer to stay in control of their finances at all times. You're sure to have a financial-tracking program on your computer. You're not an impulse buyer, unless you see something that immediately turns you on. Rely on your instincts! Scorpio is the sign of credit cards, taxes, and loans, so you are able to use these tools cleverly. Investing for Scorpio is rarely casual. You'll do extensive research and track your investments—reading the financial pages, annual reports, and profit-and-loss statements.

Sagittarius

Sagittarius is a natural gambler, with a high tolerance for risk. It's important for you to learn when to hold 'em, and when to fold 'em, as the song goes, by setting limits on your risk taking and covering your assets. You enjoy the thrill of playing the stock market, where you could win big and lose big. Money itself is rarely the object for Sagittarius—it's the game that counts. Since your sign rarely saves for a rainy day, your best strategy might be an automatic-savings plan that deducts a certain amount without your knowing it. Regular bill-paying plans are another strategy to keep you on track. You could benefit from an inspirational money manager who gets you fired up about an investment plan.

Capricorn

You're one of the strongest money managers in the zodiac, which should serve you well this year when Jupiter, the planet of luck and expansion, is blessing Capricorn. You're a born bargain hunter and clever negotiator, a saver rather than a spender. You are the sign of self-discipline, which works well when it comes to sticking with a budget and living frugally while waiting for resources to accumulate. You are likely to plan carefully for your elder years, profiting from long-term investments. You have a keen sense of value and will pick up a bargain, then turn it around at a nice profit.

Aquarius

The Aquarius trait of unpredictability extends to your financial life, where you surprise us all with your ability to turn something totally unique into a money spinner. Consider your wealthy sign mates Oprah Winfrey and Paris Hilton, who are able to intuit what the public will buy at a given moment. Some of your ideas might sound far-out, but turn out to be right on the money. Investing in high-tech companies that are on the cutting edge of their field is good for Aquarius. You'll probably intuit which ones will stay the course. You'll feel good about investing in companies that improve the environment, such as new types of fuel, or ones that are related to your favorite cause.

Pisces

The typical Pisces is probably the sign least interested in money management. However, there are many billionaires born under your sign, such as Michael Dell, David Geffen, and Steve Jobs. Generally they have made money from innovative ideas and left the details to others. That might work for you. Find a Scorpio, Capricorn, or Virgo to help you set a profitable course and systematically save (which is not in your nature). Sign up for automatic bill paying, so you won't have to think about it. If you keep in mind how much less stressful life will be and how much more you can do when you're not worried about paying bills, you might be motivated enough to stick to a sensible budget. Investmentwise, consider anything to do with water—offshore drilling, water conservation and purifying, shipping, and seafood. Petroleum is also ruled by your sign, as are institutions related to hospitals.

CHAPTER 15

Keep Father Time in His Place: Antiaging Tips

In 2008, both Jupiter and Pluto enter the sign of Capricorn, the Saturn-ruled sign associated with Father Time and the elder years. This is especially meaningful for the baby boomer generation, the millions of Americans born between 1946 and 1964. For the post–World War II generation, who are looking forward to a long and vital life span, age sixty is the beginning of middle age, not old age. This active generation will be reinventing our concept of how to spend the senior years, as they play a much more vocal and demanding role in society.

It will not be unusual to live to be over one hundred, say the experts, but baby boomers will be concerned with how well they live, not just how long. Innovative medical technologies in areas such as joint replacement and management of cardiovascular disease assure this generation of more pep and productivity, while drugs like Viagra boost their sex lives. Americans will be well able to skip retirement and continue in the workforce or choose to start a second, more rewarding career.

Astrology has many ideas for keeping baby boomers healthy and happy. Each sign is associated with a part of the body that could become vulnerable in later years. Within the personality of a sign are other clues for having a productive old age.

Aries

The Aries baby boomer is one who plans on staying forever young. You'll stay up-to-date and may identify with the younger generation rather than your peers. If something is wrong physically, you'll fix it quickly with the latest medical technology. It's important, Aries, that you learn to pace yourself and be realistic about what you can do. (You are the sign that goes snowboarding at age sixty.) Be sure to take physical precautions to safeguard yourself when doing sports. Guard your head area with the right gear and rein in your impulsiveness when in crowded or traffic situations. More patience could be the greatest gift of your elder years.

Taurus ·

As the zodiac's gourmet, Taurus needs to watch your diet and craving for sweets as you grow older, since you're more likely to overindulge and gain weight. Exercise is not your favorite activity, so trick yourself by combining a workout with a walk in a beautiful nature preserve or bike path. Since you are a great shopper, you could combine bargain hunting with a power walk in your local mall. Gardening and playing with a lively pet are pleasant ways to get moving or get a fun workout playing with young grandchildren. Combining movement with your everyday activities is the key for sedentary Taurus.

Gemini

Yours is one of the active signs that rarely has a serious weight problem. Your lungs may be vulnerable, however, so do everything you can to stop smoking, get regular flu shots, and improve the air quality in your home. Gemini thrives on social contact and mental stimulation and should remain active in the community. Expand your social network as much as possible to include young people with innovative ideas. Take courses at your local college and challenge yourself by learning new skills. It is important for Gemini to protect your nerve pathways, so be sure your chairs are ergonomic and watch for carpal tunnel syndrome if you use a computer.

Cancer

Cancer is family-oriented in the elder years and thrives on close contact with loving relatives. It is even better if your home is near water, where you can exercise with long walks on the beach and swimming. If not, join a local water-aerobics class at your local pool. Cancer can be moody, so combat any tendency to get depressed by doing creative projects and spending time with loved ones. A positive attitude is one of your best antiaging techniques.

Leo

Leo's vulnerable area is the heart, which you should check frequently as you grow older, even if you appear to be the picture of health, like Leos Arnold Schwarzenegger and Bill Clinton, who have had cardiac surgery. Adopting a heart-healthy diet will help stave off problems. Sun-ruled Leos should take preventive measures to avoid skin cancer by using a high SPF sunscreen, especially if you live in a Southern climate. Leos thrive on the attention they get from performing, so why not share skills by lecturing or teaching a local class. Share that hard-won wisdom!

Virgo

As one of the most health-conscious signs, Virgo usually sticks to a sensible diet and gets regular checkups. Staying mentally active can ward off age-related depression, so investigate your local community college, take education-oriented trips, and expand your social circle with new friends. Virgo thrives when being of service to the community and should seek opportunities to do volunteer work. Teaching or coaching young people can be especially rewarding to your sign.

Libra

Libra's key to youth is to keep the social, family, mental, and physical areas of your life in balance. Strengthen your body with balancing exercises like tai chi and yoga or artistic and social exercises like dancing. Exercises done in a sociable group are more to Libra's liking. Your back and kidneys are vulnerable areas to keep in good condition. In later years, Libra has the time to become more involved in intellectual pursuits and arts and crafts. Libra enjoys entertaining and throwing parties for friends and family. Cultivating relationships with like-minded friends by joining a club or group with a common cause is a good idea.

Scorpio

You're the sexy senior! The sign of Scorpio is associated with the sex organs and known for having an active sex life in the senior years. Your partner may well need Viagra! Scorpio is often likened to a phoenix rising from the ashes for your ability to survive illness and regain health. However, you should pay special attention to the elimination and sexual functions of the body with regular examinations and colonoscopies. Water sports and vacations near the sea are excellent therapy for stressed-out Scorpios. Getting involved in something you care passionately about keeps Scorpio young at heart.

Sagittarius

You're no stay-at-home senior! You'll enjoy the independence you have, which gives you the chance to pursue your many interests, including travel to places you've always wanted to explore and having fun times with pals. Active Sagittarius is one of the most athletic signs and may continue to play your favorite sports in senior years, right alongside your grandchildren. Now's your time to motivate the younger generation, so find ways to pass on your hard-won wisdom via teaching or writing, perhaps continuing your career on a part-time basis. Many Sagittarius will get involved in promoting an idealistic or political cause.

Capricorn

The Capricorn senior likes to stay actively involved in community life. Yours is a disciplined, organized sign that may not retire from business or may continue your career on a part-time basis. Some may pursue an entirely different career, with great success. You could well represent the seniors in your community on boards and committees. It is important for Capricorn to continue doing productive work, even if it is on a volunteer basis. Physically Capricorn is one of the longer-lived signs. It is associated with bones and knees, so protect these areas and watch a tendency toward arthritis and osteoporosis.

Aquarius

Aquarius is on the cutting edge and usually on top of the latest trends, even later in life. You won't let advanced years hold you back! You're likely to play computer games with grandchildren and even have your own Web site. You remain young if you stay involved in a cause and pursue your multiple interests. You'll share your wisdom by teaching a class, lecturing, or writing. Physically, protect yourself against airborne allergies, and exercise to prevent circulation problems. Group activities appeal to Aquarius, especially if you are promoting a cause.

Pisces

Elder Pisces is happiest when pursuing creative activities, such as filmmaking, painting, writing, or a hobby or craft in which you can express your imagination. Places near water are particularly healthful for Pisces. Water sports, especially swimming, can maintain your health. Avoid addictive substances and stick to a balanced diet of organic foods, including plenty of fish. Lymphatic drainage massage is good therapy for Pisces, which is associated with the lymphatic system. Pay special attention to the condition of your feet, and wear the appropriate shoes for each activity.

CHAPTER 16

The Mystic Properties of Your Birthstone

Who hasn't at one time or another received a special piece of jewelry with a birthstone? We enjoy the idea that wearing a special gem resonates with our personality and might even bring us luck. However, there is quite a bit of confusion over which stone is best for each sign, because we are often given birthstones according to the month of our birthday rather than our zodiac sign. You may be wondering if the amethyst is more suitable for a February-born Pisces than the aquamarine, or you might prefer the gems associated with your moon sign, which resonate with your emotional nature, or your Venus sign, which appeal to your sense of fashion and good taste.

There are many ways to approach the subject of birthstones. Lovers of precious gems could choose one that reflects the element of your sun sign. Earth signs (Taurus, Virgo, Capricorn) resonate to the bright green emerald. Fire signs (Aries, Leo, Sagittarius) belong to the flaming ruby. Water signs (Cancer, Scorpio, Pisces) might prefer the deep blue sapphire. And air signs (Gemini, Libra, Aquarius) may gravitate to the clear, brilliant diamond.

If you don't care for your birthstone, you could choose a talisman by color. Choose a stone that is associated with your sun, moon, or Venus sign. An Aries with moon in Cancer might prefer a pale lunar jewel like the pearl or moonstone. A Pisces with Venus in Aries might love to wear bright red stones like ruby or spinel.

In ancient India, Egypt, and Babylonia, rare and beautiful gemstones were thought to have magical properties. People are said to have consulted astrologers for advice on wearing the appropriate gem for each occasion. Ancient Egyptians carried scarabs and tiny figures of their gods for protection and luck. These were carved in semi-precious stones like lapis lazuli, carnelian, and turquoise. In India, one of the most powerful talismans was an amulet designed with precious stones representing the known planets at the time. Another astrological connection was the wearing of gems associated with a planet on that planet's special day. Mars-ruled rubies would be worn on the Mars day, Tuesday, for instance. It is still possible to find special astrological talismans created by astrologer-jewelers, who will make up a special pendant or necklace displaying your horoscope's special stones in a beautiful design.

In the Judeo-Christian tradition, the astrological association with gemstones dates from the sacred twelve-gem breastplate of Aaron, recorded in Exodus. Each gem symbolized one of the twelve tribes of Israel. Later these gems became connected with the twelve signs of the zodiac. However, it was not until the eighteenth century that people began to wear their special birthstones. For more information on the history and mystery of gemstones, including their astrological use, read *The Curious Lore of Precious Stones* by George Frederick Kunz.

Here are some suggestions for choosing stones associated with a given zodiac sign. Bear in mind that there are no hard-and-fast rules; you might find yourself attracted to a certain gem without fully understanding why. That might well be the gem you are supposed to wear, regardless of your sign.

Aries

Though most sources give the birthstone for April as the diamond, Aries may feel more affinity for Mars-ruled stones with red hues, such as ruby, spinels, fire opals, garnets, coral, and carnelian.

Taurus

Emeralds are most associated with Taurus. However, Taurus might gravitate toward some of the earthy agates and green stones such as tourmaline, jade, serpentine (which is believed to draw good fortune), and green quartz.

Gemini

Pearls and agates are associated with Gemini, but you might prefer fascinating gems like alexandrite or tanzanite, which change color according to the angle of light. Or watermelon tourmaline, which has dual colorations. Interesting rutilated quartzes with fine hairlike inclusions are associated with communication and might be perfect for your sign.

Cancer

July has often been linked with the ruby; however, that fiery stone might be better suited to Leos born in late July. Cancer seems to resonate more with the elegant blue sapphire, moonstone, chalcedony, and the deep blue flashes of laboradorite and rainbow moonstone.

Leo

The yellow-green peridot and all golden stones belong to sun-ruled Leos. You may also love the ruby, yellow diamonds, amber, and citrine. Go for the golden tones!

Virgo

Sapphires, which come in many colors, carnelian, onyx, and pink jasper are associated with Virgo. You may also respond to the earthy agates and the green tones of emerald and jade.

Libra

Opal, which was once considered exclusive to Libra, comes in many variations. In fact, the opal was deemed unlucky for any other sign. This beautiful stone comes in many color variations, from the deeper Australian opals to the pale Russian opals. You might try the blue-and-pink Peruvian opal or the mysterious, earthy boulder opal. Libra is also associated with the color pink, as in rose quartz, pink sapphires, pink diamonds, and kunzite. Apple green chrysoprase is another beautiful choice.

Scorpio

This mysterious sign was given the topaz, which comes in blue or golden variations. You might also respond to the deep tones of smoky quartz, tiger's eye, black onyx, rainbow obsidian, black diamonds, or black South Sea pearls.

Sagittarius

Visionary Sagittarius responds to turquoise, the mystical stone of Native Americans and Tibetans. No medicine man's outfit was complete without a turquoise. It was treasured by the Persians, who believed that turquoise could protect from evil and bring good fortune. Also consider lapis lazuli, blue topaz, and ruby.

Capricorn

The burgundy red garnet is the usual stone for Capricorn, but garnets are now available in many other colors, such as the green tsavorite garnet. Also consider the beautifully marked green malachite. Onyx in all its color variations is compatible with Capricorn.

Aquarius

Aquarius is associated with the purple amethyst, a type of quartz that was once thought to prevent drunkenness. This sign might respond to some of the newer stones on the market, such as laboradorite, a gray stone that flashes electric blue, or to some of the other purple stones, such as sugilite, tanzanite, or purple jade. The colorful quartzes, which are able to conduct electricity, could be your gem. Diamonds of all kinds also resonate with Aquarius, according to the glamorous Aquarius Gabor sisters and Carol Channing, who sang "Diamonds Are a Girl's Best Friend."

Pisces

The blue-green aquamarine and the earthy bloodstone are usually associated with Pisces. During the sixteenth century, bloodstone was believed to cure hemorrhages caused by the plague. Jasper is also a Pisces stone, now available in many beautiful colors such as "picture jasper" and "poppy jasper," which look like miniature paintings. Pisces also responds to jewels from the sea: pearls and coral and ocean blue sapphires. Elizabeth Taylor, a great Pisces jewel collector, owns the famous Peregrina pearl as well as many deep blue sapphires.

CHAPTER 17

Give the Perfect Gift to Every Sign

So often we're in a quandary about what to give a loved one, someone who has everything, that hard-to-please friend, or a fascinating new person in your life, or about the right present for a wedding, birthday, or hostess gift. Why not let astrology help you make the perfect choice by appealing to each sun sign's personality. When you're giving a gift, you're also making a memory, so it should be a special occasion. The gift that's most appreciated is one that touches the heart, reminds you both of a shared experience, or shows that the giver has really cared enough to consider the recipient's personality.

In general, the water signs (Cancer, Pisces, Scorpio) enjoy romantic, sentimental, and imaginative gifts given in a very personal way. Write your loved one a poem or a song to express your feelings. Assemble an album of photos or mementos of all the good times you've shared. Appeal to their sense of fantasy. Scorpio Richard Burton had the right idea when he gave Pisces Elizabeth Taylor a diamond bracelet hidden in lavender roses (her favorite color).

Fire signs (Aries, Leo, Sagittarius) appreciate a gift presented with lots of flair. Pull out the drama, like the actor who dazzled his Aries sweetheart by presenting her with trash cans overflowing with daisies.

Air signs (Gemini, Libra, Aquarius) love to be surprised with unusual gifts. The Duke of Windsor gave his elegant Gemini duchess, Wallis Windsor, fabulous jewels engraved with love notes and secret messages in their own special code.

Earth signs (Taurus, Virgo, Capricorn) value solid, tangible gifts or ones that appeal to all the senses. Delicious gourmet treats, scented body lotions, the newest CDs, the gift of a massage, or stocks and bonds are sure winners! Capricorn Elvis Presley once received a gold-plated piano from his wife.

Here are some specific ideas for each sign:

Aries

These are the trendsetters of the zodiac, who appreciate the latest thing! For Aries, it's the excitement that counts, so present your gift in a way that will knock their socks off. Aries is associated with the head, so a jaunty hat, hair ornaments, chandelier earrings, sunglasses, and hair-taming devices are good possibilities. Aries love games of any kind that offer a real challenge, like war video games, military themes, or rousing music with a beat. Anything red is a good bet: red flowers, red gems, and red accessories. How about giving Aries a way to let off steam with a gym membership or aerobic-dancing classes? Monogram a robe with a nickname in red.

Taurus

These are touchy-feely people who love things that appeal to all their senses. Find something that sounds, tastes, smells, feels, or looks good. And don't stint on quality or comfort. Taurus know the value of everything and will be aware of the price tag. Taurus foodies will appreciate chef-worthy kitchen gadgets, the latest cookbook, and gourmet treats. Taurus is a great collector. Find out what their passion is and present them with a rare item or a beautiful storage container such as an antique jewelry box. Green-thumb Taurus would love some special plants or flowers, garden tools, beautiful plant containers. Appeal to their sense of touch with fine fabrics—high-thread-count sheets, cashmere, satin, and mohair. One of the animal-loving signs, Taurus might appreciate a retractable leash or soft bed for the dog or cat. Get them a fine wallet or checkbook cover. They'll use it often.

Gemini

Mercury-ruled Gemini appreciates gifts that appeal to their mind. The latest book or novel, a talked-about film, a CD from a hot new singer, or a high-tech gadget might appeal. A beautiful diary or a tape recorder would record their adventures. Since Geminis often do two things at once, a telephone gadget that leaves their hands free would be appreciated. In fact, a new telephone device or superphone would appeal to these great communicators. Gloves, rings, and bracelets accent their expressive hands. Clothes from an interesting new designer appeal to their sense of style. You might try giving Gemini a variety of little gifts in a beautiful box or a Christmas stocking. A tranquil massage at a local spa would calm Gemini's sensitive nerves. Find an interesting way to wrap your gift. Nothing boring, please!

Cancer

Cancer is associated with home and family, so anything to do with food, entertaining at home, and family life is a good bet. Beautiful dishes or serving platters, silver items, fine crystal and linen, gourmet cookware, cooking classes or the latest DVD from a cooking teacher might be appreciated. Cancer designers Vera Wang and Giorgio Armani have perfected the Cancer style and have many home products available, as well as their elegant designer clothing. Naturally, anything to do with the sea is a possibility: pearls, coral, or shell jewelry. Boat and water-sports equipment might work. Consider cruise wear for traveling Cancers. Sentimental Cancer loves antiques and silver frames for family photos. Cancer people are often good photographers, so consider frames, albums, and projectors to showcase their work. Present your gift in a personal way with a special note.

Leo

Think big with Leo and appeal to this sign's sense of drama. Go for the gold (Leo's color) with gold jewelry, designer clothing, or big attention-getting accessories. Follow their signature style, which could be superelegant, like Jacqueline Onassis, or superstar, like Madonna or Jennifer Lopez. This sign is always ready for the red carpet and stays beautifully groomed, so stay within these guidelines when choosing your gift. Feline motifs and animal prints are usually a hit. The latest grooming aids, high-ticket cosmetics, and mirrors reflect their best image. Beautiful hairbrushes tame their manes. Think champagne, high-thread-count linens, and luxurious loungewear or lingerie. Make Leo feel special with a custom portrait or photo shoot with your local star photographer. Be sure to go for spectacular wrapping, with beautiful paper and ribbons. Present your gift with a flourish!

Virgo

Virgo usually has a special subject of interest and would appreciate relevant books, films, lectures, or classes. Choose health-oriented things: gifts to do with fitness and self-improvement. Virgo enjoys brainteasers, crossword puzzles, computer programs, organizers, and digital planners. Fluffy robes, bath products, and special soaps appeal to Virgo's sense of cleanliness. Virgo loves examples of good, practical design: efficient telephones, beautiful briefcases, computer cases, desk accessories. Choose natural fibers and quiet colors when choosing clothes for Virgo. Virgo has high standards, so go for quality when choosing a gift.

Libra

Whatever you give this romantic sign, go for beauty and romance. Libra loves accessories, decorative objects, whatever makes him or his surroundings more aesthetically pleasing. Beautiful flowers in pastel colors are always welcome. Libras are great hosts and hostesses, who might appreciate a gift related to fine dining: serving pieces, linens, glassware, flower vases. Evening or party clothes please since Libra has a gadabout social life. Interesting books, objets d'art, memberships to museums, and tickets to cultural events are good ideas. Fashion or home-decorating magazine subscriptions usually please Libra women. Steer away from anything loud, garish, or extreme. Think pink, one of their special colors, when giving Libra jewelry, clothing, or accessories. It's a very romantic sign, so be sure to remember birthdays, holidays, and anniversaries with a token of affection.

Scorpio

Scorpios love mystery, so bear that in mind when you buy these folks a present. You could take this literally and buy them a good thriller DVD, novel, or video game. Scorpios are power players, so a book about one of their sign might please. Bill Gates, Jack Welch, Condoleezza Rice, and Hillary Clinton are hot Scorpio subjects. Scorpios love black leather, suede, fur, anything to do with the sea, power tools, tiny spy tape recorders, and items with secret compartments or intricate locks. When buying a handbag for Scorpio, go for simple shapes with lots of interior pockets. Sensuous Scorpios appreciate hot lingerie, sexy linens, body lotions, and perfumed candles. Black is the favored color for Scorpio clothing—go for sexy textures like cashmere and satin in simple shapes by designers like Calvin Klein. This sign is fascinated with the occult, so give them an astrology or

tarot-card reading, beautiful crystals, or an astrology program for the computer.

Sagittarius

For these outdoor people, consider adventure trips, designer sportswear, gear for their favorite sports. A funny
gift or something for their pets pleases Sagittarius. For
clothing and accessories, the fashionista of this sign tends to
like bright colors and dramatic innovative styles. Otherwise,
casual sportswear is a good idea. These travelers usually
have a favorite getaway place; give them a travel guide,
DVD, novel, or history book that would make their trip
more interesting. Luggage is also a good bet. Sleek carry-
ons, travel wallets, ticket holders, business-card cases, and
wheeled computer bags might please these wanderers. Anything that makes travel more comfortable and pleasant is
good for Sagittarius, including a good book to read en
route. This sign is the great gambler of the zodiac, so gifts
related to their favorite gambling venue would be
appreciated.

Capricorn

For this quality-conscious sign, go for a status label from
the best store in town. Get Capricorns something good for
their image and career. They could be fond of things Span-
ish, like flamenco or tango music, or of country-and-western
music and motifs. In the bookstore, go for biographies of
the rich and famous, or advice books to help Capricorn get
to the top. Capricorns take their gifts seriously, so steer
away from anything too frivolous. Garnet, onyx, or malachite jewelry, Carolina Herrera fragrance and clothing, and
beautiful briefcases and wallets are good ideas. Glamorous
status tote bags carry business gear in style. Capricorns like
golf, tennis, and sports that involve climbing, cycling, or

hiking, so presents could be geared to their outdoor interests. Elegant evening accessories would be fine for this sign, which often entertains for business.

Aquarius

Give Aquarius a surprise gift. This sign is never impressed with things that are too predictable. So use your imagination to present the gift in an unusual way or at an unexpected time. With Aquarius, originality counts. When in doubt, give them something to think about, a new electronic gadget, perhaps a small robot, or an advanced computer game. Or something New Age, like an amethyst-crystal cluster. Aquarius like innovative materials with a space-age look. They are the ones with the wraparound glasses, the titanium computer cases. This air sign loves to fly—an airplane ticket always pleases. Books should be on innovative subjects, politics, or adventures of the mind. Aquarius goes for unusual color combinations—especially electric blue or hot pink—and abstract patterns. They like the newest, coolest looks on the cutting edge of fashion and are not afraid to experiment. Think of Paris Hilton's constantly changing looks. Look for an Aquarius gift in an out-of-the-way boutique or local hipster hangout. They'd be touched if you find out Aquarius's special worthy cause and make a donation. Spirit them off to hear their favorite guru.

Pisces

Pisces respond to gifts that have a touch of fantasy, magic, and romance. Look for mystical gifts with a touch of the occult. Romantic music (a customized CD of favorite love songs) and love stories appeal to Pisces sentimentalists. Pisces is associated with perfume and fragrant oils, so help this sign indulge with their favorite scent in many forms. Anything to do with the ocean, fish, and water sports appeals to Pisces. How about a whirlpool, a water-therapy spa treatment, or a sea salt rub. Appeal to this sign with treats for the feet: foot massages, pedicures, ballet tickets, and dance lessons. Cashmere socks and metallic evening sandals are other Pisces pleasers. A romantic dinner overlooking the water is Pisces paradise. A case of fine wine or another favorite liquid is always appreciated. Write a love poem and enclose it with your gift.

CHAPTER 18

The Meaning of Numbers

What exactly is a number 9 day, and how did it get to be that number? If you've been reading the dailies, you've no doubt seen such numerological references. Usually you'll find these numbers on the days when the moon is transiting from one sign to another.

If you're familiar with numerology, you probably know your life-path number, which is derived from your birth date. That number represents who you were at birth and the traits that you'll carry throughout your life. There are numerous books and Web sites that will provide you with details on what the numbers mean regarding your life path.

The numbers used in the dailies are found by adding the numbers related to the astrological sign (1 for Aries, 2 for Taurus, etc.), the year, the months, and the day. For example, June 14, 2008 for a Libra would be 7 for Libra, plus 1 (adding together the numbers in 2008), plus 6 for June, plus 7 (1+6) for the day. That would be 7+1+6+5 (sign+year+month+day)=19=1 (1+9=10 [1+0=1]).

So on that number 1 day, you might be advised that you're getting a fresh start, a new beginning. You can take the lead on something new. Stress originality and creativity. Explore and discover. You're inventive and make connections that others overlook.

Briefly, here are the meanings of the numbers, which are included in more detail in the dailies themselves.

1: taking the lead, getting a fresh start, a new beginning
2: cooperation, partnership, a new relationship, sensitivity
3: harmony, beauty, pleasures of life, warm, receptive

4: getting organized, hard work, being methodical, rebuilding, fulfilling your obligations
5: freedom of thought and action, change, variety, thinking outside the box
6: a service day, being diplomatic, generous, tolerant, sympathetic
7: mystery, secrets, investigations, research, detecting deception, exploration of the unknown, of the spiritual realms
8: your power day, financial success, unexpected money, a windfall
9: finishing a project, looking beyond the immediate, setting your goals, reflection, expansion

—Rob MacGregor

Rob MacGregor is the author of seventeen novels and ten nonfiction books, including *Psychic Power*, *Star Power for Teens*, and *Romancing the Raven*. For more information, go to www.robmacgregor.net.

CHAPTER 19

All About Cancer: Your Personality, Family, Career, Relationships, and Lifestyle

Have you tapped in to your Cancer power? Knowing and using your positive Cancer sun-sign traits (and downplaying the negative ones) could be your key to achieving more happiness and success in all areas of your life. That's because every part of your life has a strong Cancer influence. That includes what and whom you like, your family relationships, your strengths on the job, even the decor of your home. The more you understand the Cancer in you, the better you can use your personal solar power to help you make good decisions. You can use it every day from something as basic as choosing what to wear to more important issues such as getting along with your boss or spicing up your love life.

So get ready for your close-up! In the following chapters, you'll be empowered with tools to control your destiny and make your dreams come true by moving in harmony with your natural inclinations.

Before we begin, here's how we determine what a Cancer personality is. Astrologers describe a Cancer using a type of recipe. The basic personality of a Cancer is determined by blending several ingredients. First there's your Cancer element: water. Cancer operates like a cardinal sign: an active doer. Then there's your sign's polarity, which adds a reactive, feminine, yin dimension. Let's not forget your planetary ruler: the moon, the planet of emotion. Add your sign's place in the zodiac: fourth, in the house of the home, family, roots. Finally, stir in your symbol, the Crab, with a hard protective shell and soft vulnerable interior.

This recipe influences everything we say about Cancer. For example your sun sign occupies the place of home and family, making Cancer a home-loving type. With the Moon as a ruler, you operate intuitively. Like the Crab, you're likely to be a bit self-protective and concerned with security. But your individual astrological personality contains a blend of many other planets, colored by the signs they occupy, plus factors such as the sign coming over the horizon at the exact moment of your birth. However, the more Cancer planets in your horoscope, the more likely you'll follow your sun sign's prototype. On the other hand, if many planets are grouped together in a different sign, they will color your horoscope accordingly, sometimes making a low-key, mellow sun sign come on much stronger. So if the Cancer traits mentioned here don't describe you, there could be other factors flavoring your cosmic stew. (Look up your other planets in the tables in this book to find out what they might be!)

The Cancer Man: Intuitive Power

The Cancer man operates very much like his symbol, the Crab. You're a sidewalker who moves indirectly at a situation, never confronting it head-on, but always obliquely, subtly, and cleverly. Some might call you shrewd, others surreptitious. But what you are doing is reacting to your keen intuitive understanding of the hidden motives and agendas of others. You'll tune in to your powerful sixth sense before you listen to objective reason.

You sometimes wear a hard outer shell to protect yourself from the harsh realities of life. But inside you're vulnerable and tender, afraid of being exploited if you show this nurturing side to the world. Usually, it comes forth in a professional way, through your choice of a career where you can express your feelings safely in a creative context. Many Cancer men choose nurturing fields in medicine, child care, psychology, hotel work, family businesses, or restaurants. Or they'll extend their nurturing to a family tribe, like the Cancer writer Ernest Hemingway, who was called "Papa" by all who knew him personally.

You have an uncanny ability to read the feelings of others, which gives you great emotional power and understanding. You know exactly how to nurture people by giving them what they need when they need it. On the other hand, you know where to inflict the most hurt—often by withholding what is needed. But your negative side, which can be cool and cruel, is actually a form of resentment if you yourself have not been nurtured enough. If you can learn how to release the past and any hurts rendered to you, and how to nurture yourself, you have a much better chance to reach your full potential. Many Cancers have found psychotherapy extremely helpful in doing this.

A Cancer man's mother is especially important to him, even more so than to other men. If this relationship is lacking, you may try to replace it by mothering (or smothering) others or by looking for someone else to mother you.

The Cancer man, though virile and sensual, rarely embodies the stereotypical masculine attitude. There is always a special communication of tenderness in your treatment of women, which makes you one of the zodiac's great lovers. You can tap into a woman's emotional needs and treat her with great understanding and sensitivity. This subtle vulnerability is evident in Cancer celebrities such as Robin Williams, Tom Cruise, Harrison Ford, and Geraldo Rivera. The shy blue-eyed gaze of England's Prince William is ever so effective with the opposite sex. The Cancer man's special sensitivity is far more attractive to women than the muscle-flexing of macho types.

In a Relationship

Like the crab, the Cancer man hangs on. You're extremely possessive of whatever and whoever belongs to you. You'll hang on to old memories, old sweaters, often your first dollar. In a committed relationship or marriage, you're at last free to show your tender, caring, protective side. Your home is supremely important to you. It's the place where you feel most secure. Here you can thrive in the supportive atmosphere of a long-term love. Cancer President George W. Bush prefers the Texas ranch he calls home to the high-profile life of the White House. You treasure the mother of your children, who probably resembles your own mother in some way. You are usually not attracted to independent women (unless your mother was independent), preferring the more maternal, nurturing type or a romantic, creative partner. You'd like her to be interested in domestic life and be an excellent cook. (If your partner is on the go all the time, she'll come home to a crabby mate.) Since you are usually materially successful, your home can be a private paradise for enjoying the good life together.

The Cancer Woman: Moon Maiden

Ruled by the moon and associated with the breast, motherhood, and nurturing, the Cancer woman is one of the most feminine of the zodiac. As an active cardinal sign, you know how to capitalize creatively on your deeply sensitive feelings by finding ways to satisfy or feed others. Many Cancer women have become successful in business by providing the right product at the right time, like cosmetics tycoon Estée Lauder. However, you can be quite acquisitive, hoarding money or objects as if to store up for hard times. It has been said that nothing upsets a Cancer woman more than an empty refrigerator or an empty closet.

Because of your deep feelings and uncanny intuition, you easily grasp the inner motivations of others. This knowledge becomes your shell of protection. Cancer women in high places often extend their shell to become mother figures for their country, such as the late Princess Diana, Imelda Marcos, or Nancy Reagan. The wisest and wealthiest members of your sign use their intuition for personal and professional benefit.

You are especially affected by the moon's phases, especially during the full moon, when you could become super-sensitive and overreact to imagined slights. Let creative projects come to the rescue, turning your negative energies into positive ones again. You can find emotional fulfillment by providing food and shelter to others; cooking a delicious family dinner is excellent therapy for the Cancer moody blues.

Family influences are more potent with Cancer than with many other signs. It is especially important that you try to conquer or reprogram negative relationships. This way you can express your creative talents fully. You keep strong family ties throughout life and you are often able to combine your career with your home life either by working at home or in a family business.

In a Relationship

You need a partner who is devoted and demonstrative, who will give you tangible proof of his love, and who will provide you with the stable home life you need. Your choice of a mate is especially important. A good relationship can draw you out of your shell and provide the emotional security you crave.

Usually, you are quite possessive of your husband and anxious to fulfill his needs. And if his needs include a beautiful home and strong family ties, you will make him happy indeed. Many of you marry someone wealthy, powerful, and protective, and then provide an indispensable support system for him. That could include transforming your shy self into a public person and perfect hostess if your husband's role demands it, like Nancy Reagan and the late Princess Diana did. You make a perfect wife for a chief executive, as you are able to embody the feminine power role. You can be seen as a maternal figure, a supportive coruler with your mate. There are several stellar examples of Cancer women who became as famous and powerful as their husbands: Leona Helmsley, Imelda Marcos, and the late Princess Diana come to mind.

Cancer in the Family

The Cancer Parent

As the mother figure of the zodiac (even if you're the dad), you're in your element as a parent. You're at your best cuddling a tiny vulnerable child. This nurturing quality may extend to all children, who arouse your deepest caring instincts. You can be fiercely protective of your brood and also possessive, hanging on to the mother role long after your children have left the nest. Often the Cancer parent will have a dynasty, sustaining their parental role by bringing the children into a family business. One of your greatest lessons will be to let go when the time comes, and to find constructive outlets for your nurturing energies as you evolve out of the parental role.

The Cancer Stepparent

Since a broken home is probably one of the most traumatic events that can happen to a Cancer, you will be full of compassion for your stepchildren. You will intuitively understand their unspoken feelings and their need for emotional support. Much depends, however, on how secure you yourself feel in the new family situation, and if you are getting the emotional support you require from your mate. If not, you may have difficulty sharing your mate with a previous family. If you can be open with your feelings, this situation can be remedied. Establishing open communications can sidestep power struggles and emotional manipulation. You'll easily win the children over when your caring, protective nature is channeled in the right direction. Then you can provide a warm, welcoming, extended family.

The Cancer Grandparent

Grandparenthood is a liberating experience for Cancer. Now you're free to enjoy young children without chores or responsibilities. You can fuss over the babies to your heart's content. You'll actually love babysitting the toddlers, pampering them with presents. Family get-togethers, when your brood gathers over a delicious meal, will be important seasonal events. You'll keep close ties with everyone in the family. Your grandchildren will always have a home with you, and there usually will be some young visitor toddling about. Especially concerned that your dynasty's future will be secure, you probably have provided a substantial nest egg. As you grow older, you'll pass on your family traditions, recipes, and stories to each new generation.

CHAPTER 20

The Cancer Lifestyle: How to Make Your Cancer Sign Shine

Astrology's personal insights follow through to the way you dress and live. Here's how to polish your Cancer image with tips tailored specifically for your sign, improve your atmosphere by using your best colors and surrounding yourself with Cancer-loving sounds. Find out how to create a living environment that reflects your personality, where you'll feel totally at home. And how to make the most of your sign's special fashion flair. Even your vacations might be more fun and relaxing if you tailor them to your sun sign's natural inclinations.

The Cancer Fashion Image

Cancer has an intuitive fashion sense that cues you on the right dress for every occasion. Like the late Princess Diana, you look best in fluid, romantic lines that play up your intense femininity. Soft, flowing, shimmering evening wear brings out the luminous moon maiden in you. Wear silver and pearls, iridescent fabrics, and wavy hair to play up this quality. Accent your expressive eyes with subtle makeup and take care of your sensitive skin, which can react to emotional upsets or overexposure to the sun.

Cancer women, like Pamela Anderson, often have (or acquire via cosmetic surgery) spectacular breasts, which you can play up with discreetly plunging necklines. (Choose undergarments that play up your best assets and give you the support you need.)

Cancer's Fashion Colors

As one of the zodiac's most emotional signs, you'll feel and look your best when you wear your Cancer colors, which are soft, subtle shades, nothing garish or shouting. All the moonbeam shades of pearly white, silver, and taupe are yours. Wear colors of the sea, plus moss green, midnight blue, and coral. Cancer designers like Giorgio Armani and Vera Wang are specialists in using subtle colors and filmy fabrics to evoke romantic moods and create a dreamlike atmosphere.

Your Cancer Fashion Role Models

There are many chic fashion leaders and designers under your sun to inspire you. These designers understand the many moods and the perfect styles for your sign: Giorgio Armani, Vera Wang, Oscar de la Renta, and Norma Kamali. Trendy Cancers like Lindsay Lohan, Jessica Simpson, Liv Tyler, and Courtney Love always look best when they are accenting their beautiful eyes and luminous skin, and when they project an ethereal moonbeam quality. Cancer fashion models have always ruled the runway. In recent years, the Brazilian sensation Gisele Bundchen's curvaceous body and undulating walk capture the sensual mood of the moment.

Cancer at Home

Does your home atmosphere express who you really are? If not, you probably don't feel as comfortable as you should in your environment, which could adversely affect your health and well-being. Astrology offers you many ways to attune your environment to your natural tendencies. There are colors, styles, places, and music that will help you create the setting that complements your sun sign, one where you're sure to feel truly relaxed and at home.

There's a good reason why some of the world's most famous decorators have been born under the sign of Cancer. Yours is the sign associated with the fourth house in the astrological chart, the place that governs family ties and the home, where you feel most secure. As a Cancer, you take to home decorating like a crab to water, and you instinctively know how to create a nurturing shell for yourself and others.

You couldn't do better than follow the advice of the late Sister Parish, who was the First Lady of decorating for the rich and famous. "Sister's" infallible Cancer intuition helped her create the kinds of rooms where everyone felt at home. She created a mood that was comforting, secure, and relaxing by using crystal, candlelight, silver, and mirrors; the room looked especially good at night, when Cancer shines brightest. Not for her the cold minimalist look! Sister enhanced the personality of the owner with carefully selected accessories and sentimental touches. She was not afraid to express emotion in her rooms, and neither should you be. Recently fashion designers Giorgio Armani and Vera Wang have translated their aesthetic into furniture and accessories for the home, using subtle subdued colors to create a restful relaxing atmosphere.

You tend to accumulate sentimental treasures, so be sure there is storage space for favorite items and memorabilia you've saved over the years. Since you love to cook, your kitchen and dining room should be equipped to prepare frequent family feasts. It will probably be the favorite gathering place in your home. A large dining table will be needed to accommodate your extended family and friends.

One room should be done in tranquil, restful colors—a place for solitary meditation. Incorporate the water element in some way in your decor, perhaps with a tiny waterfall or fountain, an aquarium, or a painting of a favorite beach. A swimming pool or a Jacuzzi tub are water-loving Cancer luxuries. Why not turn a bathroom into a home spa as a private place to relax and rejuvenate?

More than any other sign, you understand how to use color to evoke emotion. Your favorites are sure to be the soft, subtle moonlight shades, though Sister Parish was known to use dramatic dark walls, spectacular at night.

Generally, you can't go wrong using all the colors of the sea and ships in your environment: Atlantic blue, surf white, pearly pastels, and plenty of silver touches.

Background Music

Your kind of music stirs deep feelings or reminds you of happy times. Though you gravitate to blues and love songs, you should collect upbeat music that lifts your spirits as well as cool jazz that soothes your nerves. Make special tapes of your favorite songs, themed to evoke moods for romance, relaxation, or high energy, as the perfect background music to intimate occasions, festive meals, and family parties.

Cancer Travel Guide

Water-loving Cancers are in their element on cruises, at seaside resorts, or in tropical island paradises. Rather than an impersonal resort, you might prefer a home-away-from-home with a family feeling. Or invite a relative or intimate friend for company. Investigate renting your own villa or condominium at a resort rather than staying in a big hotel. This would give you both privacy and a place to entertain new friends. Cancer will actually enjoy shopping at the local food markets and serving regional specialties.

One of the zodiac's great shoppers, you'll probably bring home souvenirs for everyone in the family. Stash an extra collapsible suitcase or ballistic nylon tote bag in your baggage to hold all your finds. Most Cancers love to take photos, so bring a small camera with you at all times. The new disposable cameras are perfect for casual snapshots, and eliminate worry about theft.

Since stomach upsets are your travel foe, take along proper medication. Another sensitive Cancer area is your skin, so include a high-SPF sunscreen in all your travel kits.

Cancer likes to be upon or under the waves; ocean liners

are the perfect floating vacation homes, ideal for family vacations. Or you may rent a sailboat to cruise the Caribbean or the Greek Islands. Scuba vacations also appeal. Go where the reefs are unspoiled: Australia, Belize, Samoa. Exotic places like Nairobi, Singapore, Istanbul, Venice, and the highlands of Scotland suit your many travel moods.

CHAPTER 21

Cancer Health and Well-Being

Astrology can clue you in to the tendencies that contribute to good or ill health (especially when it comes to controlling your appetite). So follow these tips on how best to lose those extra pounds, and make this your healthiest year ever.

Get the Emotional Support You Need

Dieting can be difficult for Cancers, who love good food, find emotional solace with goodies, and fill up with comfort foods in tough times. There are sure to be conflicts between the Cancer who wants to be fashionably thin but also to please the family with Grandma's favorite dishes. Cancer food conflicts sometimes lead to eating disorders, as with Princess Diana. Remember that you must be nurtured emotionally as well as physically. A diet therapy group might help you deal with issues surrounding food and give you the support you need to stick to a diet. Find nonfood ways to baby yourself, such as a visit to a spa, walks along the beach, beauty treatments to help you feel good about yourself while you lose weight.

Get the family behind you when you diet. You'll never lose weight if they insist on eating caloric favorites in front of you. Challenge yourself to create diet-conscious variations of family recipes so the whole family can eat healthy.

Water Is Your Best Therapy

Your natural water-sign element is also your best therapy. Sometimes just a walk by a pond or a brief stop by a fountain can do wonders to relieve emotional stress and tension. You will more likely stick to an exercise routine if it's in or near water. Pool aerobics, swimming, fishing, sailing, and all other water sports provide ideal ways for you to stay fit.

Protect Your Vulnerable Areas

Health-wise, Cancer is associated with the breast area. Cancer women should have regular checkups, according to your age and family health history of breast-related illness and be sure to wear a well-fitting supportive bra.

Cancer is also prone to digestive difficulties, especially gastric ulcers and eating disorders. When emotionally caused digestive problems from those stomach-knotting insecurities crop up, baby yourself with extra pampering. The comforts of home have special health benefits for Cancer, so try to live in a cozy, harmonious atmosphere. If you feel blue, a visit with loved ones, old friends, and family could provide the support you need. Planning special family activities that bring everyone closer together will further benefit your health and well-being.

CHAPTER 22

Your Cancer Career Guide: What It Takes to Succeed in 2008

Find the Right Career for You

Cancer has a special combination of talents and abilities that can make you a natural winner. Develop and nurture these sun-sign strengths, and you'll be likely to find a career you truly enjoy, one where you'll be most successful. The great philosopher and teacher Joseph Campbell gave you the best advice: Follow your bliss!

Your Ideal Work Environment

Cancer has proven to be one of the most financially success-ful signs. From behind your thick protective shell, you can figure out just what a job requires, or intuit what the public wants and needs, then put your creativity to work finding ways to fulfill those needs. It's no wonder that many billion-aires were born under your sign! Your natural acquisitive-ness makes you a shrewd judge of quality. And, as self-protective as your symbol, the Crab, you will build your personal nest egg at the same time as you're increasing company profits.

Your emotional sensitivity can be your greatest strength, if you use it properly. It gives you a powerful way to con-nect with the public wants and needs. Then apply your natural creativity to market your wares.

Follow your natural Cancer tendencies. Cancer often thrives in the security of a family business, or brings the family into a successful business. Creative fields give the needed self-expression: photography, theater, music, fashion. The food, shelter, home-maintenance, and child-related businesses are other natural Cancer meccas, as well as interior design and architecture. Many successful Cancers have made their fortunes in hotels, restaurants, and real estate. Marine businesses such as shipping, yacht sales, and marine biology are water-sign havens that would put you in the seaside environment you love.

The Cancer Leader

There is no such thing as an uninvolved Cancer, especially one at the helm of a profitable business. You are extremely possessive of your means of security, and you hang on to your position despite all odds. As a boss, you operate intuitively rather than openly, which could lead others to suspect a hidden agenda. Your secretiveness can project paranoia, but you usually make up for this with a very protective attitude toward your underlings. Your emotional sensitivity is a plus when negotiating a deal, helping you intuit when to sign on the dotted line and when the competition is about to act. Though your moods may be baffling to associates, they have learned never to underestimate you and to wait out your downtime for a few days until your mood changes.

Cancer's emotional sensitivity is your greatest strength and enables you to connect with what the public wants and needs. Richard Branson's Virgin Records began when he saw an opportunity to sell pop records at a discount. Later he started Virgin Airlines when he sensed that the public wanted more personal services at reasonable prices than other airlines were providing. Estée Lauder was a self-made cosmetics tycoon who had a finger on the pulse of women's needs and buying habits. She knew that offering a free sample of her creams and perfumes would entice the customer to buy more product. As the business began to thrive, she brought her family into the company, which is run by her relatives today.

The Cancer Team Player

You work best in a traditional, nurturing atmosphere. Here you can express your creativity and surprise everyone with your organizational talent and perseverance. Once you feel secure, you really produce. It is very important for Cancer to work with supportive and congenial people, because you are easily upset by criticism and office politics. While you may appear quiet and shy, you are really taking everyone's measure. This is your way of protecting yourself before you reveal your tender, caring side.

You'd like your office to be a home away from home, where you are taking care of people and fulfilling their needs. Though you may have up-and-down days, you should guard against bringing your personal problems into the workplace. Emphasize your excellent sense of marketing and your shrewd eye for quality, plus your innate good taste.

The Cancer Way to Get Ahead

As a Cancer, you bring some important assets to the table. It's up to you to decide how to best utilize your talents and abilities to bring you the very highest return on the investment of your time and energy. When you job hunt, choose a company with a supportive atmosphere and creative opportunities. Play up your finest attributes:

- Creativity
- Intuitive insight into the market
- Perseverance
- Shrewd judgment
- Caring, nurturing qualities
- Organizational talent

CHAPTER 23

Cancer on the Red Carpet

Are you a fan of tabloids and gossip columns? Your fascination with the rich and famous could have a fringe benefit. It's also a terrific way to learn more about astrology. A celebrity's attraction for the public tells much about the planetary influences of a given time and the special star quality of his or her sun sign. You may even have a celebrity astro twin who shares both your birthday and the same year.

You're sure to have many of the same traits as your famous sun-sign siblings. Cancer's ultrafeminine charisma is a stellar quality of Jessica Simpson, Princess Diana, and Lindsay Lohan. Your financial savvy is evident in the lives of John D. Rockefeller and Richard Branson. Does your leadership style compare with that of Nelson Mandela or George W. Bush?

The lives of the famous can be fascinating textbooks with full-color illustrations of the different planetary combinations. If someone intrigues you, explore his personality further by looking up his other planets using the tables in this book. Then apply the effects of Venus, Mars, Saturn, and Jupiter to his sun-sign traits. It's a fun way to get up close and personal with your famous friend, maybe learn some secrets not revealed to the public.

Then why not move on from the red carpet to world leaders and current newsmakers? You can find accurate data online at Internet sites such as www.Stariq.com or www.astrodatabank.com, which have the charts of world events and headline makers. Then compare notes with other fans, including many professional astrologers who frequent the forums on these sites.

Cancer Celebrities

Jane Russell (6/21/21)
Mariette Hartley (6/21/40)
Meredith Baxter (6/21/47)
Juliette Lewis (6/21/73)
Prince William (6/21/82)
Bill Blass (6/22/22)
Kris Kristofferson (6/22/36)
Klaus-Maria Brandauer (6/22/44)
Meryl Streep (6/22/49)
Lindsay Wagner (6/22/49)
Tracy Pollan (6/22/60)
Carson Daly (6/22/73)
Alfred Kinsey (6/23/1894)
Selma Blair (6/23/72)
Michelle Lee (6/24/42)
Peter Weller (6/24/47)
Nancy Allen (6/24/50)
Carly Simon (6/25/45)
George Michael (6/25/63)
Pearl S. Buck (6/26/1892)
Peter Lorre (6/26/1904)
Chris Isaak (6/26/56)
Derek Jeter (6/26/74)
Ross Perot (6/27/30)
Vera Wang (6/27/49)
Isabelle Adjani (6/27/55)
Tobey Maguire (6/27/75)
Mel Brooks (6/28/26)
Pat Morita (6/28/32)
Kathy Bates (6/28/48)
Mary Stuart Masterson (6/28/66)
John Cusack (6/28/66)
Ruth Warrick (6/29/15)
Gilda Radner (6/29/46)
Lena Horne (6/20/17)
Mike Tyson (6/30/66)
Charles Laughton (7/1/1899)
Estée Lauder (7/1/1908)

Olivia de Havilland (7/1/16)
Farley Granger (7/1/25)
Leslie Caron (7/1/31)
Karen Black (7/1/42)
Geneviève Bujold (7/1/42)
Deborah Harry (7/1/45)
Dan Aykroyd (7/1/52)
Princess Diana (7/1/61)
Pamela Anderson (7/1/67)
Liv Tyler (7/1/77)
Imelda Marcos (7/2/31)
Richard Perry (7/2/37)
Ron Silver (7/2/46)
Jerry Hall (7/2/56)
Lindsay Lohan (7/2/86)
Geraldo Rivera (7/3/43)
Betty Buckley (7/3/47)
Montel Williams (7/3/56)
Aaron Tippin (7/3/58)
Tom Cruise (7/3/62)
Jaime Pressley (7/3/77)
Louis Armstrong (7/4/1900)
P.T. Barnum (7/5/1810)
Edie Falco (7/5/63)
Nancy Reagan (7/6/21)
Merv Griffin (7/6/25)
Ned Beatty (7/6/36)
George W. Bush (7/6/46)
Sylvester Stallone (7/6/46)
Geoffrey Rush (7/6/51)
Pierre Cardin (7/7/22)
Ringo Starr (7/7/40)
John D. Rockefeller (7/8/1839)
Anjelica Huston (7/8/51)
Marianne Williamson (7/8/52)
Kevin Bacon (7/8/58)
Barbara Cartland (7/9/1901)
Brian Dennehy (7/9/39)
O. J. Simpson (7/9/49)
John Tesh (7/9/52)
Jimmy Smits (7/9/55)

Tom Hanks (7/9/56)
Kelly McGillis (7/9/57)
Courtney Love (7/9/64)
David Brinkley (7/10/20)
Jessica Simpson ((7/10/80)
Tab Hunter (7/11/31)
Giorgio Armani (7/11/34)
Sela Ward (7/11/56)
Richie Sambora (7/11/59)
Lisa Rinna (7/11/65)
L'il Kim (7/11/75)
Henry David Thoreau (7/12/1817)
Milton Berle (7/12/1908)
Bill Cosby (7/12/37)
Richard Simmons (7/12/48)
Cheryl Ladd (7/12/51)
Rolanda Watts (7/12/59)
Kristi Yamaguchi (7/12/71)
Patrick Stewart (7/13/40)
Harrison Ford (7/13/42)
Ingmar Bergman (7/14/18)
Harry Dean Stanton (7/14/26)
Polly Bergen (7/14/30)
Linda Ronstadt (7/15/46)
Jesse Ventura (7/15/51)
Brigitte Nielsen (7/15/63)
Orville Redenbacher (7/16/1907)
Ginger Rogers (7/16/11)
Ruben Blades (7/16/48)
Michael Flatley (7/16/58)
Phoebe Cates (7/16/63)
Corey Feldman (7/16/71)
Art Linkletter (7/17/12)
Diahann Carroll (7/17/35)
Donald Sutherland (7/17/35)
Camilla Parker Bowles (7/17/47)
Lucie Arnaz (7/17/51)
David Hasselhoff (7/17/52)
Hume Cronyn (7/18/11)
Red Skelton (7/18/13)
Nelson Mandela (7/18/18)

Ann Landers and Abigail van Buren (7/18/18)
John Glenn (7/18/21)
James Brolin (7/18/40)
Richard Branson (7/18/50)
Pat Hingle (7/19/24)
Diana Rigg (7/20/38)
Ernest Hemingway (7/21/1899)
Robin Williams (7/21/52)
Alex Trebek (7/22/40)
Danny Glover (7/22/47)
Don Henley (7/22/47)
Rob Estes (7/22/63)

CHAPTER 24

Star Wars or Passionate Supernovas? How Cancer Partners with Every Other Sign

After learning all about your own sun sign, it's time to consider how you interact with others. Knowing how your sun sign works with other signs can give you valuable insight into the future of all your relationships. Once you understand how another sun sign is likely to view yours, you'll be in a much better position to judge whether this combination will burn and crash or have lasting happiness potential.

The celebrity couples are used as examples to help you visualize each sun-sign combination. Note that some legendary couples have stood the test of time, others blazed brightly and then burned out, and a few existed only in the fantasy world of film or television (but still captured our imagination). Is there a magic formula for compatibility? Traditional astrological wisdom holds that signs of the same element, in your case other water signs (Scorpio and Pisces), are naturally compatible. So are signs of complementary elements, such as earth signs with water signs. In these relationships communication supposedly flows easily and you'll feel most comfortable with each other. However, there are no hard-and-fast rules with sun-sign combinations. Many lasting marriages happen between incompatible sun signs, while some ideally matched couples fizzle after a few years.

When sparks fly, and an irresistible magnetic pull draws you together, when disagreements and challenges fuel intrigue, mystery, passion, and sexy sparring matches, don't rule the relationship out. That person may provide the diversity, excitement, and challenge you need for an unforgettable romance, a stimulating friendship, or a successful business partnership!

Cancer/Aries

THE ATTRACTION:

Cancer will give Aries hero worship and nurturing, plus shrewd business sense and a solid home base to operate from. Aries gives Cancer romance, positive energy, and courage.

THE ISSUES:

Aries detests complaining or whining, so you'll have to suffer in silence. Sulking and possessive behavior are other Aries turnoffs. You may balk when Aries pushes, finding the behavior too insensitive and self-centered.

SIGN MATES:

Cancer President Gerald Ford and Aries Betty Ford

Cancer/Taurus

THE ATTRACTION:

In theory, this should be one of the best combinations. Taurus can't get too much affection, which Cancer provides. And Taurus protects Cancer from the cold world, with solid secure assets. Both are home loving, emotional, and sensual.

THE ISSUES:

Cancer's dark mood plus Taurus's stubbornness could create some muddy moments. Both partners should look for constructive ways to let off steam rather than brooding and sulking over grievances.

SIGN MATES:

Cancer James Brolin and Taurus Barbra Streisand

Cancer/Gemini

THE ATTRACTION:

This is a very public pair with charisma to spare. Gemini charm sets off Cancer poise with the perfect light touch. Cancer adds warmth and emotional appeal to Gemini. You can go places together.

THE ISSUES:

It's not easy for Gemini to deliver the emotional intimacy Cancer demands. There are too many other exciting options. Cancer possessiveness versus Gemini restlessness could sink this one if you don't have strong mutual interests or projects.

SIGN MATES:

Cancer Tracy Pollan and Gemini Michael J. Fox

Cancer/Cancer

THE ATTRACTION:

Ideally, here is someone who understands your moods, gives you the mothering care you crave, and protects you from the cold cruel world. Your home can be a loving sanctuary for your extended family and a secure nest for each other.

THE ISSUES:

You both take slights so personally that disagreements can easily get blown out of proportion. And if you are both in a down mood at the same time, your relationship can explode. You'll need outside activities for balance and time away from each other to regain perspective. Creative expression can save the day by providing an outlet for your emotions.

SIGN MATES:

Cancers Donna Dixon and Dan Aykroyd

Cancer/Leo

THE ATTRACTION:

These neighboring signs come through for each other like good buddies. Cancer gives Leo total attention, backup support, and the VIP treatment the Lion craves. Here is someone who won't fight for the spotlight. Leo gives you confidence, and this sign's positive mental outlook is good medicine for your moods.

THE ISSUES:

Cancer's blue moods and tendency to cling tenaciously can weigh Leo down. High-handed Leo behavior can steamroll your sensitive Cancer feelings.

SIGN MATES:

Cancer Kevin Bacon and Leo Kyra Sedgwick

Cancer/Virgo

THE ATTRACTION:

You two vulnerable signs protect and nurture each other. Moody Cancer needs Virgo to refine and focus emotions creatively. Virgo gives Cancer protective care and valuable insight. The charming romantic tenderness of Cancer nurtures the shy side of Virgo. You'll have good communication on a practical level, respecting each other's shrewd financial acumen.

THE ISSUES:

Cancer's extreme self-protection could arouse Virgo suspicions. Why must Cancer be so secretive? Virgo's protectiveness could become smothering, making Cancer overdependent. Virgo must learn to offer suggestions instead of criticism.

SIGN MATES:

Sopranos costars Cancer Edie Falco and Virgo James Gandolfini

Cancer/Libra

THE ATTRACTION:

You'll bring out each other's creativity, as Cancer's sensitivity merges with the balanced Libra aesthetic sense. Libra's innate sense of harmony could create a serenely elegant atmosphere where Cancer flourishes. You'll create an especially beautiful and welcoming home together.

THE ISSUES:

Libra's detachment could be mistaken for rejection by Cancer, while your Cancer hypersensitivity could throw the Libra scales off-balance. Emotions and emotional confrontations are territories Libra avoids, so Cancer may look elsewhere for sympathy and nurturing.

SIGN MATES:

Cancer Richie Sambora and Libra Heather Locklear

Cancer/Scorpio

THE ATTRACTION:

Cancer actually enjoys Scorpio intensity and possessiveness—it shows how much they care! And like Prince Charles and Camilla Parker Bowles (or Diana), this pair cares deeply about those they love. Strong emotions are a great bond that can survive heavy storms.

THE ISSUES:

Mysterious and melancholy Scorpio moods can leave Cancer feeling isolated and insecure. And the more Cancer clings, the more Scorpio withdraws.

SIGN MATES:

Cancer President George W. Bush and Scorpio Laura Bush
Cancer Harrison Ford and Scorpio Callista Flockhart

Cancer/Sagittarius

THE ATTRACTION:

Sagittarius gets a sensual partner who will keep the home fires burning and the coffers full, while Cancer gets a strong dose of optimism that could banish the blues. The carefree, outgoing, outdoor Sagittarius lifestyle expands the sometimes narrow Cancer point of view and gets you physically active.

THE ISSUES:

This joy ride could reach a dead end when Sagittarius shows little sympathy for the Cancer need for mothering or runs roughshod over sensitive Cancer feelings.

SIGN MATES:

Cancer Tom Cruise and Sagittarius Katie Holmes

Cancer/Capricorn

THE ATTRACTION:

A serious sense of duty, family pride, and a basically traditional outlook bring you together. The zodiac mother (Cancer) and father (Capricorn) establish a strong home base. Cancer's tender devotion brings out Capricorn's earthy and sensual side. This couple gets closer over the years.

THE ISSUES:

Melancholy moods could muddy this picture. Develop a strategy for coping if depression hits. Capricorn is a lone wolf who may withdraw emotionally. Cancer could look elsewhere for comfort and consolation.

SIGN MATES:

Cancer Pamela Anderson and Capricorn Kid Rock
Cancer Prince William and Capricorn Kate Middleton

Cancer/Aquarius

THE ATTRACTION:

The key to success for this one-of-a-kind couple is basic ideals. If you two share goals and values, there is no limit to how far you can go. Cancer is turned on by the security of a high position and offers Aquarius strong support and caring qualities that touch everyone's heart, the perfect counterpoint to Aquarius charisma. Former President Ronald Reagan and his wife, Nancy, are a case in point.

THE ISSUES:

Cancer is best one on one, while Aquarius loves a crowd. Cancer has to learn to share love with many. Aquarius has to learn to show warmth and emotion rather than turn off Cancer moods.

SIGN MATES:

Cancer Nancy Reagan and Aquarius President Ronald Reagan

Cancer/Pisces

THE ATTRACTION:

You both love to swim in emotional waters, where your communication flows easily. Cancer protective attention and support help Pisces gain confidence and direction. Pisces gives Cancer dreamy romance and creative inspiration. A very meaningful relationship develops over time.

THE ISSUES:

You two emotionally vulnerable signs know where the soft spots are and can really hurt each other. Pisces has a way of slipping through clingy Cancer clutches, possibly to dry out after too much emotion. Learn to give each other space. Find creative projects to defuse negative moods and to give a sense of direction.

SIGN MATES:

Cancer David Gest and Pisces Liza Minnelli

CHAPTER 25

The Big Picture for Cancer in 2008

Welcome to 2008, Cancer! It promises to be an intriguing year, so let's take a closer look.

In late 2007, Saturn left Leo and your second house of finances and moved into your third house. You learned a lot about your beliefs concerning money while Saturn was in Leo; you also became more aware of discipline and responsibility concerning your finances. Now Saturn is in Virgo, where it will transit for 2.5 years.

During Saturn's transit through Virgo, your conscious thoughts will become more structured and disciplined. You may feel burdened at times, particularly if you have siblings. A brother or sister, for instance, may need your help and emotional support. You may encounter restrictions or delays in terms of your community or neighborhood. Your communication ability will be more focused and organized.

Jupiter, the planet that symbolizes expansion and success, entered Capricorn and your seventh house at the end of 2007 and will remain there until early 2009. During this transit, your partnerships—both romantic and business—expand and broaden. A deeper commitment in a relationship is possible. On January 25, Pluto enters Capricorn, joining Jupiter in your seventh house. Throughout the year, Pluto moves back into Sagittarius when it turns retrograde, then finally enters Capricorn again in late November. The combination of Jupiter and Pluto suggests that a romantic or business partnership will transform your life profoundly, in a positive sense. This partnership could be with a foreign-born individual or someone who works in the law, higher education, or publishing.

Uranus, the planet symbolic of sudden, unexpected change, continues its transit through Pisces and your ninth house, forming a beneficial angle to your sun. You may be traveling overseas this year, and the opportunity could come up suddenly. Make sure you have a bag packed; be ready to go and have your passport in order! Uranus also attracts unusual individuals who are often brilliant, idiosyncratic, or unusual in some way. If you get involved with someone while traveling overseas, the relationship will be exciting, for sure, but may not last forever.

Neptune continues its long transit through Aquarius and your eighth house. By now, you should have a pretty good idea what kinds of experiences Neptune attracts—the strange, mystical, and spiritually inspired. There could be some confusion concerning your spouse's income or any resources you share with others.

Best Time for Romance

Mark the dates between June 18 and July 12, when Venus is in your sign. Your romantic quota soars. You're also artistic then, and others see you in a flattering light. You feel confident, and your sex appeal rises. Great backup dates for romance fall between September 23 and October 18, when Venus is transiting your fifth house of love and forming a beautiful angle to your sun.

Other excellent dates for romance fall between May 11 and 13, and September 3 and 5, when the sun and Jupiter see eye to eye and there's a nice flow of energy between them.

Best Time for Career Decisions

Make career decisions between April 4 and 30, when Venus is transiting your tenth house of careers. This should be quite a smooth time professionally. In fact, things may be going along so smoothly that you'll be tempted to kick back and relax. Don't. Seize the opportunity.

Mercury Retrogrades

Every year, there are three periods when Mercury—the planet of communication and travel—turns retrograde. During these periods, it's wise not to negotiate or sign contracts, to travel, submit manuscripts, or make major decisions. Granted, we can't live our lives entirely by Mercury retrogrades! However, if you have to travel during the periods listed below, then expect changes in your itinerary. If you have to sign a contract, expect to revisit it.

It's also a good idea to back up computer files before Mercury turns retrograde. Quite often, computers and other communication devices act up. Be sure your virus software is up-to-date, too. Pay special attention to the house in which Mercury retrograde falls. It will tell you the area of your life most likely to be impacted. The periods to watch for in 2008 are:

January 28–February 18: retrograde in Aquarius, your eighth house of shared resources.

May 26–June 19: retrograde in Gemini, your twelfth house—what's hidden, the personal unconscious, karma.

September 24–October 15: retrograde in Libra, your fourth house of home, family, your parents.

Eclipses

Every year, there are four eclipses, two solar and two lunar. Solar eclipses trigger external events that allow us to see something that eluded us before. When an eclipse hits one of your natal planets, it's especially important. Take note of the sign and house placement. Lunar eclipses bring up emotional issues related to the sign and house into which they fall.

Here are the dates to watch for:

February 6: Solar eclipse at 17 degrees Aquarius, your eighth house of shared resources, taxes, insurance, and esoteric topics. Those of you born between July 7 and 11 are likely to feel the greatest impact.

February 20: Lunar eclipse at 10 degrees Virgo, in your third house of communication, siblings, the conscious mind.

August 1: Solar eclipse, 9 degrees Leo, in your second house of finances. If you're born between June 29 and July 3, this eclipse will impact you strongly.

August 16: Lunar eclipse at 24 degrees Aquarius, your eighth house of shared resources.

Luckiest Days in 2008

Every year, Jupiter forms a beneficial angle with the sun, usually a conjunction, when both planets are in the same sign. In 2008, the angle is a lovely trine and it occurs during two time periods: May 11–13 and September 3–5. If you're going to buy a Lotto ticket, do it during these periods!

Now let's take a look at what 2008 has in store for you day by day.

CHAPTER 26

Eighteen Months of Day-by-Day Predictions—July 2007 to December 2008

Moon sign times are calculated for Eastern Standard Time and Eastern Daylight Time. Please adjust for your local time zone.

JULY 2007

Sunday, July 1 (Moon in Capricorn) With the moon in your seventh house, you deal with partnerships, either personal or business. Loved ones and partners play an important role. Women play a prominent role. Be careful that others don't manipulate your feelings.

Monday, July 2 (Moon in Capricorn to Aquarius 1:25 a.m.) Your organizational skills are highlighted. Control your impulses; avoid scattering your energy. Persevere to get things done. Be methodical and thorough. You're building a creative base.

Tuesday, July 3 (Moon in Aquarius) You could be dealing with matters related to taxes, insurance, or investments. Shared resources play a role. Look beyond the immediate; play your hunches. Experiences may be intense.

Wednesday, July 4 (Moon in Aquarius to Pisces 6:53 a.m.) You could encounter an emotional outburst. Try to be understanding; avoid confrontations. Do a good deed for someone. Focus on making people happy. Find your rhythm.

Thursday, July 5 (Moon in Pisces)   Break away from your routine. Pay attention to your dreams. Ideas are ripe; your imagination is highlighted. Look for universal knowledge and eternal truths.

Friday, July 6 (Moon in Pisces to Aries 10:57 a.m.) Play it your way. You have a chance to expand your focus and to gain fame and power. It all could start from your home base.

Saturday, July 7 (Moon in Aries)   Initiate projects, brainstorm, or launch new ideas. Business is highlighted. Your life is public. Your power of persuasion is strong, especially if you're passionate about what you're doing.

Sunday, July 8 (Moon in Aries to Taurus 1:54 p.m.)   Yesterday's powerful energy keeps flowing. You get a fresh start. Don't follow others. Exploration, discovery, and creativity are key words for your day. Creative people play a role. In romance, make room for a new love.

Monday, July 9 (Moon in Taurus)   Mercury goes direct. Your communications with others will go smoothly. You get your point across. Misunderstandings are resolved. Forgive and forget.

Tuesday, July 10 (Moon in Taurus to Gemini 4:10 p.m.)   Ease up on your routines. Spread your good news. Have some fun in preparation for the challenges ahead. Spend time at home with your family.

Wednesday, July 11 (Moon in Gemini)   The moon is in your twelfth house. You may feel like withdrawing and working behind the scenes. See a therapist. Things related to your past and childhood come to your attention. Communicate your deepest feelings to another person.

Thursday, July 12 (Moon in Gemini to Cancer 5:40 p.m.) Communications, information, and writing play a role. Be versatile and changeable. Variety is the spice of life, but don't spread yourself too thin. You overcome obstacles with ease.

Friday, July 13 (Moon in Cancer) The moon is in your first house or on the ascendant. You're recharged for the month ahead, and you're more appealing to the public. You're physically vital; relations with the opposite sex go well. Your feelings and thoughts are aligned.

Saturday, July 14 (Moon in Cancer to Leo 10:44 p.m.) Venus moves into your third house. Your relations with someone in your neighborhood could turn romantic. Any writing or communications will be subjective. You express yourself with warmth and affection.

Sunday, July 15 (Moon in Leo) The moon enters your second house. Stay home. You feel comfortable in your home environment surrounded by familiar objects. Put off any big purchases for another few days.

Monday, July 16 (Moon in Leo) Strut your stuff. Showmanship is the key word. The focus is on advertising or publicizing yourself. Drama, perhaps involving children, is highlighted. You're impulsive, honest, and open.

Tuesday, July 17 (Moon in Leo to Virgo 5:40 a.m.) Take the initiative to move in a new direction. Don't follow others. Be independent and creative. Don't be discouraged by naysayers. Trust your hunches. A flirtation becomes more serious.

Wednesday, July 18 (Moon in Virgo) The moon moves into your third house. Keep conscious control of your emotions when communicating with others. Your thinking may be unduly influenced by things in the past. Watch for an invitation to a social gathering. It could involve neighbors or relatives.

Thursday, July 19 (Moon in Virgo to Libra 3:54 p.m.) Spiritual values are emphasized. Your intuition is highlighted. Your attitude determines everything. Insist on all the information, not just bits and pieces. Play your hunches. Don't forget a special anniversary or birthday.

Friday, July 20 (Moon in Libra) The moon moves into your fourth house, the native home for Cancer. Retreat to a private place for meditation. Spend time at home with your loved ones. Attend to home repairs.

Saturday, July 21 (Moon in Libra) Stay close to home. You feel emotionally possessive of those close to you. Don't speculate on real estate.

Sunday, July 22 (Moon in Libra to Scorpio 4:19 a.m.) Dance to your own tune. Find your rhythm. Domestic purchases are highlighted. Attend to a sick family member or friend. Focus on making people happy.

Monday, July 23 (Moon in Scorpio) It's a day for researching, looking behind closed doors, digging up secrets. Intense emotional experiences and high passions could prevail. Forgive and forget.

Tuesday, July 24 (Moon in Scorpio to Sagittarius 4:31 p.m.) Remain goal-oriented. You're being watched by people in powerful positions. Open your mind to a new approach that could bring in big money. Look for ways to expand your base.

Wednesday, July 25 (Moon in Sagittarius) The moon enters your sixth house of daily work and health. Your personal health occupies your attention. Keep your resolutions about exercise. Visit someone who is ill. It's a service-oriented day.

Thursday, July 26 (Moon in Sagittarius) Don't limit yourself. Look to the big picture. Think abundance and prosperity. Jupiter, the beneficent planet, rules your day. Plan a long trip, or pursue a publishing project.

Friday, July 27 (Moon in Sagittarius to Capricorn 2:23 a.m.)   Venus goes retrograde in your third house. You could face some physical discomfort related to your neighbors or siblings. Any relationship that you enter into could face difficulties and challenges. You should read and rewrite any communications to avoid any misunderstandings.

Saturday, July 28 (Moon in Capricorn)   The moon moves into your seventh house. Attend to legal matters, such as signing a contract; even a marriage vow could play a role. Loved ones and partners are key to your day. There could be confrontations, but you're at your best when you're at home.

Sunday, July 29 (Moon in Capricorn to Aquarius 9:14 a.m.)   You're at the right place at the right time. Seek an outlet for your creative energy. Be methodical and thorough in your plans. Missing papers or objects are located.

Monday, July 30 (Moon in Aquarius)   Look beyond the immediate. Play your hunches. Dance to your own tune; follow your heart. You attract powerful people to your cause. Your wishes and dreams come true.

Tuesday, July 31 (Moon in Aquarius to Pisces 1:41 p.m.)   Be understanding and kind; try to avoid confrontations. Be diplomatic, especially with people making unfair demands on your time. Like yesterday, you should dance to your own tune.

AUGUST 2007

Wednesday, August 1 (Moon in Pisces)   The moon is in your ninth house. You feel like getting away. Alter your routine; attend a workshop or seminar. A foreign person or place could play a role.

Thursday, August 2 (Moon in Pisces to Aries 4:43 p.m.)   Freedom of thought and action is the key phrase of the day. Communicate and get your ideas across. Prepare for change. Like yesterday, try to approach the day with an unconventional mind-set. Experiment.

Friday, August 3 (Moon in Aries)   Initiate a new project or relationship. Your power of persuasion is strong, especially if you're passionate about what you're trying to convey. Have an adventure.

Saturday, August 4 (Moon in Aries to Taurus 7:16 p.m.)   Mercury moves into your second house. Deal with money matters; pay bills and collect what's owed to you. You tend to equate your financial assets with emotional security. Watch your spending.

Sunday, August 5 (Moon in Taurus)   The moon is in your eleventh house. You get along with friends who can be helpful. Focus on your wishes and dreams. Examine your overall goals. Make sure that they express who you really are.

Monday, August 6 (Moon in Taurus to Gemini 10:02 p.m.)   Jupiter goes direct in your sixth house. That means you could be seeing some expansion in your daily work: more responsibilities, more pay, more prestige. Watch your diet. You could put on a couple extra pounds if you're not careful.

Tuesday, August 7 (Moon in Gemini)   Mars moves into your twelfth house. You have the energy to deal with your inner self at this time. Withdraw and deal with unconscious attitudes that could relate to your past and childhood. A secret sexual affair is a possibility. Be careful. You may be more accident prone than usual.

Wednesday, August 8 (Moon in Gemini)   The moon is in your twelfth house, an indication that you should back off. Keep your feelings secret; work behind the scenes. Make use of your intuition. Follow a hunch. You could pursue your interest with a mystical or spiritual practice.

Thursday, August 9 (Moon in Gemini to Cancer 1:37 a.m.) Your attitude determines everything. Make time to listen to others. Relax and enjoy yourself. Recharge your batteries. Spend time with family members.

Friday, August 10 (Moon in Cancer) The moon is in your first house. You're in the public eye. The recharging that began yesterday continues and gets you ready for the rest of the month. Relations with the opposite sex go well as your feelings and thoughts are aligned.

Saturday, August 11 (Moon in Cancer to Leo 6:42 a.m.) Freedom of thought and action highlights your day. Find a new perspective. Get ready for change; attend a workshop or seminar. Approach your day with an unconventional point of view.

Sunday, August 12 (Moon in Leo) Drama is highlighted. A romance heats up; passion and possessiveness play as factors. You're impulsive, honest, and creative. It's a good day to take a gamble. Let others know what you've got!

Monday, August 13 (Moon in Leo to Virgo 2:04 p.m.) Maintain your emotional balance. Knowledge is essential to success. Gather information and search beneath the surface, but don't make any absolute decisions. Go with the flow.

Tuesday, August 14 (Moon in Virgo) The moon is in your third house. You express a strong point of view in many of your communications. Contact with neighbors and relatives works to your favor. A female relative plays a role.

Wednesday, August 15 (Moon in Virgo) Strive for universal appeal. Look beyond the immediate. Clear up odds and ends, and get ready for the challenges you'll face tomorrow. Don't start anything new. Accept whatever comes your way.

Thursday, August 16 (Moon in Virgo to Libra 12:05 a.m.) The moon is in your fourth house, the natural home of Cancers. It's a good day for recalling your dreams. Take the day off and stay home! Spend time with those close to you. Retreat to a private place.

Friday, August 17 (Moon in Libra) Romance is highlighted. Relationships are at the forefront. Sensuality, personal grace, and magnetism play a role. Attend a concert, a gallery opening, or the theater. Harmony and peace prevail.

Saturday, August 18 (Moon in Libra to Scorpio 12:14 p.m.) Ease up on your routines. Relax and enjoy yourself. Spend time talking to friends and neighbors; work on a hobby. Expect an invitation from a friend or loved one.

Sunday, August 19 (Moon in Scorpio) Mercury moves into your third house, its natural home. Communicate with neighbors and siblings. Take time to write in a journal or to publicize what you're doing.

Monday, August 20 (Moon in Scorpio) Experiment or take a risk. Let go of old structures; get a new point of view. Approach the day with an unconventional mind-set, and you could reap long-term benefits.

Tuesday, August 21 (Moon in Scorpio to Sagittarius 12:45 a.m.) The moon is in your sixth house. Make sure that you don't overlook the details in whatever you're doing. Help others, especially people close to you. But avoid acting like a martyr. Take time to exercise; watch your diet.

Wednesday, August 22 (Moon in Sagittarius) Make use of your sense of humor to lighten things up. Expand the possibilities. Don't limit yourself to your comfortable routine. It may be time to look beyond the horizon.

Thursday, August 23 (Moon in Sagittarius to Capricorn 11:20 a.m.) Play it your way. Business meetings go well. People in power are watching you. Be courageous.

Open your mind to a new approach that could bring in big bucks.

Friday, August 24 (Moon in Capricorn)   The moon is in your seventh house. Focus on relationships, both personal and business. Loved ones are important, but there could be confrontations, especially with women. You'll find it difficult to maintain a detached and objective perspective.

Saturday, August 25 (Moon in Capricorn to Aquarius 6:35 p.m.)   You're at the top of your cycle. Be independent and creative. Don't be afraid to turn in new directions. Refuse to be discouraged by naysayers. In romance, a flirtation turns serious.

Sunday, August 26 (Moon in Aquarius)   The moon is in your eighth house. Your experiences may be intense. Explore your interest in metaphysical subjects. Powerful people could influence your beliefs and ideas on the spirit realm.

Monday, August 27 (Moon in Aquarius to Pisces 10:35 p.m.)   Your charm and wit attract attention. Your intuition and imagination are highlighted. Be happy, positive, and upbeat. Attitude determines everything. Take time for family matters.

Tuesday, August 28 (Moon in Pisces)   There's a lunar eclipse in your ninth house. It's a day for new beginnings. You may feel restless and yearn for something new. Use your imagination; be compassionate. Universal knowledge and eternal truths are at the heart of your search.

Wednesday, August 29 (Moon in Pisces)   Look for a change of scenery. Key words for the day are change, variety, and freedom. People take note of your writing and communications skills.

Thursday, August 30 (Moon in Pisces to Aries 12:25 a.m.)   The moon moves into your tenth house. Look for an elevation in prestige related to your career. You're warmer toward fellow workers. But avoid any emotional displays, and don't blur the boundaries between your personal and professional lives.

Friday, August 31 (Moon in Aries)   Initiate projects, launch new ideas, or even attend a sports event. Emotions can be volatile, especially if you're passionate about your subject. Have an adventure; do something thrilling. Be careful about accidents.

SEPTEMBER 2007

Saturday, September 1 (Moon in Aries to Taurus 1:36 a.m.)   The moon is in your eleventh house. Focus on your wishes and dreams. Examine your overall goals. Make sure that they are an expression of who you really are. You join a group of like-minded individuals with a common goal. Social consciousness wins the way.

Sunday, September 2 (Moon in Taurus)   Saturn moves into your third house. You find the structure for a writing project or another means of communicating. You revise your connection with certain neighbors. Or you bring more structure to your relationship with siblings.

Monday, September 3 (Moon in Taurus to Gemini 3:31 a.m.)   Search beneath the surface for answers. Gather information, but don't make any absolute decisions until tomorrow. Knowledge is essential for success. Express your desires, but watch out for self-deception.

Tuesday, September 4 (Moon in Gemini)   The moon is in your twelfth house. Withdraw from the action. Relations with the opposite sex can be difficult. Stay home where you're comfortable. Work behind the scenes. Communicate your deepest feelings to a friend.

Wednesday, September 5 (Moon in Gemini to Cancer 7:09 a.m.)   Mercury moves into your fourth house. Communications improve at home. Set up a home office. Spend time with your family. Activity related to real estate goes smoothly.

Thursday, September 6 (Moon in Cancer) The moon is in your first house. You're in the public view. You're physically vital and getting recharged for the month ahead. Your feelings are variable, but so are your thoughts. You're particularly sensitive to other people's feelings.

Friday, September 7 (Moon in Cancer to Leo 1:00 p.m.) Pluto goes direct in your sixth house. Any changes that have been delayed will begin to unfold. Watch your diet; exercise. Make sure your beliefs about your health are positive.

Saturday, September 8 (Moon in Leo) Venus goes direct, which means it's an ideal time for pursuing a romance and matters dealing with communications. Get started or continue to refurbish or redecorate your home.

Sunday, September 9 (Moon in Leo to Virgo 9:11 p.m.) Realize that you can find the outlet for your creative efforts. You can overcome obstacles easily. You're building a creative base for your future. Revise and rewrite. You're at the right place at the right time.

Monday, September 10 (Moon in Virgo) Tend to health matters. Watch your diet, and make sure you exercise. Stop worrying and fretting. Stick close to home, where you feel comfortable. You're intuitive and nurturing.

Tuesday, September 11 (Moon in Virgo) There's a solar eclipse, which means something hidden will be revealed related to a relationship with a neighbor or sibling. It could also be that something is exposed through your writing. Or something comes to light while you're on a short journey.

Wednesday, September 12 (Moon in Virgo to Libra 7:32 a.m.) Go with the flow. Maintain your emotional bal-

232

ance. Express your desires. But see things as they are, not as you wish them to be. Keep any secrets entrusted to you.

Thursday, September 13 (Moon in Libra)   The moon is in your fourth house. Your intuitive and nurturing Cancer energy is emphasized. Spend time at home with your loved ones. Change a bad habit.

Friday, September 14 (Moon in Libra to Scorpio 7:37 p.m.)   Complete a project. Clear up odds and ends. Get ready for a new challenge. Be confident, not obsequious. Look beyond the immediate. But don't start anything new.

Saturday, September 15 (Moon in Scorpio)   With the moon in your fifth house, you're feeling creative. You can tap deeply into the collective unconscious. Be yourself. Be emotionally honest. A relationship reaches great depth.

Sunday, September 16 (Moon in Scorpio)   You may feel somewhat possessive of loved ones. You feel passionate about whoever interests you. Your sexuality is heightened. Things are happening in secret!

Monday, September 17 (Moon in Scorpio to Sagittarius 8:21 a.m.)   Your intuition is heightened. Play your hunches. Remain flexible. Stay positive and upbeat. Make time to listen to others.

Tuesday, September 18 (Moon in Sagittarius)   There's a lunar eclipse in Virgo, your third house. An emotional issue that relates to a sibling or a neighbor is exposed. Talk it over; stay in control of your emotions. You also express strong feelings in something that you write.

Wednesday, September 19 (Moon in Sagittarius to Capricorn 7:52 p.m.)   It's all about freedom of thought and action. Variety is the spice of life. Experiment. Get ready for change. You overcome obstacles with ease.

Thursday, September 20 (Moon in Capricorn)   The moon is in your seventh house. It's all about partnerships.

You have a hard time remaining emotionally detached in any confrontation with a partner. Be careful that others don't manipulate your feelings. Use your native intuition. Be nurturing. You'll feel best at home.

Friday, September 21 (Moon in Capricorn) There could be dealings with elderly people. Banks and institutions may be involved. You deal with an authority figure, or you are the authority figure. Your ambition and drive are highlighted. You may feel stressed and overworked. Relax.

Saturday, September 22 (Moon in Capricorn to Aquarius 4:18 a.m.) Unexpected money arrives. You have a chance to expand and to gain recognition, fame, and power. Be courageous; remain goal-oriented.

Sunday, September 23 (Moon in Aquarius) Emotional experiences can be intense. You may feel like dancing to your own tune, especially related to a metaphysical pursuit. You have shared resources to consider. Issues related to taxes, insurance, and investments may come up.

Monday, September 24 (Moon in Aquarius to Pisces 8:56 a.m.) You get a fresh start. Express your opinions dynamically. Make room for a new love. Trust your hunches; follow your intuition. Don't be afraid to turn in a new direction.

Tuesday, September 25 (Moon in Pisces) The moon is in your ninth house. You feel a need to get away from the usual routines. Sign up for a workshop or seminar. Plan a long trip or take an armchair journey to a foreign land. Your interest in exotic ideas leads to new possibilities.

Wednesday, September 26 (Moon in Pisces to Aries 10:23 a.m.) Your charm and optimism work well for you. Relax and ease up on your routines. Listen to others, but don't forget to spread your good news. You're happiest close to home with your family and friends.

234

Thursday, September 27 (Moon in Aries)   Mercury moves into your fifth house. That's great for creative projects. You'll be able to communicate your ideas to those who can provide the help you need. In love, you relate well to that special person. You understand each other particularly well.

Friday, September 28 (Moon in Aries to Taurus 10:18 a.m.)   Mars moves into your first house. Lots of new energy comes your way. You're recharged for the month ahead. Your thoughts and emotions are well aligned. You attract the right people. You feel physically vital; relations with the opposite sex go very well.

Saturday, September 29 (Moon in Taurus)   The moon is in your eleventh house. You experience deep contact with friends. You also work well with a group, as long as you avoid any tendency toward stubbornness or feeling oversensitive. Examine your overall goals. Make sure they fit who you are and then get to work.

Sunday, September 30 (Moon in Taurus to Gemini 10:35 a.m.)   You could set out on a journey into the unknown. Spirituality is emphasized. Secrets, mystery, intrigue, and confidential information could play into your day. Maintain your emotional balance.

OCTOBER 2007

Monday, October 1 (Moon in Gemini)   The moon is in your twelfth house. You could face your past. You may feel a need to withdraw and work behind the scenes. Keep your feelings secret; avoid confrontations. You might have dealings with hospitals, jails, or institutions. Look to the future.

Tuesday, October 2 (Moon in Gemini to Cancer 12:58 p.m.)   Yesterday's energy keeps flowing. Make sure that you see things as they are and not how you wish them to be. Keep any secrets entrusted to you. Avoid self-deception.

Wednesday, October 3 (Moon in Cancer)   The moon moves to your first house. You are moody. You're sensitive to other people's feelings. The self and how you relate to others is at the heart of your day. Relax and get revitalized.

Thursday, October 4 (Moon in Cancer to Leo 6:28 p.m.)   Finish what you've started. Make room for something new. Take time to assess what you've accomplished and to see where you're going. Accept whatever comes your way, but don't start anything new.

Friday, October 5 (Moon in Leo)   Drama is highlighted. You're at center stage. Showmanship wins. You're impulsive, honest, and creative. Dress in bold colors; do something different with your hair. It's a day for extravagance. Romance and love are part of the picture.

Saturday, October 6 (Moon in Leo)   The moon is in your second house. Investments pay off. Deal with money matters, but avoid making any major purchases for another few days. You feel best at home surrounded by familiar objects.

Sunday, October 7 (Moon in Leo to Virgo 3:04 a.m.)   Relax and enjoy yourself. Recharge your batteries. Spend time in conversation with friends and neighbors. Spread your good news and listen to what others have to say.

Monday, October 8 (Moon in Virgo)   Tend to health matters. Stick close to home and pay attention to details. Watch your diet, exercise, and stop fretting. Dig deep for information. Write in a journal.

Tuesday, October 9 (Moon in Virgo to Libra 1:58 p.m.)   You're looking for change. Variety is the spice of life. Approach the day with an unconventional mind-set and get ready for change.

Wednesday, October 10 (Moon in Libra)   Service to others is the key phrase. Be diplomatic. Focus on making people happy. Do a good deed for someone, but avoid scattering your energies. Be understanding even in the face of emotional outbursts.

Thursday, October 11 (Moon in Libra)   Mercury goes retrograde and stays that way until November 1. Communications can be difficult during this period. There could be disruptions and delays, especially with groups. Work behind the scenes as much as possible for the next three weeks. Review, revise, and reevaluate your creative activities. Allow yourself plenty of time for arriving at appointments. Put off signing contracts, if possible, or examine all the details closely.

Friday, October 12 (Moon in Libra to Scorpio 2:14 a.m.) Play it your way. Business discussions work in your favor. People in power are paying attention to you. Be courageous. Appear successful even if you don't feel that way.

Saturday, October 13 (Moon in Scorpio)   You're more possessive of loved ones and protective of your children. Animals also play a role. Be yourself, be honest, and be creative.

Sunday, October 14 (Moon in Scorpio to Sagittarius 2:58 p.m.)   You're at the top of your cycle. Creative people play a role in your day. Stress your originality. Trust your hunches. Intuition is highlighted. Make room for a new love. Exploration and discovery are key words for the day.

Monday, October 15 (Moon in Sagittarius)   The moon is in your sixth house. Keep your resolutions about exercise and diet. Your personal health may occupy your attention, but don't let your fears hold you back. Stay strong. Ease up on your routines. Visit someone who's not feeling well or could use your help.

Tuesday, October 16 (Moon in Sagittarius)   Use your sense of humor, even if you must laugh at yourself. Look to the big picture. Don't limit yourself or allow the details to slow you down. Travel is indicated. A publishing project gets a boost.

Wednesday, October 17 (Moon in Sagittarius to Capricorn 3:04 a.m.) Control your impulses. Persevere. Fulfill your obligations. Emphasize quality. Your hard work pays off. You're building a creative base. You can overcome any red tape. Use your native intuition.

Thursday, October 18 (Moon in Capricorn) The moon is in your seventh house of partnerships and marriage. It's all about relationships. Loved ones and partners are important. Your nurturing nature will help you through any rough areas.

Friday, October 19 (Moon in Capricorn to Aquarius 12:52 p.m.) Focus on making people happy. Be understanding, not demanding. Be generous and tolerant. Buy something for the home that will please everyone.

Saturday, October 20 (Moon in Aquarius) The moon is in your eighth house. Your experiences are intense. A relationship may die or be reborn. Sex is at the heart of the matter. You find spiritual and emotional support.

Sunday, October 21 (Moon in Aquarius to Pisces 7:03 p.m.) Play it your way. You have a chance to expand and to gain recognition, fame, and power. Open your mind to a new approach. There could be a big payoff. Be courageous. Expect a financial coup.

Monday, October 22 (Moon in Pisces) Your imagination is highlighted. Keep track of your dreams. Your ideas are rich and ripe for development tomorrow. You may experience psychic events and synchronicities.

Tuesday, October 23 (Moon in Pisces to Aries 9:25 p.m.) You're at the top of your cycle. You get a fresh start. Express your opinions dynamically; don't be afraid to turn in a new direction. In romance, make room for a new love, but make sure you consider all the repercussions.

Wednesday, October 24 (Moon in Aries)   The energy from your fresh start yesterday flows forward with a new sense of aggressiveness. Take the initiative and launch your new ideas. Your power of persuasion is strong, especially if you really are passionate about what you're doing.

Thursday, October 25 (Moon in Aries to Taurus 9:08 p.m.)   Diversify. Insist on all the information, not just bits and pieces. Your attitude determines everything. Stay positive and upbeat. Relax, enjoy yourself, and get recharged.

Friday, October 26 (Moon in Taurus)   The moon is in your eleventh house of wishes and dreams. Examine your overall goals; make sure that they are an expression of who you are now. Your friends play an important role. For example, a friend may offer a tip or a lead that will prove extremely helpful. Your actions could raise the social consciousness of others.

Saturday, October 27 (Moon in Taurus to Gemini 8:12 p.m.)   Variety is the spice of life. A change of scenery sounds good. You might be considering a move or relocation. Don't be afraid to take risks. Get ready for change.

Sunday, October 28 (Moon in Gemini)   The moon is in your twelfth house. You may feel a need to withdraw and work behind the scenes. Something from your past may be haunting you. Face it and clear it away. Look to the future. Keep your feelings secret; avoid confrontations. Draw on your intuitive nature.

Monday, October 29 (Moon in Gemini to Cancer 8:50 p.m.)   You may encounter delays that relate to others who are not living up to their commitments. Avoid confusion and conflict. Go with the flow. See things as they are, not how you'd like them to be. Keep any secrets entrusted to you.

Tuesday, October 30 (Moon in Cancer) The moon is in your first house. You get recharged for the month. You appeal to the public, you are vital and aware. Relations with the opposite sex go well. Your feelings and thoughts are aligned.

Wednesday, October 31 (Moon in Cancer) Complete a project. Clear your desk. Discard preconceived notions. Nurture your intuition and strive for universal appeal.

NOVEMBER 2007

Thursday, November 1 (Moon in Cancer to Leo 12:48 a.m.) Mercury goes direct. Communication glitches and delays that you may have been experiencing end. Your relations with others will go smoothly. You get your point across. Misunderstandings are resolved. Forgive and forget.

Friday, November 2 (Moon in Leo) The moon is in your second house of finances and possessions. Investments pay off. Take care of payments and collections. You identify emotionally with your possessions or whatever you value. Put off any big purchases for a few days.

Saturday, November 3 (Moon in Leo to Virgo 8:45 a.m.) Take care of odds and ends. Finish up what you've started. Plan a long trip or foreign travel. Look beyond the immediate. Visualize the future. Set your goals and get to work.

Sunday, November 4—Daylight Saving Time Ends (Moon in Virgo) The moon is in your third house. Your communications are subjective. You express your emotions as well as your opinions. You relate well with neighbors and siblings. You get an invitation to attend a social gathering.

Monday, November 5 (Moon in Virgo to Libra 6:47 p.m.) Cooperation is highlighted. Be kind and understanding. Partnerships are key. The spotlight is on cooperative efforts. Don't make waves.

Tuesday, November 6 (Moon in Libra)   The moon is in your fourth house, the native home of Cancer. Stay home and work or relax in a nurturing environment. You feel especially comfortable and secure in your home environment.

Wednesday, November 7 (Moon in Libra)   Romance is highlighted. It's another good day for sticking close to home. Tend to details; seek perfection. Relax and spend time writing in a journal. Don't forget to exercise and watch your diet.

Thursday, November 8 (Moon in Libra to Scorpio 7:19 a.m.)   Venus moves into your fourth house. It's a good day for a romance at home, and for setting up a home office or redecorating your house. You're artistically aware.

Friday, November 9 (Moon in Scorpio)   The moon is in your fifth house. Be yourself. You find great emotional depth in a relationship. You're protective and nurturing of your children. Animals play a role.

Saturday, November 10 (Moon in Scorpio to Sagittarius 7:59 p.m.)   Search beneath the surface for information. There's a mystery afoot. You're digging into the unknown. Go with the flow. Keep any secrets entrusted to you. Maintain your emotional balance.

Sunday, November 11 (Moon in Sagittarius)   The moon is in your sixth house. It's all about service, duty, and health. Take responsibility for your health. Deal with stress, and adjust your sleep habits, if needed. Help others today, but don't act like a martyr.

Monday, November 12 (Moon in Sagittarius)   Make good use of your sense of humor to ease tensions. Matters dealing with publishing or the law could come up. Travel could be indicated, possibly a long trip. Look for the big picture. Don't limit yourself.

Tuesday, November 13 (Moon in Sagittarius to Capricorn 8:01 a.m.) You're at the top of your cycle. It's all about individuality, leadership, and new beginnings. Take the initiative to turn in a new direction. Don't follow others. Explore, discover, create!

Wednesday, November 14 (Moon in Capricorn) The moon is in your seventh house of partnerships and marriage. The focus is on relationships, both business and personal. Women play a prominent role. You may find it difficult to remain detached and objective. Any conflicts could be confrontational. Be careful that others don't manipulate your feelings.

Thursday, November 15 (Moon in Capricorn to Aquarius 6:31 p.m.) Mars goes retrograde in Cancer until January 29. This is a red-flag period. There could be instances of irrational action, introspection, and depression. You may have to rethink and reorient current projects. These conditions can be especially difficult for you since you were born under the sign of Cancer.

Friday, November 16 (Moon in Aquarius) The moon is in your eighth house. Your experiences are intense, especially related to your belongings, as well as to things that you share with another person, such as your spouse. Matters related to taxes, insurance, and investments could also enter the picture.

Saturday, November 17 (Moon in Aquarius) It's about sex, death, and taxes! Death, of course, can be metaphorical, as in the death of a relationship. Sexual experiences are intense. Taxes can be taxing, but must be paid, especially if they were due last April 15!

Sunday, November 18 (Moon in Aquarius to Pisces 2:15 a.m.) Focus on making people happy. Give them what they want as long as you're willing. Be generous and tolerant. Domestic matters take precedence.

Monday, November 19 (Moon in Pisces)   The moon is in your ninth house. Higher education or long-distance travel is at the heart of matters. You're seeking the truth regarding a concern and broadening your knowledge. On a more mundane level, you could have dealings with your in-laws.

Tuesday, November 20 (Moon in Pisces to Aries 6:25 a.m.)   You're playing with power, and it could lead to financial success. Open your mind to a new approach. It can pay off in a big way.

Wednesday, November 21 (Moon in Aries)   The moon is in your tenth house of profession and career. You're warm toward fellow employees and more responsive to the needs of the public. Emotions run high, but don't blur the boundaries between your personal and professional lives.

Thursday, November 22 (Moon in Aries to Taurus 7:19 a.m.)   Happy Thanksgiving! You're at the top of your cycle. Express your opinions boldly. Get out and meet new people. Have new experiences. You get a fresh start. In romance, make room for a new love.

Friday, November 23 (Moon in Taurus)   The moon is in your eleventh house. You find an identity within a group that gives you deep contact with friends. Focus on your wishes and dreams.

Saturday, November 24 (Moon in Taurus to Gemini 6:29 a.m.)   Uranus goes direct in your ninth house. That brings a burst of new energy into your life and opens the door to a relationship with an independent-minded foreign-born person. It's a good time for travel, business overseas, and exploration of your spiritual beliefs.

Sunday, November 25 (Moon in Gemini)   The moon is in your twelfth house. You might have dealings with hospitals, jails, or institutions. Don't let the past hold you back. Look to the future. You may feel a need to withdraw for an exploration of a spiritual or mystical practice.

Monday, November 26 (Moon in Gemini to Cancer 6:07 a.m.)　　Freedom of thought and action is key to your day. Physical desires play a role. Variety is the spice of life. You tend to be versatile and changeable. Don't spread yourself too thin, and don't break anyone's heart. Take risks, but understand the consequences.

Tuesday, November 27 (Moon in Cancer)　　The moon is in your first house. You get recharged for the month ahead. You're appealing to the public. You are physically vital; relations with the opposite sex go well. Your feelings and thoughts are aligned.

Wednesday, November 28 (Moon in Cancer to Leo 8:23 a.m.)　　It's all about mystery and a journey into the unknown. Intrigue, secrets, and confidential information play a role. Gather the facts, but don't make any absolute decisions until tomorrow. Spirituality is emphasized.

Thursday, November 29 (Moon in Leo)　　The moon is in your second house. Tend to investments and money matters. It's your power day, so look for a financial coup. You attract material success.

Friday, November 30 (Moon in Leo to Virgo 2:45 p.m.)　　It's all about beginnings and endings. If the emphasis is on the latter, finish up what you've started, clear your desk, clean up odds and ends. Focus on the future. Consider how you can expand.

DECEMBER 2007

Saturday, December 1 (Moon in Virgo)　　Mercury moves into your sixth house of daily work and health. Communicate more than usual with employees and coworkers. You might be scheduling doctor or dentist appointments or joining a gym.

Sunday, December 2 (Moon in Virgo)　　The moon is in your third house of communications, siblings, and neighbors. Write in a journal; your communications are emotional and expressive. In contacts with relatives, you could be affected by matters from the past. Stay home and relate to family members and neighbors.

Monday, December 3 (Moon in Virgo to Libra 1:02 a.m.)   Be independent and creative; refuse to be discouraged by naysayers. You get a fresh start. Trust your hunches; stress originality. Don't follow others, take the lead, and emphasize individuality.

Tuesday, December 4 (Moon in Libra)   The moon is in your fourth house, the native home of Cancer. You feel best at home surrounded by familiar possessions and family members. Handle home repairs, if you have the time. Retreat to a private place for meditation.

Wednesday, December 5 (Moon in Libra to Scorpio 1:32 p.m.)   Venus is in your fifth house. In your love life, you'll find great emotional depth. If you have children, you'll feel protective of them and allow time for them. In your creative life, your efforts expand and flourish.

Thursday, December 6 (Moon in Scorpio)   Your organizational skills are highlighted. Persevere to get things done. You can overcome obstacles, including bureaucratic red tape. Take time to revise and rewrite; emphasize quality.

Friday, December 7 (Moon in Scorpio)   The moon is in your fifth house. Be yourself. If you have children, you tend to be protective and nurturing. Animals may play a large role in your day, possibly including a visit to the vet. It's a good creative time for you.

Saturday, December 8 (Moon in Scorpio to Sagittarius 2:12 a.m.)   It's about service to others. Be diplomatic, focus on making people happy, and do a good deed. A domestic adjustment works out for the best. Be understanding and avoid confrontations.

Sunday, December 9 (Moon in Sagittarius)   The moon is in your sixth house of daily work and health. You could feel emotionally repressed, although you may deny that. Help others, but don't become a martyr for someone else's cause. Take time to exercise. Watch your diet.

Monday, December 10 (Moon in Sagittarius to Capricorn 1:51 p.m.)   Play it your way. Follow your hunches in business matters. You're being watched by people in power. Be courageous. You have a chance to gain recognition, fame, and power!

Tuesday, December 11 (Moon in Capricorn)   The moon is in your seventh house of partnerships and marriage. You could be dealing with legal matters, possibly a contract. A marriage could be in the picture. Women play a prominent role. Any conflict, especially with a partner, could be emotional.

Wednesday, December 12 (Moon in Capricorn)   You're at the top of your cycle. You get a fresh start. Be independent and creative. Get out and meet new people; have new experiences. Pursue your ideas and refuse to deal with people who have closed minds.

Thursday, December 13 (Moon in Capricorn to Aquarius 12:02 a.m.)   The spotlight is on working together and getting along. A family member plays an important role. Be kind and understanding, as well as nurturing. Don't make waves or take on any major tasks.

Friday, December 14 (Moon in Aquarius)   Play your hunches. Look beyond the immediate. Your sense of prophecy is heightened. You work well with a group and help others find new ways of doing things. Dance to your own tune; follow your heart.

Saturday, December 15 (Moon in Aquarius to Pisces 8:15 a.m.)   You can overcome obstacles, including bureaucratic red tape. Take time to revise and rewrite. Emphasize

246

quality. Be methodical and thorough. You're building a new creative base.

Sunday, December 16 (Moon in Pisces)   The moon is in your ninth house. You feel somewhat restless, and you look for a change of scenery or a break from your routine. Foreign travel is highlighted. You could be planning a long trip, or you may have contact with a foreign-born person.

Monday, December 17 (Moon in Pisces to Aries 1:53 p.m.)   Domestic matters play an important role. You may need to make some adjustment in your home life. Emotional outbursts are likely. Be helpful, but don't allow anyone to make unfair demands on your time.

Tuesday, December 18 (Moon in Aries)   Jupiter moves into your seventh house. A partnership allows you to expand in new areas. This expansion will last for a full year. You could also develop new relationships. Contracts could be involved.

Wednesday, December 19 (Moon in Aries to Taurus 4:38 p.m.)   Saturn goes retrograde in your third house. You could face some delay in the healing of relationships with siblings or neighbors. You could face some travel restrictions. It's a good time for revising and rewriting and reorganizing your daily routine.

Thursday, December 20 (Moon in Taurus)   Mercury goes into your seventh house. Mercury, the planet of intellect and communication, joins Jupiter, the planet of expansion, in your house of partnerships. New ideas arise. You're more versatile and adaptable to changing circumstances, which places you in a strong position.

Friday, December 21 (Moon in Taurus to Gemini 5:14 p.m.)   You're at the top of your cycle. Stress originality. Express your ideas dynamically. Trust your hunches; intuition is highlighted. Your prestige is elevated. Make room for a new love, if that's what you want.

247

Saturday, December 22 (Moon in Gemini) The moon is in your twelfth house. You work behind the scenes. It's a great day for mystical experiences or a spiritual discipline. You communicate your deepest feelings to another person, who may act as your therapist.

Sunday, December 23 (Moon in Gemini to Cancer 5:19 p.m.) Your popularity is on the rise. Love and affection come your way. Your optimism, charm, and wit win the day. Remain flexible; listen to others. You feel vital and express yourself well.

Monday, December 24 (Moon in Cancer) The moon is in your first house. Get recharged for the holidays. The physical vitality you sensed yesterday continues. Relations with the opposite sex go well. Your feelings and thoughts are aligned.

Tuesday, December 25 (Moon in Cancer to Leo 6:53 p.m.) Merry Christmas! It's all about freedom of thought and action. It's a good day for a fresh perspective, a change of scenery. You let go of your routines and get a new point of view. Variety is the spice of life.

Wednesday, December 26 (Moon in Leo) The moon is in your second house. You feel best when you are home and surrounded by familiar objects. You identify emotionally with your possessions and your values.

Thursday, December 27 (Moon in Leo to Virgo 11:45 p.m.) There's a feeling of mystery in the air. Something is hidden, and you seek to find out what's going on behind closed doors. Gather information, but keep any secrets that are entrusted to you. Avoid self-deception. Maintain emotional balance.

Friday, December 28 (Moon in Virgo) The moon is in your third house. You get along well with neighbors and siblings. A holiday gathering brings people together. Memories of other holidays may influence your thoughts. You communicate your thoughts in writing to someone important and express your opinions.

Saturday, December 29 (Moon in Virgo) Attend to health matters, exercise, and watch your diet, especially if the holiday cheer has been excessive. Relax. Write your thoughts in a journal or letter. Stick close to home, where you're comfortable. Tend to details about the house.

Sunday, December 30 (Moon in Virgo to Libra 8:38 a.m.) Venus moves into your sixth house. That's good for romance at work, where things are going well. Women are helpful. Your health is good, but you're concerned about your appearance. You want to look better.

Monday, December 31 (Moon in Libra) The year ends with the moon in your fourth house, the native home of Cancer. You feel emotionally possessive. Spend time at home with your loved ones. A parent plays a role. Meditate in your special place. Then celebrate.

HAPPY NEW YEAR!

JANUARY 2008

Tuesday, January 1 (Moon in Libra to Scorpio 8:33 p.m.) The year begins with the moon shifting from Libra to Scorpio and entering your fifth house. Your creative adrenaline starts pumping overtime this evening. Dust off that manuscript, screenplay, or portfolio, and finish it off. With the holidays behind you, focus on what's ahead.

Wednesday, January 2 (Moon in Scorpio) Your creative roll continues. You're looking for the bottom line on a project, and you hit gold. Your kids may provide creative insights that prove helpful. Your love life seems to be heating up, and overall, life looks good.

Thursday, January 3 (Moon in Scorpio) With Mercury and Venus still in Capricorn, linking up with Jupiter in your seventh house, your partnerships are the focus. There's a lot of discussion about partnerships and a possible contract in the works. You may be negotiating before the day's end. You're in good shape for this one, Cancer.

Friday, January 4 (Moon in Scorpio to Sagittarius 9:14 a.m.)   The moon enters your sixth house. Things at work could feel a bit odd. You suddenly see the big picture concerning a work issue and may have to take steps to rectify the situation. Follow your intuition.

Saturday, January 5 (Moon in Sagittarius)   You can get away for the weekend and feel fine about doing it. Your desk at work has been cleared off, and you're itching to travel. Indulge yourself, Cancer. You and your partner need some time alone.

Sunday, January 6 (Moon in Sagittarius to Capricorn 8:43 p.m.)   The moon joins Jupiter, Mercury, and Venus in Capricorn in your seventh house. That's quite a lineup of planets; it puts special emphasis on relationships and partnerships. You might consider signing a contract. The outcome looks favorable.

Monday, January 7 (Moon in Capricorn)   Mercury enters Aquarius and your eighth house. During the next three weeks, you'll be involved in discussions concerning joint finances and resources. You should look at things like taxes and insurance and make sure that your bills in these areas are up-to-date.

Tuesday, January 8 (Moon in Capricorn)   You and your partner are in the mood to talk about where your relationship goes from here. Is a deep commitment on the horizon? Take an honest look at your emotions. The new moon augurs well for a new chapter in any partnership.

Wednesday, January 9 (Moon in Capricorn to Aquarius 6:13 a.m.)   As the moon enters Aquarius, you're conscious of the undercurrents that ripple through your life.

250

You ask profound questions. Don't expect immediate answers.

Thursday, January 10 (Moon in Aquarius) You may sign up for a workshop or seminar on an esoteric subject that intrigues you. You could look for ways to shave off what you're going to owe on taxes for 2007. Talk to your accountant.

Friday, January 11 (Moon in Aquarius to Pisces 1:44 p.m.) The moon enters Pisces, a sign compatible with your sun sign. This transit increases your intuition and deepens your subjective view of everything. Try not to get trapped in the usual Cancer dilemma: head versus heart. Make a decision and stick with it.

Saturday, January 12 (Moon in Pisces) You may spend the day with in-laws or visitors from out of town. It may not be what you want to do, but you feel obligated. Make the best of it.

Sunday, January 13 (Moon in Pisces to Aries 7:24 p.m.) Even though it's Sunday, touch base with your clients or a boss, through e-mail. There may be a problem or issue you need to resolve this week; it's best to get a jump on it!

Monday, January 14 (Moon in Aries) Set your agenda early. You'll be impatient with others, anxious to get things done, and you won't tolerate any differences of opinion. You may have to delegate tasks to those you trust.

Tuesday, January 15 (Moon in Aries to Taurus 11:13 p.m.) The Taurus moon is very much to your liking. All that earth energy grounds you, coaxes you to put your abstract ideas into practical terms that others can understand. Be careful that you don't overindulge in rich foods.

Wednesday, January 16 (Moon in Taurus) You and friends get together to brainstorm, celebrate, or just enjoy one another's company. You solidify plans that move you closer to attaining a wish or dream that you have.

Thursday, January 17 (Moon in Taurus)   Read a book that appeals to your humanity. When you're not reading, you'll look at your own home and family through much different eyes.

Friday, January 18 (Moon in Taurus to Gemini 1:30 a.m.)   The moon enters Gemini and your twelfth house; you may feel like spending time alone. Solitude is rarely a problem for you; relax with a book or watch a DVD.

Saturday, January 19 (Moon in Gemini)   You're on a quest for information. The Internet proves to be a valuable resource for your search, but so do your friends and network of acquaintances. Be alert for synchronicities. They'll guide you in the right direction.

Sunday, January 20 (Moon in Gemini to Cancer 3:06 a.m.) Recharge your energy for tomorrow when the moon enters your sign. Make room for the new by cleaning out your closets, your garage, your attic. The universe loves symbolic gestures.

Monday, January 21 (Moon in Cancer)   Stick close to home. Memories may surface concerning your childhood, and you'll feel nostalgic. Your mother or another nurturing female in your life has advice or insights for you.

Tuesday, January 22 (Moon in Cancer to Leo 5:22 a.m.)   If you're in contract negotiations, try to wrap things up before January 28, when Mercury turns retrograde in your eighth house. Your focus is on money and resources you share with others, as well as your own earning and spending habits.

Wednesday, January 23 (Moon in Leo)   Balance your checkbook and take stock of your finances. If you don't like what you see, come up with a plan for cutting back on certain expenses and putting more of your income into savings.

Thursday, January 24 (Moon in Leo to Virgo 9:49 a.m.) Venus enters Capricorn and your seventh house. The period between now and February 17 marks a romantic time for you. If you're not involved with anyone, you may be before this transit is finished. With Venus here, any contracts you sign before January 28 should be favorable for you.

Friday, January 25 (Moon in Virgo) Pluto enters Capricorn and your seventh house. The combination of Pluto, Venus, and Jupiter in the same sign is sure to ignite your partnerships. Jupiter seeks to expand existing relationships and to attract new partnership opportunities. Pluto transforms and Venus is about romance.

Saturday, January 26 (Moon in Virgo to Libra 5:36 p.m.) Late this afternoon, the moon enters Libra and your fourth house. You feel the need to beautify your home and personal surroundings. A fresh coat of paint in your home office, the rearrangement of furniture, or the addition of fresh flowers or art might do the trick.

Sunday, January 27 (Moon in Libra) Your home really is your castle. You putter away at beautifying your surroundings, perhaps in anticipation of the arrival of friends or family this evening. One of your parents figures into events. A Gemini or Aquarius proves helpful.

Monday, January 28 (Moon in Libra) The first Mercury retrograde of 2008 begins in Aquarius, your eighth house. Until February 18, it's best not to sign contracts or to apply for any kind of loan. Be sure that your tax and insurance payments are in order. If you have to travel, expect sudden changes in your schedule.

Tuesday, January 29 (Moon in Libra to Scorpio 4:35 a.m.) As the moon enters Scorpio, your love life revs up. You're feeling particularly emotional and perhaps even

253

somewhat vulnerable. Listen to your intuition regarding matters of the heart, and you won't go wrong.

Wednesday, January 30 (Moon in Scorpio)   Mars turns direct, releasing pent-up energy that allows you to move forward in your therapy, dream analysis, or meditative practice. In early March, it moves into your sign, which is sure to increase your physical and sexual energy.

Thursday, January 31 (Moon in Scorpio to Sagittarius 5:08 p.m.)   With the moon entering Sagittarius and your sixth house, you're on fire. You grasp the big picture concerning a work or health issue and may have to make certain decisions in these areas.

FEBRUARY 2008

Friday, February 1 (Moon in Sagittarius)   You head for the gym, a yoga class, or even an aerobic class. Body consciousness is the order of the day. You may want to scrutinize your diet and cut back on carbs, red meat, and desserts. A vitamin regimen may be in order.

Saturday, February 2 (Moon in Sagittarius)   Despite the fact that it's Saturday, you're working at home, catching up on whatever went uncompleted from last month. It's just as well. Today you have more information and greater insight concerning the projects.

Sunday, February 3 (Moon in Sagittarius to Capricorn 4:52 a.m.)   The moon enters your seventh house of partnerships. With Mercury still retrograde, there's room for misunderstandings with a partner or even a close friend. Take time to explain what you mean or feel. The other person will appreciate it, and the risk for miscommunication won't be as great.

Monday, February 4 (Moon in Capricorn)   The moon joins Jupiter and Venus in your seventh house. This combination of planets may exaggerate feelings of vulnerability in relationships. Or it may broaden romantic notions that you have. Either way, the day could feel a bit strange.

Tuesday, February 5 (Moon in Capricorn to Aquarius 2:10 p.m.)   Insurance or estate matters occupy you. It may be that someone in your family or even a friend needs help or advice, or you're the one who needs the advice or expertise. Either way, this is the area of the day's focus.

Wednesday, February 6 (Moon in Aquarius)   Yesterday's focus snaps into clarity, with a solar eclipse in Aquarius and your eighth house. Solar eclipses can signal new beginnings; you may find that new people enter your life and that you have new experiences related to metaphysics. A past-life memory could survive.

Thursday, February 7 (Moon in Aquarius to Pisces 8:47 p.m.)   This moon is a gentle one for you, a fellow water sign that may spur a yearning for travels to a distant place. Maybe the grass looks greener elsewhere. Before you buy into that notion, solve your problems at home.

Friday, February 8 (Moon in Pisces)   Take a virtual trip. It'll whet your hunger for foreign travel and enable you to pick several places that you would like to see, which are within your budget.

Saturday, February 9 (Moon in Pisces)   Visitors are in town; you meet them someplace this evening. These individuals may be from another country or have spiritual beliefs that intrigue you. Listen and learn, Cancer. Your intuition gets it.

Sunday, February 10 (Moon in Pisces to Aries 1:18 a.m.)   It's a career day, and things could be challenging. It's not anything you've done—more a matter of circumstances than anything else. Roll with the punches.

Monday, February 11 (Moon in Aries)   With your focus on career matters, you don't have the time or energy for issues that may come up at home. You don't have to be a

255

super person, you know. Just do what you can. Scorpio proves helpful in accepting delegated tasks.

Tuesday, February 12 (Moon in Aries to Taurus 4:35 a.m.)   You enjoy the Taurus moon, all that friendly earth energy grounding your hunches and intuitive feelings. You spend time with friends or a group of people whose passions support your own.

Wednesday, February 13 (Moon in Taurus)   Your theater or writing group throws a party or pioneers some sort of social activity that engages everyone involved. You feel grounded and practical; those feelings are reflected in everything you undertake.

Thursday, February 14 (Moon in Taurus to Gemini 7:20 a.m.)   Happy Valentine's Day! It's a perfect day to spend time alone with your partner. Plan something special that involves only the two of you. Have a notebook handy when you go to bed. It's an excellent time for dream recall and finding information or insight you need from your dreams.

Friday, February 15 (Moon in Gemini)   If you're feeling a money crunch, it's all in your head. Strive to be as organized and responsible as possible in regard to money. Stay away from bookstores!

Saturday, February 16 (Moon in Gemini to Cancer 10:30 a.m.)   With the moon in your sign, all the inner angst vanishes; you're on top of the world. Not too much can dent your self-confidence and resolve. If a sibling has gotten in touch with you recently, it may portend an issue that surfaces on February 20.

Sunday, February 17 (Moon in Cancer)   With the moon in your sign, Venus entering Aquarius and your seventh house, and Mercury about to turn direct, you're in an excellent position to apply for a mortgage or loan. Just don't sign the contract until after February 18. If you aren't involved in a relationship, there's a strong possibility that you meet someone at a workshop or seminar.

Monday, February 18 (Moon in Cancer to Leo 1:52 p.m.)   Mercury turns direct. Pack your bags, buy your plane ticket, and get out of town! Sign contracts; apply for loans. You get the idea here. Travel and communication are all in forward motion.

Tuesday, February 19 (Moon in Leo)   Checks you've been expecting start to arrive. Stash some money away because your holidays bills are beginning to show up in your mailbox. Even if you've got money in your account to cover them, you'll feel more secure if you've got additional funds to draw on.

Wednesday, February 20 (Moon in Leo to Virgo 7:07 p.m.)   Today's lunar eclipse in Virgo and your third house bring up an emotional issue related to siblings, neighbors, or travel plans. Another possibility is that your conscious mind is inundated with so many emotions it's difficult to think clearly.

Thursday, February 21 (Moon in Virgo)   Your attention to details pays off. By the end of the day, you spot an error or flaw that was overlooked earlier. You and a neighbor may get involved in a project of some kind: beautification, crime watch, whatever you feel the community needs.

Friday, February 22 (Moon in Virgo)   The Virgo moon's earth energy fits nicely with your water-sign sun. It helps to ground your intuition and emotions. Your reactions to situations are based in reality rather than in the realm of your imagination.

Saturday, February 23 (Moon in Virgo to Libra 2:45 a.m.)   The moon enters Libra and your fourth house. This moon forms a challenging angle to your sun, but still manages to light up your love life at home this evening. And who knows? With Mercury moving direct, your conversation could be profound and illuminating.

Sunday, February 24 (Moon in Libra)   You get into one of those moods in which you simply have to do something with your home. Fresh paint and brighter colors, a new piece of furniture, rearranging furniture, cleaning up your home office—all are possibilities. You may prepare for tomorrow's romantic interlude with your new love interest.

Monday, February 25 (Moon in Libra to Scorpio 1:06 a.m.)   The moon enters your fifth house. Think romance, creativity, and whatever you do for pleasure. The Scorpio moon always adds more intensity to your sun sign; it brings a deeper intuitive awareness as well.

Tuesday, February 26 (Moon in Scorpio)   It's important to keep your options open. Someone steps forward with an offer that will be difficult to refuse. Another water-sign individual may be involved. Stay alert and be prepared to act.

Wednesday, February 27 (Moon in Scorpio)   Your life is pretty interesting. Uranus in Pisces brings surprises related to education and publishing. The moon in Scorpio is deepening your passions. Pluto linked up with Jupiter in Capricorn is transforming your personal and business partnerships. Are you able to keep up with it all, Cancer?

Thursday, February 28 (Moon in Scorpio to Sagittarius 1:23 a.m.)   As you head into the end of the week, you suddenly realize what needs to be done. It's the big picture you've been looking for. Your coworkers may not all agree with you, but once you make your passionate pitch, you find all the supporters you need.

Friday, February 29 (Moon in Sagittarius)   Clear off your desk before you leave work, and you'll have a great weekend. Otherwise, you'll obsess about things all weekend. In fact, you may want to get out of town with your partner or kids.

MARCH 2008

Saturday, March 1 (Moon in Sagittarius to Capricorn 1:33 p.m.)   Romance and contracts. Those are your concerns. And with Venus linked up with Uranus in Pisces in your ninth house, you can expect the unexpected. In fact, be prepared for a nice surprise!

Sunday, March 2 (Moon in Capricorn)   With every planet except Saturn moving direct, the timing is excellent for long-range planning, in any area that suits you. Set your priorities. Keep your goals realistic, and don't stress out over goals you don't reach.

Monday, March 3 (Moon in Capricorn to Aquarius 11:25 p.m.)   Find a good book for an Aquarius moon day. Dive in, and when you surface, you'll have plenty of questions that are typical for the moon transiting your eighth house.

Tuesday, March 4 (Moon in Aquarius)   Mars enters your sign. This event happens only once every two years and lasts about nine weeks. During this period, your energy will be nothing short of remarkable, and you'll have the drive and ambition to move ahead personally and professionally. Your sexuality will deepen; your intuition will be on target.

Wednesday, March 5 (Moon in Aquarius)   Friends and group activities are the focus. You meet with your team to discuss strategies and goals. Don't hesitate to present your visionary ideas. They'll be well received; you'll get some excellent feedback that may improve your ideas.

Thursday, March 6 (Moon in Aquarius to Pisces 5:54 a.m.)   You can taste spring in the air; it stimulates your imagination, intuition, and the dreamy side of your personality. Take time to nurture your dreams.

Friday, March 7 (Moon in Pisces)   Belief is where it all starts, Cancer. You grasp this intuitive truth and begin a

259

journey through your own beliefs. Which beliefs about yourself or the world hold you back? Which beliefs have helped you move forward?

Saturday, March 8 (Moon in Pisces to Aries 9:24 a.m.)   The Aries moon isn't your favorite, unless you have fire-sign planets in your birth chart. But it does stimulate career and professional matters. Even though it's Saturday, you hear from a boss or peers and learn that one of the higher-ups is going to recognize you for your ability. You've earned the praise!

Sunday, March 9—Daylight Saving Time Begins (Moon in Aries)   During an interaction with your parents or someone else in authority, there could be some tension over a misunderstanding. Clear and honest communication clears the air.

Monday, March 10 (Moon in Aries to Taurus 12:15 p.m.)   The Taurus moon is to your liking. Not only does it trigger social activities with friends, but it helps ground your intuitive energy and makes you stubborn when you should be!

Tuesday, March 11 (Moon in Taurus)   Tomorrow, Venus enters Pisces and your ninth house. You may feel the effects already, particularly if you travel overseas. Romance with a foreign-born individual is possible. It's equally possible that publishing news comes your way.

Wednesday, March 12 (Moon in Taurus to Gemini 1:55 p.m.)   Venus enters Pisces. This planet rules romance as well as the arts and money. It's possible that in the next three weeks, your business expands overseas or your product is sold overseas. Whatever the case, you receive money from foreign sales.

Thursday, March 13 (Moon in Gemini)   The Gemini moon is gregarious and intellectual. You display these character traits, and you aren't sure whether you want to spend time alone or get together with friends. Either way, you enjoy yourself.

Friday, March 14 (Moon in Gemini to Cancer, 4:38 p.m.)   Mercury joins Venus in Pisces, your ninth house. The combination certainly indicates lots of communication with a lover, spouse, or partner. In fact, until April 2, your conscious mind is fully engrossed with romance.

Saturday, March 15 (Moon in Cancer)   It's a power day. You're in a great position to succeed at whatever you do, even if it's just relaxing. It would behoove you to have something definite on your slate so that you can use this terrific energy in a focused way.

Sunday, March 16 (Moon in Cancer to Leo 9:04 p.m.)   With both Venus and Mercury in fellow water sign Pisces, your intuition is remarkable. Your publishing and educational opportunities are particularly strong for the next several weeks. Take advantage of this window of opportunity. Timing, as they say, is everything.

Monday, March 17 (Moon in Leo)   The moon would love some company in your second house. But Saturn left late last year. So the moon is alone, stoking the fires of your intuition. You know, intuitively, that your finances are fine. But the moon here creates security issues regarding your finances.

Tuesday, March 18 (Moon in Leo)   Reread yesterday's entry and realize that there is plenty of prosperity to go around.

Wednesday, March 19 (Moon in Leo to Virgo 3:25 a.m.)   The Virgo moon feels good when it urges you to pay attention to details—whether in a contract, in communication, or simply in the privacy of your own life. It's time to finish that novel you stashed away.

Thursday, March 20 (Moon in Virgo)   You may volunteer for a community organization that promotes a worthy

261

cause. Before you commit, be sure you have the time and interest. You may sign up for a day at a spa that promotes alternative therapies and treatments.

Friday, March 21 (Moon in Virgo to Libra 11:45 a.m.) Home is where you want to be. A family member may need extra support and help.

Saturday, March 22 (Moon in Libra) You get the feeling that it's time to spruce up your house. You're a whirlwind. Whether you're repainting, rearranging, or completely renovating a room, you're in your element, Cancer.

Sunday, March 23 (Moon in Libra to Scorpio 10:07 p.m.) When the moon enters your fifth house, your focus is on love, pleasure, creativity, and your kids. Specifically, you're after the deepest level of truth you can find about a relationship. It may take some research and investigation, but you find your answers over the next two days.

Monday, March 24 (Moon in Scorpio) With Mercury, Venus, Mars, the moon, and Uranus in water signs, your intuition is exceptionally strong, and your emotions are running fast and furiously. You have a hunch about an investment or piece of property. Do your homework, gather the facts, and then make your decision.

Tuesday, March 25 (Moon in Scorpio) Your passions run high. For better or worse, be careful on whom you turn those passions. You're in a powerful spot; the force of your words could hurt someone else.

Wednesday, March 26 (Moon in Scorpio to Sagittarius 10:12 a.m.) With so many planets still in water signs, the fire-sign moon sticks out like the proverbial sore thumb. Your bluntness with an employee or coworker could offend the person, so try to think before you speak. On the other hand, if the situation calls for bluntness to snag the person's attention, don't hold back!

Thursday, March 27 (Moon in Sagittarius)   Armed with a broad vision of where things stand at work and with your health, you make informed decisions. One such decision may be whether you go the conventional route or seek nontraditional venues.

Friday, March 28 (Moon in Sagittarius to Capricorn 10:44 p.m.)   You may want to take the day off and get out to do something physical for yourself. A brisk walk may stimulate your creative adrenaline, so why not start with that?

Saturday, March 29 (Moon in Capricorn)   You're in a goal-oriented mood. Whether you turn your focus to your daily work, profession, health, relationships, or some other aspect of your life, create realistic goals. Watch your nutrition.

Sunday, March 30 (Moon in Capricorn)   Whether you're dieting or just watching your nutritional intake, it behooves you to research vitamins and herbs. On the Internet, you'll discover helpful information on every kind of supplement you might need.

Monday, March 31 (Moon in Capricorn to Aquarius 9:35 a.m.)   Share your knowledge and insights with others. You'll have plenty of opportunities to do that. In fact, you may be overwhelmed with requests!

APRIL 2008

Tuesday, April 1 (Moon in Aquarius)   With spring really in the air, your world is humming with possibilities. You help someone with taxes or insurance matters and then feel the need to work on your own taxes and insurance matters. If you don't already have a living will, make sure that you have one drawn up.

Wednesday, April 2 (Moon in Aquarius to Pisces 4:56 a.m.)   Mercury enters Taurus and your eleventh house. This transit is very compatible with your sun sign and should bring about stimulating conversations with friends and a joint writing or communication project of some sort.

Thursday, April 3 (Moon in Pisces) With the moon in compatible Pisces, in your ninth house, you may be considering a return to college or graduate school. You could also be planning a trip overseas.

Friday, April 4 (Moon in Pisces to Aries 8:28 p.m.) It's not your favorite lunar transit, with all this fire, impatience, and restlessness. But it stimulates your career in some way. You may spend social time this evening with bosses and peers. Don't pitch any agendas!

Saturday, April 5 (Moon in Aries) How far can you take your agenda? Since it's Saturday, probably not very far, unless you're willing to surrender your Saturday to work. Better to put this energy into touching base with the authority figures in your life! The new moon in Aries portends a new chapter in your professional life.

Sunday, April 6 (Moon in Aries to Taurus 9:20 p.m.) Venus enters Aries. Until April 30, professional concerns move smoothly. Things may seem so smooth, in fact, that you're tempted to just slide through the weeks, doing as little as possible to get by. Resist that urge.

Monday, April 7 (Moon in Taurus) There are times to be stubborn and times to be flexible. Today it's the former. A friend or acquaintance pushes your buttons, and you dig in your heels and refuse to budge from your position. By Wednesday, that feeling passes.

Tuesday, April 8 (Moon in Taurus to Gemini 9:27 p.m.) Hunker down and enjoy your solitude, Cancer. You actually don't mind being alone. In fact, there are many times when you prefer your own company to that of other people. While you're alone, use your time wisely.

Wednesday, April 9 (Moon in Gemini) You reorganize your work area. Then you go home and do the same thing to your house. Regardless of what you're attempting to enhance—your prosperity, romance, happiness—you'll succeed if you follow the feng shui rules of placement and color.

Thursday, April 10 (Moon in Gemini to Cancer 10:43 p.m.)   Even though the moon doesn't enter your sign until late this evening, you feel the shift in energy long before it arrives. Tonight, prioritize what you would like to accomplish tomorrow so that you can use this terrific energy to have a carefree weekend.

Friday, April 11 (Moon in Cancer)   Regardless of what else you do this weekend, be sure that your tax return is ready to mail, if you haven't already done so. If you owe taxes, be sure to send the return with feelings of gratitude that you make enough money to pay the taxes!

Saturday, April 12 (Moon in Cancer)   You haunt old shops in search of an antique—a piece of furniture, a book, or maybe an article of clothing. It's your nostalgic frame of mind that is urging you to this kind of exploration. Your mother may join you on this journey.

Sunday, April 13 (Moon in Cancer to Leo 2:29 a.m.) With Mercury and Venus both in fire sign Aries and the moon entering fire sign Leo, you've got plenty of energy and drive to tackle professional and financial issues. You may need a partner to do some of the groundwork, so don't be hesitant about delegating.

Monday, April 14 (Moon in Leo)   In some way, your personal beliefs and values are called into play. You may have to defend what you believe through your actions. Or events could unfold that prompt you to take action regarding a future plan you have for retirement or investments.

Tuesday, April 15 (Moon in Leo to Virgo 9:07 a.m.)   Tax day. Get to the post office early. Then work on that novel or screenplay that has consumed your time recently. It's your secret world, Cancer—the place where you call the shots.

Wednesday, April 16 (Moon in Virgo)   A communication project takes over your life. It could be something as mundane as updating your e-mail list of contacts or as exciting as diving back into the novel you're writing. Pay attention to the details. With Saturn still retrograding in Virgo, it's easy to miss the finer points.

Thursday, April 17 (Moon in Virgo to Libra 6:11 p.m.)   Home really is where your heart lies; you don't want to leave it. Perhaps your love life has heated up to the point where to leave would be to break the spell. Or maybe it's just that someone at home needs your support. Mercury enters Taurus, a sign that could bring about a flirtation with someone you already know as a friend.

Friday, April 18 (Moon in Libra)   In two days, the full moon in Scorpio may bring about an intense romantic encounter. Think about that potential. Are you ready for a relationship to which you must commit completely?

Saturday, April 19 (Moon in Libra)   Music and art soothe your soul. Well, they probably soothe your soul every day, but today the bar for audio and visual beauty is raised. There could be a little tension between your obligations and responsibilities at home and those in your career.

Sunday, April 20 (Moon in Libra to Scorpio 5:02 a.m.)   The full moon in Scorpio brings about some sort of passionate romantic encounter. Your partner doesn't have to be your soul mate (although that's a possibility). The point is self-revelation and discovery.

Monday, April 21 (Moon in Scorpio)   Your muse is at your beck and call. Focus on the creative project that's most important to you. You may want to prioritize the demands of this project. Ultimately, that will make it easier to navigate the ins and outs.

Tuesday, April 22 (Moon in Scorpio to Sagittarius 5:08 p.m.) How far can you take an idea? How much support can you garner among your coworkers? The answers to both questions are positive and intrinsic to the day's activities. Mercury in Taurus gives you the verbal skills to get your point across and helps to gather support.

Wednesday, April 23 (Moon in Sagittarius) You've got a handle on the big picture of a work-related issue. You still have to tie up loose ends to resolve the issue, but you're on your way, Cancer. As it says in the *I Ching,* "Perseverance furthers."

Thursday, April 24 (Moon in Sagittarius) With Mars still transiting your sign, and both Mercury and Jupiter in compatible earth signs, you're able to expand on an idea or project to broaden its mass appeal. Your concept is well received by coworkers and bosses.

Friday, April 25 (Moon in Sagittarius to Capricorn 5:48 p.m.) The moon enters Capricorn and your seventh house. Even though the earth energy of this sign is compatible with the water element of your sun sign, the moon is opposed to your sun. That can create tension, particularly with Mars still in your sign. Breathe, Cancer. Anything can be overcome through patience and intent.

Saturday, April 26 (Moon in Capricorn) You and your partner build on your relationship's solid foundation to deepen your commitment to each other. Whether you move in together or actually tie the knot, the course is appropriate for both of you. You get advice from an earth-sign friend.

Sunday, April 27 (Moon in Capricorn to Aquarius 5:28 p.m.) A romance may be brewing with someone you have met through friends or through a group to which you belong. You'll have a keener sense of the particulars after Venus enters Taurus on April 30. Keep your eyes open.

Monday, April 28 (Moon in Aquarius) Early next month, Jupiter turns retrograde in Capricorn, your seventh house. While a retrograde for this planet isn't as disruptive as a Mercury retrograde, it does mean the planet goes into a dormant state. So iron out your partnership challenges.

Tuesday, April 29 (Moon in Aquarius) You're looking for tax breaks already this year. Consult with your attorney to find out what you can write off. If nothing else, it will bring you peace of mind.

Wednesday, April 30 (Moon in Aquarius to Pisces 2:11 a.m.) Venus enters Taurus. Over the next three weeks, your love life should heat up. Any relationship that begins under this transit should be pleasant, sensual, and perhaps more intense than you anticipate. If you're involved already, you're in for a romantic and pleasant three weeks!

MAY 2008

Thursday, May 1 (Moon in Pisces) The moon joins Uranus in Pisces, in your ninth house. It happens every month, so you should be accustomed to some of the manifestations that occur when these two planets pair up. Your emotional reactions are unusual, idiosyncratic, unexpected. Take nothing for granted.

Friday, May 2 (Moon in Pisces to Aries 6:51 a.m.) Mercury enters Gemini and your twelfth house, and Saturn turns direct in Virgo. These transits stimulate different areas of your chart but combine in such a way that your communications skills are triggered in a positive way. You'll have time to work in private for long, uninterrupted stretches.

Saturday, May 3 (Moon in Aries) With Mars in your sign and the moon in Aries, you've got plenty of energy to plow through whatever needs to get done quickly. It's related to your career or a professional issue; even though it's Saturday, you tackle whatever it is.

Sunday, May 4 (Moon in Aries to Taurus 7:58 a.m.) The moon joins Venus in Taurus, lighting up your love life, possibly with a friend or someone you meet through friends. Your social schedule suddenly picks up steam. You'll have your choice of parties and festivities to attend.

Monday, May 5 (Moon in Taurus) The Taurus moon is like an old friend. You feel a certain element of physical and emotional comfort; it's reflected most of all in your dealings with friends. There's a certain sensuality that accompanies this moon. And since it's a new moon, it opens up fresh opportunities for the realization of wishes and dreams.

Tuesday, May 6 (Moon in Taurus to Gemini 7:18 a.m.) Pay close attention to your dreams. Insights and information will come to you concerning an issue or an area of particular concern. You may want to consider a dream project in which you compile a list of personal symbols and metaphors. Your own dream dictionary, Cancer.

Wednesday, May 7 (Moon in Gemini) Conversation and discussion with a close friend or family member highlight the day. Forgiveness and healing are involved in these discussions, which means you should take the time to say what you feel. Past issues are cleared up.

Thursday, May 8 (Moon in Gemini to Cancer 7:03 a.m.) The moon joins Mars in your sign. This powerful combination may attract a sexual relationship that sweeps through your life with the force of a tsunami. You may have to back off a little for breathing space, Cancer. Enjoy this while it lasts.

Friday, May 9 (Moon in Cancer) Jupiter turns retrograde in Capricorn, your seventh house. This indicates that you look within to scrutinize a current partnership. Also, Mars enters Leo, your second house. For the next seven weeks, your energy is focused on earning money. There could be unexpected royalty checks or perhaps repayment of a loan.

Saturday, May 10 (Moon in Cancer to Leo 9:11 a.m.) Money, money, money. You may receive a check in the mail or the repayment of a loan, or the bank makes an error in your favor. You may spend some time balancing your accounts, making sure that your figures are correct.

Sunday, May 11 (Moon in Leo) With the moon still in bold, dramatic Leo, you may decide your wardrobe is too drab and old-fashioned to suit the new you. Shop with a friend who has great fashion sense. Decide ahead of time how much you can afford, and have the cash to pay for what you buy.

Monday, May 12 (Moon in Leo to Virgo 2:49 p.m.) Any of the earth-sign moons are comfortable for you. Today's moon highlights your relationship with a neighbor or sibling. You do something unexpected for one of these individuals, and they are immensely grateful.

Tuesday, May 13 (Moon in Virgo) Details, details. Read all the fine print. Be attentive, but not obsessive. A Capricorn or a Taurus is helpful or has insights concerning a relationship with a sibling or neighbor.

Wednesday, May 14 (Moon in Virgo to Libra 11:48 p.m.) With Mars in a fire sign, Mercury and the moon in air signs, and Venus in an earth sign, you could feel somewhat puzzled. Once you understand the problem, the solution seems to come to you out of the blue. Trust your hunches.

Thursday, May 15 (Moon in Libra) You could be looking for a piece of art that will enhance your home. Or perhaps new blinds or curtains or even flooring are in order. One way or another, you're going to beautify your personal surroundings.

Friday, May 16 (Moon in Libra)   You engage in a delicate balancing act. Like a tightrope walker, you strive to stay on the straight and narrow, but external events force you to do otherwise. There are no accidents, Cancer. Today's distractions could become tomorrow's missions.

Saturday, May 17 (Moon in Libra to Scorpio 11:00 a.m.)   Your passions and emotions run deep. Be careful that you don't drown in them. Pour some of this passion into a creative project or into doing something special with your kids.

Sunday, May 18 (Moon in Scorpio)   Your new romantic interest is a surprising mix of qualities. You connect with this person on such an intuitive level that at times, you don't have to talk to be understood. A single glance or touch is all that it takes.

Monday, May 19 (Moon in Scorpio to Sagittarius 11:20 p.m.)   The full moon brings your passions and sensuality right to the forefront of your life and consciousness. You and your partner share a romantic evening that takes your relationship to a whole new level.

Tuesday, May 20 (Moon in Sagittarius)   Your perspective is so broad that you're able to see where you're going and how you'll get there. The trick is to remember it all. Write it down. Record it. Do whatever you have to do to preserve the insight.

Wednesday, May 21 (Moon in Sagittarius)   In just five days, Mercury turns retrograde for the second time this year. Finish up projects, make phone calls about travel plans and checks that are owed you, and negotiate and sign contracts. In other words, clear your desk so that when Mercury turns retrograde, you aren't left holding the bag.

Thursday, May 22 (Moon in Sagittarius to Capricorn 11:56 a.m.)   The moon is in the seventh house, and that lights up your love life and your partnerships. Jupiter is opposed to Mars, which can cause you to take risks you

271

might not take otherwise. Your energetic approach to everything you undertake is a recipe for success. Don't speed. There's a traffic cop on every corner!

Friday, May 23 (Moon in Capricorn)   It's another high-energy day. Be aware that you may bite off more than you can handle effectively. If you strive to take a more measured approach to everything, you'll feel better at the end of the day!

Saturday, May 24 (Moon in Capricorn to Aquarius 11:52 p.m.)   Venus enters Gemini and your twelfth house. Until June 18, a secret romance is possible. You're good at keeping secrets, but that will be more difficult to do after Venus enters your sign on June 18.

Sunday, May 25 (Moon in Aquarius)   With the moon, Venus, Mercury, and Neptune all in air signs, your brain literally hums with ideas. You engage in discussions with anyone who has something substantial to say; you are capable of winning others to your way of thinking.

Monday, May 26 (Moon in Aquarius)   Mercury turns retrograde in Gemini and Neptune turns retrograde in Aquarius. Of the two, the Mercury retrograde will have the most immediate impact. If you're involved in a secret romance, for instance, there could be misunderstandings, or the news gets out despite your best efforts to keep it secret.

Tuesday, May 27 (Moon in Aquarius to Pisces 9:39 a.m.)   With the moon entering fellow water sign Pisces and joining Uranus in your ninth house, you're in rare form. Your mood is buoyant and optimistic; your magnetism attracts unusual, idiosyncratic people. You may have the itch to travel; try to hold off on making firm plans until after Mercury turns direct on June 19.

Wednesday, May 28 (Moon in Pisces)   You and friends get together for an evening of great debate and philosophical discussion. It's the kind of thing you love to do when you're with people whose company you enjoy. The topic? World affairs, politics, or spirituality.

Thursday, May 29 (Moon in Pisces to Aries 3:53 p.m.) As you head toward the beginning of summer, there are professional issues that have to be dealt with before you can take time off. Figure out what they are, and be firm about meeting a deadline for completing them.

Friday, May 30 (Moon in Aries) You're a tad impatient with yourself and the people around you. Take a couple deep breaths. You don't have to go on the warpath to get things done. Cool efficiency and organization will take you farther.

Saturday, May 31 (Moon in Aries to Taurus 6:19 p.m.) Remember this moon? The one that fits like a comfortable shoe? Treat yourself to the company of like-minded individuals today. You'll get fresh insights and ideas from the time spent with friends.

JUNE 2008

Sunday, June 1 (Moon in Taurus) What fun for you, Cancer, with the moon in a compatible sign. It's another day with friends or with people who share your passions and interests. You may have to be stubborn about an issue or situation, and the Taurus moon makes it easier for you to do.

Monday, June 2 (Moon in Taurus to Gemini 6:07 p.m.) Mercury is still retrograde, but just the same, you're working on a writing project that may involve other people. Don't submit the final draft until after Mercury turns direct on June 19.

Tuesday, June 3 (Moon in Gemini) You and a sibling or neighbor have a misunderstanding. A bit of patience and a sincere attempt to clear things up is what's called for in this situation. Get busy, Cancer. Never burn your bridges!

Wednesday, June 4 (Moon in Gemini to Cancer 5:17 p.m.) The moon is in your sign. Whenever this happens, you suddenly have more physical and emotional energy at your disposal. It's as if the universe has handed you a gift that you can use in whatever way you choose.

Thursday, June 5 (Moon in Cancer) Your intuition is remarkable. You get hunches about people, situations, and places. If you follow this guidance, the end results boggle your mind. How can your intuition be so on target? Easy. You're a Cancer. The intuitive path is one you are meant to follow.

Friday, June 6 (Moon in Cancer to Leo 6:01 p.m.) This moon sign stimulates the money sector of your chart, and that can't be all bad, right? You tend to be concerned about financial security when the moon is in Leo; examine your beliefs and attitudes concerning how you earn and spend.

Saturday, June 7 (Moon in Leo) You may feel bold and flashy. It's a rarity for you, but events call for it. You need to stand up for what you think is right and true; once you've done that, you've pretty much met your obligations.

Sunday, June 8 (Moon in Leo to Virgo 10:02 p.m.) If you know a Gemini whose birthday is today, create a major celebration for this individual. And while you're at it, maybe some sort of block party is due. There's no better time than summer to get to know your neighbors.

Monday, June 9 (Moon in Virgo) If you've been feeling that you're undisciplined or irresponsible in some area of your life, take stock of your life. It's not karma, just that Virgo moon demanding that you do your share and pull your load.

Tuesday, June 10 (Moon in Virgo) Read the fine print and negotiate to your heart's content, but do not sign on the dotted line. Mercury doesn't turn direct until June 19. On June 18, Venus moves into your sign, marking one of the most romantic periods of the year. Be prepared. Do whatever you have to do to get ready emotionally, spiritually, and physically.

Wednesday, June 11 (Moon in Virgo to Libra 5:56 a.m.)
With the moon entering Libra and your fourth house, your concerns focus on balance and fairness related to your family. One of your parents may play into this picture as well. This moon is placated through beauty of all kinds—consider music, art, or a wonderful novel.

Thursday, June 12 (Moon in Libra)   You may decide to renovate something at home. This means repainting a room (or several rooms), rearranging furniture (or buying new furniture), or even hiring a contractor to add a room onto your house. However this plays out, remember that Mercury is still retrograde, so don't sign any contracts until after June 19.

Friday, June 13 (Moon in Libra to Scorpio 4:54 p.m.)   With Venus still in Gemini and the moon entering your fifth house of romance, any relationship that begins will center on mental camaraderie first. Without strong communication, you won't be interested. Listen to your intuition concerning a new romantic interest.

Saturday, June 14 (Moon in Scorpio)   With such intense emotions running wild, you feel as if you're in a rushing tide that's pushing you forward. Other people might chafe at such focused feelings. But you actually revel in the sensations and situations the day brings. But then, you're unusual in that you're extremely comfortable with your emotions and intuition.

Sunday, June 15 (Moon in Scorpio)   You may deal with insurance matters. Whether it's paying your insurance bills or rectifying a statement, don't let the fine details escape you. You're gearing up for Venus entering your sign, one of the more romantic periods all year.

Monday, June 16 (Moon in Scorpio to Sagittarius 5:20 a.m.)   As the moon enters Sagittarius and your sixth house, there could be some tension or disagreements with coworkers or employees. Delay making any decision concerning the issues involved until after Mercury turns direct on June 19.

Tuesday, June 17 (Moon in Sagittarius)   You grasp the bigger picture in your work life. If you don't like what you see, decide how you might change it. Do you need more education, different skills, or a different career path altogether?

Wednesday, June 18 (Moon in Sagittarius to Capricorn 5:52 p.m.)   Venus enters your sign. Until July 12, your love life should soar. Even if you're not involved with anyone, you probably will be before this transit ends. This transit also stimulates your creativity. So get busy doing what you love, Cancer.

Thursday, June 19 (Moon in Capricorn)   Breathe. Mercury turns direct! Pack your bags, sign your contracts, make your travel plans, and send out e-mails. You're free to do all the things you've delayed doing for the last several weeks.

Friday, June 20 (Moon in Capricorn)   You're exceptionally good at planning and strategizing. The strategies may involve contracts and professional partnerships. It could also involve a romantic relationship, but this is less likely unless you're getting married or signing a prenuptial contract.

Saturday, June 21 (Moon in Capricorn to Aquarius 5:34 a.m.)   The moon joins Neptune in Aquarius. This happens once a month, and while some patterns remain consistent, others don't. This combination might prompt you to idealize a partner, a friend, or even a sibling or a child. With Jupiter retrograde in your seventh house of partnerships, you may be taking a second, more honest look at a relationship.

Sunday, June 22 (Moon in Aquarius)   The focus is on other people's money. Sounds strange, right? But you may be helping out a friend or relative with tax returns, insurance, or wills. And since it's Sunday, be sure to save time to enjoy yourself. Relaxation is an art.

Monday, June 23 (Moon in Aquarius to Pisces 3:33 p.m.)   The moon joins Uranus in your ninth house. The itch to travel is almost unbearable. Indulge yourself, but check out your finances to see what you can reasonably afford. Chances are good that you're in better shape than you think.

Tuesday, June 24 (Moon in Pisces)   With the moon at a nice angle to your sun, you're in a dreamy, intuitive mood. Take note of images or feelings that surface spontaneously. They may answer some concern that you have. Be sure to keep a notepad or your Blackberry handy to record any impressions you get.

Wednesday, June 25 (Moon in Pisces to Aries 10:50 p.m.)   A career day. You're on fire with something you have learned or an idea that you have. Garner the support that you need from your peers before pitching this to the higher-up's.

Thursday, June 26 (Moon in Aries)   Uranus turns retrograde in Pisces, your ninth house. You may not even notice this. Uranus is a slow-moving planet and the impact of its retrograde motion is apt to be subtle. For the next several months, you'll be looking inward, examining your personal philosophy and worldview. Your education or overseas travel plans may change. You may embark on a spiritual quest, Cancer. Just the kind of things you love to do!

Friday, June 27 (Moon in Aries)   A fire-sign individual—Aries, Leo, or Sagittarius—is helpful with a professional matter. Perhaps this person helps raise excitement for a new team project. On the romance front, you're in rare form with Venus in your sign.

277

Saturday, June 28 (Moon in Aries to Taurus 2:51 a.m.)
With the moon in compatible Taurus, Venus in your sign, and Jupiter and Saturn in signs compatible with yours, the stars are stacked in your favor. Use your time wisely; don't be afraid to take chances.

Sunday, June 29 (Moon in Taurus)   The sensuous Taurus moon attracts a flirtation with someone you previously considered friend. The attraction could be mutual, Cancer. Are you ready to plunge into a romance?

Monday, June 30 (Moon in Taurus to Gemini 4:04 a.m.)   The moon enters your twelfth house. This is usually a good time to steal away by yourself and do whatever you have to do to complete projects. Home improvement, self-improvement, work improvement—whatever you tackle, you have the luxury of solitude.

JULY 2008

Tuesday, July 1 (Moon in Gemini)   Mars enters Virgo. This transit certainly stimulates communication between you and your siblings and neighbors. Until August 19, you may get more involved in your community or neighborhood, but just be sure you can afford the commitment in time and energy that will be required.

Wednesday, July 2 (Moon in Gemini to Cancer 3:54 a.m.)
With the new moon entering your sign, Mars and Saturn in compatible Virgo, and Venus still in your sign until July 12, you are in a good place. Whether it's romance, work, your family and friends, or your spiritual life, everything seems to be working just the way you like it.

Thursday, July 3 (Moon in Cancer)   Your July Fourth preparations are under way! If you're dieting, allow yourself a little leeway. Instead of putting out chips and pizza for your guests, try veggie platters and high-protein foods. But even more to the point, don't allow the change in your routine to stress you out.

Friday, July 4 (Moon in Cancer to Leo 4:16 a.m.)
Happy Independence Day! You're on show. You relish the special attention from family and friends, even from those who don't share your personal beliefs and philosophies. In fact, given the diverse personalities and backgrounds, the entire day goes exceptionally well.

Saturday, July 5 (Moon in Leo)   If you're worried that you don't have enough money to cover your bills, put together a strategy to develop a more prosperous attitude. Worrying never helped anybody.

Sunday, July 6 (Moon in Leo to Virgo 7:04 a.m.)   The moon joins Saturn in Virgo and your third house. Saturn can stabilize your emotions or depress you. It's up to you. You write the script of your life, Cancer.

Monday, July 7 (Moon in Virgo)   Your emotions are focused. You may feel that your responsibilities are greater—with less compensation—but intuitively you know the reasons for this. You're in the groove all day; this evening, get out and about with people in your community.

Tuesday, July 8 (Moon in Virgo to Libra 1:32 p.m.)   Romance is on your mind. That's no surprise. Your new relationship is the center of your life, and it's tough to think about anything else. But think you must, Cancer. There are work and contractual obligations that have to be dealt with.

Wednesday, July 9 (Moon in Libra)   You and your partner take in an art exhibit, a film, or perhaps a concert. You're striving for balance and equilibrium. Your intuitive feelings are quite strong; so follow them and you won't make a wrong move.

Thursday, July 10 (Moon in Libra to Scorpio 11:35 p.m.)   Mercury enters your sign, joining Venus in your first house. This powerful combination brings your conscious thoughts squarely on your love life. You and your partner should discuss things honestly.

Friday, July 11 (Moon in Scorpio)   Regardless of what you come across or experience, the bottom line surfaces. This can be a good thing if it's a bottom line you're looking for. A little research and investigation go a long way.

Saturday, July 12 (Moon in Scorpio)   Venus enters Leo, a wonderfully warm and exuberant sign. Your love life picks up for the next several weeks, and so do your finances. It's possible to make money from an artistic project; so take advantage of this opportunity.

Sunday, July 13 (Moon in Scorpio to Sagittarius 11:50 a.m.)   You prepare for a presentation at work tomorrow. You really don't feel like working, but because you're worried about everything going right, you spend several hours on this project. This evening, give yourself a break.

Monday, July 14 (Moon in Sagittarius)   Your presentation goes extremely well. You not only have the big picture, but know exactly how to express it so others will support and understand it. Bosses now take notice.

Tuesday, July 15 (Moon in Sagittarius)   The moon is opposite your sun, which happens once a month. It's in your seventh house, and that tends to put emphasis on your partnerships. You and your partner should talk about your respective visions for the relationship.

Wednesday, July 16 (Moon in Sagittarius to Capricorn 12:20 a.m.)   Whenever the moon joins Jupiter in Capricorn, things can either get blown out of proportion or give great insights concerning your feelings and hunches. Which it is depends on you. You also have a need to create long-range plans.

Thursday, July 17 (Moon in Capricorn)   With Saturn in your third house, it's easy for you to rebuild bridges between you and a relative or a neighbor. It also strengthens your communication abilities—a boon for any writer! Give some thought to the kind of structures you would like to build in your life.

Friday, July 18 (Moon in Capricorn to Aquarius 11:41 a.m.) The full moon in Aquarius should illuminate an issue you have related to resources you share with someone else. If you're engaged, you and your partner may want to sit down and go over your finances. Discuss how you plan to share your financial resources or whether you prefer to keep your money separate.

Saturday, July 19 (Moon in Aquarius) You may have a blind spot where a friend is concerned. Go with your feelings instead of your intellect on this one. You and a group of like-minded individuals may be involved in some sort of charity or relief project.

Sunday, July 20 (Moon in Aquarius to Pisces 9:09 p.m.) As the moon enters Pisces and your ninth house, you may sign up for college or graduate school classes for this fall. Or perhaps you've been admitted to a college already. Whichever it is, your focus is on higher education.

Monday, July 21 (Moon in Pisces) Relax and dream, Cancer. Even if you're at work, your imagination hums right along, concocting visions and strange stories that somehow reflect your deeper self. Be sure to write everything down.

Tuesday, July 22 (Moon in Pisces) Your imagination is running at full-tilt; you may have a hard time keeping up with the pace of your ideas! Be sure to have a notepad, computer file, or recorder close by so that none of these terrific ideas gets away from you. If you're traveling, your experiences are apt to be quite pleasant.

Wednesday, July 23 (Moon in Pisces to Aries 4:23 a.m.) With Mercury in your sign and Mars in compatible Virgo, you've got plenty of grounding for whatever you tackle. It may be a career matter that demands your attention. Try to clear off your desk by the end of the week so you can enjoy your weekend!

Thursday, July 24 (Moon in Aries) You get together with one or both of your parents. You catch up on family news and issues. There could be some brief tension, but it's nothing serious. You also should spend a little time on a work-related project you have to deal with next week.

Friday, July 25 (Moon in Aries to Taurus 9:15 a.m.) With the moon entering compatible Taurus, you're in for a social whirl. Invitations come from friends and any groups to which you belong. If you've got a product to promote, get out there and promote the heck out of it!

Saturday, July 26 (Moon in Taurus) Mercury enters Leo and your second house. Over the next several weeks, a lot of your communications will deal with your finances, earnings, and spending habits. Your values or beliefs could be more in the public eye.

Sunday, July 27 (Moon in Taurus to Gemini 11:56 a.m.) The Gemini moon enters your twelfth house. This isn't the easiest moon for you, but as a water sign, you have a strong intuitive grasp of this particular house. You have an opportunity to examine your repetitive psychological patterns and to correct them. You get insight from your dreams.

Monday, July 28 (Moon in Gemini) You and a close friend or family member have an honest discussion about things in the past. The discussion may not heal old wounds, but it's an important first step. You also may find a book or an Internet site that helps you understand an issue of some concern.

Tuesday, July 29 (Moon in Gemini to Cancer 1:12 p.m.) The moon enters your sign and stays there the rest of the week. You probably stick close to home and spend time with family members. Events could include one or both of your parents. Perhaps the best energy for this moon is to have a family barbecue at your place!

Wednesday, July 30 (Moon in Cancer)   With the moon still in your sign, you may be involved in a home-improvement project that's consuming more of your time than you initially thought it would. You're intent on finishing the job, and you enlist the help of friends or family. Make it a celebration.

Thursday, July 31 (Moon in Cancer to Leo 2:22 p.m.)   The moon joins Mercury in Leo, in your second house. You could feel a bit vulnerable, and take a deep look at what makes you feel secure emotionally. Once you know, you can take steps to bring that particular thing into your life.

AUGUST 2008

Friday, August 1 (Moon in Leo)   The solar eclipse in Leo impacts your second house of finances. External events reveal something about your finances that you didn't perceive earlier. Since solar eclipses signal beginnings as well as endings, you may find new, better opportunities for earning money. You also could be laying out quite a large amount of cash for a big-ticket item. If possible, postpone the purchase until your finances stabilize.

Saturday, August 2 (Moon in Leo to Virgo 4:59 p.m.)   Your communication skills are heightened. You may need to convince a neighbor or a relative to see your side of an issue or concern. This person appreciates your attention to details and takes your advice.

Sunday, August 3 (Moon in Virgo)   The moon has joined Mars in Virgo, adding determination and aggression to your personality. You get what you want, and it actually comes to you quickly and without hurdles. When you really want or need to manifest something, this is how you do it, Cancer!

Monday, August 4 (Moon in Virgo to Libra 10:28 p.m.)   The moon enters Libra and your fourth house.

283

This moon can be an irritant to you because it forms a challenging angle to your sun. At the same time, you feel more romantic and in need of beauty.

Tuesday, August 5 (Moon in Libra)   Venus joins Mars in Virgo, a rather interesting mix for romance with someone you meet in your community. This combination continues until August 19, when Mars enters Libra. Before that happens, Mercury also joins this lineup in Virgo, in your third house. Take a look at August 10 for what that promises.

Wednesday, August 6 (Moon in Libra)   You and a partner or close friend head for a new museum exhibit or an art film. You're in the mood for beauty, and that includes virtually anything you perceive to be beautiful—from a landscape to a person. Indulge yourself.

Thursday, August 7 (Moon in Libra to Scorpio 7:27 a.m.)   The Scorpio moon is more compatible with your sun sign and adds spice and passion to your day. It also revs up your love life, or your creative adrenaline, or both! However this energy manifests itself, you're in for a treat when it comes to romance, creativity, and your relationships with your children.

Friday, August 8 (Moon in Scorpio)   Your creative adrenaline pumps hard and fast. The bottom line is whether you can keep up with the ideas that pour out of you. And that depends on how committed you are to expressing what's in your soul!

Saturday, August 9 (Moon in Scorpio to Sagittarius 7:11 p.m.)   The moon enters your sixth house of daily work. You may feel bombarded with responsibilities or duties and obligations, but you also have a handle on the big picture. And that big picture helps you make the right decisions.

Sunday, August 10 (Moon in Sagittarius)   Mercury joins Venus and Mars in Virgo, in your third house. This impressive lineup certainly urges you to pay attention to what's going on around you, particularly in your community. Your mind, love life, and physical and sexual energy are zeroed in on perfecting what you have.

Monday, August 11 (Moon in Sagittarius) You adjust your exercise routine to fit your busy lifestyle. This routine could include a period of meditation and visualization, in addition to the actual physical activity. You're concerned about your appearance and could end up selecting a whole new style of clothing.

Tuesday, August 12 (Moon in Sagittarius to Capricorn 7:43 a.m.) Your partner or spouse is eager to spend time with you. The two of you begin to discuss long-range plans. Your commitment to each other is a given. You just have to work out the details.

Wednesday, August 13 (Moon in Capricorn) If you're in the midst of contract negotiations, be sure to ask for what you feel you deserve. You're in a strong position and able to grasp the finer details. Follow your hunches on this one.

Thursday, August 14 (Moon in Capricorn to Aquarius 6:57 p.m.) Other people share their time and resources with you concerning a project. It could be that you need help with insurance or banking matters. Or you may be the one helping someone else.

Friday, August 15 (Moon in Aquarius) Your visionary abilities pop into high gear. You're able to spot a gap in the market and feel certain your product will fill it. Not too bad for a day's work.

Saturday, August 16 (Moon in Aquarius) The lunar eclipse is in Aquarius and your sixth house. Expect emotional issues to surface around work or health over the next few weeks. If you receive a questionable health report, get another opinion. There's plenty of room for error under the influence of this eclipse.

Sunday, August 17 (Moon in Aquarius to Pisces 3:47 a.m.) If you're a writer in search of a publisher, the Pisces moon, in your ninth house of publishing, could be very good news for you. An agent or editor is interested in your material. Are you ready?

Monday, August 18 (Moon in Pisces) Your itch to travel is pronounced; you may be doing some research on-line about destinations. Or you may head off to college or graduate school in the fall and need to finalize last-minute details.

Tuesday, August 19 (Moon in Pisces to Aries 10:11 a.m.) Mars enters Libra and your fourth house. This transit lasts until October 3 and energizes your home and family life. Since Mars represents our physical aggression and sexuality, your sex life should spark up. Strive for patience. You could be a bit short-tempered.

Wednesday, August 20 (Moon in Aries) You have a professional window of opportunity. Push for your agenda, and resist the urge to do everything yourself. Allow your considerable intuition full power.

Thursday, August 21 (Moon in Aries to Taurus 2:38 p.m.) You get together with friends to campaign for a particular candidate or to promote a product or idea. However the day pans out, it's about friends and people of like minds doing something for the greater good of their world.

Friday, August 22 (Moon in Taurus) Even though it's Friday, you're on top of things. You're on the Internet or on the phone or both, putting together an advertising campaign for your company's newest product or for your own creative work. The public is receptive to your ideas. Take advantage of the opportunity.

Saturday, August 23 (Moon in Taurus to Gemini 5:49 p.m.) Late this afternoon, the moon enters Gemini and your twelfth house, signaling a time to retreat into your own head. You dive into books you've been saving for a rainy day. Save the parties until the moon enters your sign.

Sunday, August 24 (Moon in Gemini)   It's a good day to update your e-mail list and contact clients. Even if you don't have anything pressing to report, your clients appreciate the contact. You get together this evening with a close friend or sibling for some honest and insightful conversation.

Monday, August 25 (Moon in Gemini to Cancer 8:19 p.m.)   This evening the moon enters your sign, always a powerful time for you. With Mercury and Venus in compatible Virgo, Jupiter in compatible Capricorn, and Uranus in compatible Pisces, the universe is stacked in your favor. Use your time wisely over the next two days.

Tuesday, August 26 (Moon in Cancer)   Jupiter expands your business and personal partnerships in astonishing, positive ways. The big question is how willing you are to bend to the changing times. Your best bet is to allow the fluidity of your imagination and intuition greater freedom.

Wednesday, August 27 (Moon in Cancer to Leo, 10:51 p.m.)   The moon enters your second house. Patience and responsibility are required in terms of your finances. Don't despair! By August 30, your financial situation will look considerably better. Sometimes, even money concerns are just a matter of perspective.

Thursday, August 28 (Moon in Leo)   Mercury enters Libra and your fourth house. Until November 4, your home is a hub of activity. You have more visitors than usual, there's lot of conversation about books, ideas, and travel, and everyone feels a need for balance and fairness. During part of this transit, Mercury turns retrograde. So prepare.

Friday, August 29 (Moon in Leo)   Your values take center stage. Are you an animal-rights activist who eats meat or wears fur? Are you critical of the government, but don't vote? You get the idea. Take an honest look at where you stand.

Saturday, August 30 (Moon in Leo to Virgo 2:19 a.m.) Venus joins Mercury in Libra, your fourth house. This transit, lasting until late September, certainly spices up your love life and generally smoothes things out at home. You may do some home improvements during this time, attempting to add more beauty and harmony to your surroundings.

Sunday, August 31 (Moon in Virgo) Details and precision are the focus. These qualities apply to your relationship with relatives or neighbors. If you're a writer or in the communication or travel business, this transit prompts you to be precise and efficient.

SEPTEMBER 2008

Monday, September 1 (Moon in Virgo to Libra, 7:45 a.m.) There's a lot going on this month with the stars. Jupiter turns direct on September 7, releasing positive energy for partnerships. On September 24, Mercury turns retrograde in your fourth house. Back up computer files several days before, wrap up contracts, and firm your travel plans.

Tuesday, September 2 (Moon in Libra) One of your parents plays into events. He or she may have advice that you should hear and take to heart. Your home-beautification project seems to keep expanding from one room to the next. The more harmonious your surroundings at home, the better you feel and the healthier you are!

Wednesday, September 3 (Moon in Libra to Scorpio, 4:03 p.m.) With the moon in compatible Scorpio, your intuition deepens, and your eye for research and investigation is extraordinary. You enjoy digging for answers, perhaps something as complex as research for an educational purpose or something as simple as delving into your family's genealogy.

Thursday, September 4 (Moon in Scorpio)   With the moon in your fifth house of romance, you're in the mood for love. You and a partner up the ante in your relationship. Are you ready to commit? If you're not involved with anyone, pour that energy into a creative endeavor.

Friday, September 5 (Moon in Scorpio)   Bottom-line day, Cancer. Whatever you've been involved in reaches the moment of truth. You should like what you see. But keep it to yourself.

Saturday, September 6 (Moon in Scorpio to Sagittarius 3:12 a.m.)   With the moon entering Sagittarius and your sixth house, it's time to move ahead on work-related projects. You've got the wind at your back and fire in your heart. You're primed for the job.

Sunday, September 7 (Moon in Sagittarius)   Jupiter turns direct in Capricorn, your seventh house. This movement should be very nice for your partnerships. If you're self-employed, it's possible that your business or product will be sold overseas. If you're a writer, your books may enjoy foreign sales. On a personal level, your optimism increases, and you feel that you can achieve whatever you set your sights on.

Monday, September 8 (Moon in Sagittarius to Capricorn 3:46 p.m.)   Pluto, after retrograding back into Sagittarius, moves direct and in late November enters Capricorn, where it will remain until 2023. The direct movement releases energy you can use in your daily work to transform your environment.

Tuesday, September 9 (Moon in Capricorn)   Whenever the moon joins Jupiter in your seventh house, emotional issues can be blown out of proportion, particularly when they relate to partnerships. In a more positive vein, anything you imagine may be larger than life.

Wednesday, September 10 (Moon in Capricorn)   You're able to make long-range plans in an effective manner. In fact, you and your partner may be discussing plans about a life together. On other fronts, sign contracts before September 24 when Mercury turns retrograde.

Thursday, September 11 (Moon in Capricorn to Aquarius 3:20 a.m.)   Other people's resources come into play. This could involve anything from insurance, mortgages, and loans to preparing a living will. You may be concerned about big questions: is there life after death, is it possible to communicate with the dead, and is reincarnation a fact?

Friday, September 12 (Moon in Aquarius)   You sign up for a course or workshop in past-life recall. While you're delving into this topic, pick up a copy of a book about reincarnation.

Saturday, September 13 (Moon in Aquarius to Pisces 12:05 p.m.)   A water sign—Pisces, Scorpio, or another Cancer—plays an important part in the day's activities that revolve around educational and publishing issues or your plans for an overseas trip. With both Venus and Mercury still in Libra, your fourth house, you come to grips with balance and fairness in dealing with your family.

Sunday, September 14 (Moon in Pisces)   With the moon in gentle Pisces, you may come across a stray that captures your heart. With the moon at such a harmonious angle to your sun, your compassion is high.

Monday, September 15 (Moon in Pisces to Aries 5:39 p.m.)   The moon enters your tenth house late this afternoon, indicating a possible glitch in professional matters as the moon changes sign. It's nothing serious and, if you take care of it immediately, is forgotten quickly. Just don't get irritable. You need to be a team player, a challenge when the moon is in Aries.

Tuesday, September 16 (Moon in Aries)   With Mercury and Venus still in Libra, your fourth house, and the moon opposite those planets in your tenth, there could be some inner tension related to professional or personal responsibilities. This happens to all of us from time to time, but you're so diligent that it bothers you more than it does most people.

Wednesday, September 17 (Moon in Aries to Taurus 8:57 p.m.) The Taurus moon is comfortable for you. You have a lot of interaction with friends. This evening you and some like-minded individuals get together to work on a political campaign or another project about which you feel passionate.

Thursday, September 18 (Moon in Taurus) You may think that flexibility is called for, but it isn't. The Taurus moon makes you emotionally stubborn, unwilling to yield your position.

Friday, September 19 (Moon in Taurus to Gemini 11:17 p.m.) How far can you take your mind? Sounds strange, but you're stretching mental muscles you didn't know you had. Your communication skills are strong, but you prefer to do it mainly through e-mail or by phone. Your solitude is too precious to share with anyone but those you love the most.

Saturday, September 20 (Moon in Gemini) Your psychological patterns and the stuff of your unconscious surface. Use your insight as creative fodder. You may want to try meditating. Not only is meditation well suited for the temperament of a Cancer, but it will help to ground you when you need it.

Sunday, September 21 (Moon in Gemini) Books and information rule the day. Whether you're gathering facts or just poking around for your own education, you're in a mental groove, Cancer. Sign up for a course or seminar in a topic that really interests you. If you didn't complete your college or grad school education, you may want to consider returning.

Monday, September 22 (Moon in Gemini to Cancer 1:49 a.m.) The moon enters your sign. Set aside time to pamper yourself or to spend time with a group of close friends or family members. Your energy is strong, your intuition powerful. Tomorrow, things get even better!

Tuesday, September 23 (Moon in Cancer) Venus enters compatible Scorpio, in your fifth house. If your love life has been stuck in the doldrums, expect a dramatic change before October 18. You're going into the best time all year for love and romance.

Wednesday, September 24 (Moon in Cancer to Leo 5:14 a.m.) There is a bit of a chink in things. Mercury turns retrograde in Libra, your fifth house. The best way to keep this from putting a damper on romance is to communicate exactly how you feel, removing any possibility of misunderstanding.

Thursday, September 25 (Moon in Leo) With the moon in your second house, your finances and values figure into your concerns. If you feel that you're earning a living in away that isn't genuinely compatible with your deepest values, lay out a plan for changing it. If you need additional educational skills, enlist the aid of friends to help you obtain those skills.

Friday, September 26 (Moon in Leo to Virgo 9:53 a.m.) Here's another compatible moon for you, Cancer. You're on top of fine details, and the payoff comes down the line when your boss realizes just how valuable you really are.

Saturday, September 27 (Moon in Virgo) With the moon linking up with Saturn in your third house, your ability to say what you think in a practical, effective manner is just about perfect. You can describe your intuition in terms that other people understand. Despite the Mercury retrograde, you're moving ahead with vacation plans for the holidays. Just don't buy your tickets yet.

Sunday, September 28 (Moon in Virgo to Libra 4:06 p.m.)   The moon joins Mercury retrograde in Libra, your fourth house. If you're noticing that appliances or computers are acting up, it's Mercury's movement. Just grin and bear it. The best use of this retrograde period is to revise, rewrite, and reconsider.

Monday, September 29 (Moon in Libra)   If you can imagine it, you can achieve it. Your focus is on long-range goals for your family. Do you like the area where you're living? If not, can you improve the conditions or is a move in order?

Tuesday, September 30 (Moon in Libra)   Tomorrow, the moon joins Venus in Scorpio, your fifth house. Buckle your seat belt, Cancer. Your love life is about to get even better!

OCTOBER 2008

Wednesday, October 1 (Moon in Libra to Scorpio 12:27 a.m.)   The moon joins Venus in Scorpio in your fifth house of romance. This beautiful recipe for love and romance should please you to no end. If you're not involved, and have no wish to be at this time, this combination is a shot of adrenaline.

Thursday, October 2 (Moon in Scorpio)   Hang in there, Cancer. Mercury turns direct again on October 15. Your home life won't be chaotic for much longer. Try not to start any new home-improvement projects under this retrograde. Instead, touch up the improvements you've done already.

Friday, October 3 (Moon in Scorpio to Sagittarius 11:15 am.)   Mars enters Scorpio, a sign that it corules, and is at a beneficial angle to your sun. Mars represents your physical and sexual energy. Until November 16, use this energy in your creative projects and in your love life!

Saturday, October 4 (Moon in Sagittarius)   The moon joins Pluto in Sagittarius in your eighth house. This can be a powerful emotional combination. Be careful that you don't try to control the people around you. You'll be tempted, but it would be best for you to resist this particular temptation.

Sunday, October 5 (Moon in Sagittarius to Capricorn 11:49 p.m.)   A business partner would like to move ahead on your pending deal. It's fine to discuss the particulars, but don't sign contracts until after Mercury turns direct on October 15. You're in a period of expansion with your partnerships, both professional and personal, but timing is everything.

Monday, October 6 (Moon in Capricorn)   The moon has joined Jupiter in Capricorn. Your partner or spouse has a surprise for you. Friends touch base through e-mail. A Mercury retrograde often brings old friends back into your life. It also can reignite issues you thought were resolved.

Tuesday, October 7 (Moon in Capricorn)   Just another eight days before Mercury turns direct. With the moon, Jupiter, and Saturn all in earth signs and Venus and Uranus in compatible water signs, the focus is on practicality, imagination, and intuition. You feel an intuitive connection with someone and sense some sort of past-life connection.

Wednesday, October 8 (Moon in Capricorn to Aquarius 12:03 p.m.)   The moon joins Neptune in Aquarius, in your eighth house. There is usually some emotional confusion with this combination. It could revolve around certain psychological patterns in yourself that you're beginning to notice. Don't fret about your insights. Self-knowledge is what you need.

Thursday, October 9 (Moon in Aquarius)   You may look for some end-of-the-year tax breaks. Consult your accountant or tax attorney. If you don't already have a retirement fund, open one.

Friday, October 10 (Moon in Aquarius to Pisces 9:31 p.m.)   The Pisces moon works a strange magic on you, Cancer. You feel dreamy, undecided, imaginative, tender, victimized, heroic, and compassionate. Pick an emotion and run with it. See where it leads you.

Saturday, October 11 (Moon in Pisces)   Publishing or educational issues are the focus. If you have a manuscript that you've been trying to get published, the news is positive. With the moon linked up with unpredictable Uranus, your emotional reactions are apt to be unusual.

Sunday, October 12 (Moon in Pisces)   You feel conflicted about an emotional situation. Your heart urges you to move in one direction; your head demands that you move in another direction. Sit quietly for a few minutes and allow the various options to percolate. If your intuition speaks to you about which choice is the right one, follow that guidance. Otherwise, just let events unfold.

Monday, October 13 (Moon in Pisces to Aries 3:07 a.m.)   Career matters are highlighted. You and a boss or peer tackle a long-standing project that has been on the back burner. Once Mercury turns direct on October 15, this project takes on an entirely new flavor.

Tuesday, October 14 (Moon in Aries)   You've got drive and stamina; you pour it into a professional project. If you're on a deadline, you meet it. You may not be much of a team player, but you know what has to be done and you don't want to depend on others. This full moon brings to light something related to your career.

Wednesday, October 15 (Moon in Aries to Taurus 5:31 a.m.)   Mercury turns direct. Pack your bags and head for the mountains or the ocean. Any problems you've been having with computers, appliances, and communication should ease up.

Thursday, October 16 (Moon in Taurus)   People gather at your place for a celebration of some kind. Don't drive yourself nuts with preparations. Advertise your company's product or do promotion for your own creative works.

Friday, October 17 (Moon in Taurus to Gemini 6:26 a.m.)   As the moon enters Gemini and your twelfth house, you may decide to kick back and stay close to home. It's a perfect time to recharge your batteries for when the moon enters your sign on October 19.

Saturday, October 18 (Moon in Gemini)   Venus enters Sagittarius and your sixth house today. Until November 12, an office flirtation heats up. A romance may be in the offing. Are you ready, Cancer? Whether you're looking for fun or commitment, try not to place restrictions on this relationship.

Sunday, October 19 (Moon in Gemini to Cancer 7:41 a.m.)   The moon enters your sign. You're energized. Plan that overseas trip you've been considering.

Monday, October 20 (Moon in Cancer)   You usually aren't the type to seize center stage, and today is no different in that regard. But when the spotlight seeks you out, you certainly rise to the occasion. You have plenty of sex appeal and charisma.

Tuesday, October 21 (Moon in Cancer to Leo 10:36 a.m.)   This moon's energy can manifest itself through your values, your actions, or both. A situation arises that will test you and what you hold dear.

Wednesday, October 22 (Moon in Leo)   You and a fire-sign individual dive into something that's important to both of you. It may be a charity project for which you volunteer time.

Thursday, October 23 (Moon in Leo to Virgo, 3:41 p.m.)   As the moon enters earth sign Virgo, joining Saturn in your third house, you finally find the structure you need for a communication project. Whether you're dealing with the written or spoken word, the structure is paramount to the success of your project.

Friday, October 24 (Moon in Virgo) You're quite the perfectionist. You may think of yourself as the proverbial diamond in the rough and hope to smooth out your personality and shine it up. But the bottom line is that there's nothing wrong with you, Cancer.

Saturday, October 25 (Moon in Virgo to Libra 10:48 p.m.) With the moon entering Libra and Venus still in vivacious Sagittarius, you're in rare form. Ready for new friends and a whole new chapter in your social life. It's possible that an office flirtation has become a full-blown romance.

Sunday, October 26 (Moon in Libra) Balance, fairness, and the dynamics of relationships are the focus. Specifically, these qualities are applied to your family and your career. You could feel torn between professional and personal responsibilities and need to remember that you can't be all things to all people.

Monday, October 27 (Moon in Libra) Your socializing reaches new peaks. Whether it's gossip traded at the office watercooler or your e-mail buzzing with the news, you're in the center of the social hub. You're the connector for various groups of acquaintances and friends.

Tuesday, October 28 (Moon in Libra to Scorpio 7:48 a.m.) The moon joins Mars in Scorpio, your fifth house. This powerful combination of planets certainly heats up your love life. Your physical attraction to your partner or new romantic interest brings unusual surprises and twists and turns in the plot of your love life.

Wednesday, October 29 (Moon in Scorpio) You turn your energy on your creativity. There's one project in particular—photography, writing, acting, or art—that has captured your passions. Dive in and let the rest of the world pass you buy.

Thursday, October 30 (Moon in Scorpio to Sagittarius 6:41 p.m.) The moon joins Venus in Sagittarius, your sixth house. Romance at work is taking over your life. Be careful that you don't go so overboard that you overlook job responsibilities. On the other hand, Venus in the sixth house often means a smooth time at work. So maybe a romantic distraction is just fine.

Friday, October 31 (Moon in Sagittarius) Happy Halloween! What a perfect moon for the night when the dead and the living supposedly can communicate. Get out your Ouija board. And while you're at it, put on that costume from last year and let the trick-or-treaters have a good laugh!

NOVEMBER 2008

Saturday, November 1 (Moon in Sagittarius) Neptune turns direct in Aquarius, your eighth house. The effects of this movement are subtle because Neptune moves at a snail's crawl. The forward motion releases energy that could manifest itself in psychic experiences.

Sunday, November 2—Daylight Saving Time Ends (Moon in Sagittarius to Capricorn 6:13 a.m.) Change is in the wind. Three planets are entering new signs in November, and that always ushers in a whole new energy grid. Get together with your partner for quality time. Start making plans for the holidays.

Monday, November 3 (Moon in Capricorn) Your contract negotiations pay off. You get just about everything you asked for. If you're in the middle of divorce proceedings, this moon should prove to be an asset. It helps you compartmentalize your emotions. Even though the presence of the past is strong, the present is your point of power.

Tuesday, November 4 (Moon in Capricorn to Aquarius 7:02 p.m.) Mercury enters Scorpio, joining Mars in your fifth house. The combination of these two planets indicates that your sexual attraction to a partner is based on your mental camaraderie. If the mental communication is lacking, everything else will seem flat as well.

Wednesday, November 5 (Moon in Aquarius) You and your visionary friends come up with a cutting-edge idea. You may have to draw in someone else who has knowledge and expertise in the development and marketing of your idea. Or you may want to toss the idea around a while longer and wait until the moon is in your sign before you decide how to make it a reality.

Thursday, November 6 (Moon in Aquarius) You get involved with a volunteer or charity project. It may be related to an organization whose ideals appeal to your compassion. Look to a Gemini or Libra for additional insights concerning a metaphysical question.

Friday, November 7 (Moon in Aquarius to Pisces 5:44 a.m.) With the moon, Mercury, Uranus, and Mars all in a water sign, you're in good shape. Your intuition offers up valuable nudges and impulses that you may want to follow if only to see where it all leads.

Saturday, November 8 (Moon in Pisces) Your emotions feel overwhelming. You need to relax and let everything go. Go out and paint the town red to relieve stress.

Sunday, November 9 (Moon in Pisces to Aries 12:27 p.m.) The moon in Aries certainly can make you temperamental and restless. Maybe that restlessness is about the proximity of the holidays and the fact that you haven't started shopping yet. Get to work.

Monday, November 10 (Moon in Aries) There's one way to get the job done right: work alone. Even if the job or activity is supposed to be a team effort, you may not get much support from the team. So do your own thing.

Tuesday, November 11 (Moon in Aries to Taurus 3:06 p.m.) You and a group of like-minded individuals get together to brainstorm creative ideas. Whether your direction is the arts or computer science, metaphysics or psychology, you begin to find your niche. Keep at it. Your strong intuition puts you way ahead of the pack.

Wednesday, November 12 (Moon in Taurus) Venus enters Capricorn, joining Jupiter in your seventh house. When the two best planets in the zodiac are in your partnership house, you can count on good fortune, happiness, and success.

Thursday, November 13 (Moon in Taurus to Gemini 3:13 p.m.) Chill. If you absolutely have to have company, make it the company of a close family member or friend. Avoid groups.

Friday, November 14 (Moon in Gemini) Hang out at home or head to your nearest bookstore to find an interesting book. You don't have to be a complete hermit, but some of yesterday's energy is still with you. Two or three qualifies as a party.

Saturday, November 15 (Moon in Gemini to Cancer 2:53 p.m.) The moon is in your sign, and you get a high dose of self-confidence, sensuality, magnetism, and all sorts of other positive qualities. This is the last day that Mars is in Scorpio, forming a harmonious angle to your sun, so get out there and attract romance and creativity into your life.

Sunday, November 16 (Moon in Cancer) Mars enters Sagittarius, joining Venus in your sixth house. This combination of planets certainly indicates the possibility of romance and a sexual relationship with someone you meet through work or through health-related activities. Be careful that you don't get short-tempered with your partner.

Monday, November 17 (Moon in Cancer to Leo 4:08 p.m.) The moon enters your second house, forming a beneficial angle to Mars and Venus in your sixth house. It's possible that your finances are stimulated in a major way. You may soon see your way clear of debt.

Tuesday, November 18 (Moon in Leo)   Your exuberance can easily overwhelm you. It's as if you woke up with the world on your side, and the imbalance throws you off. Take it in stride. You're in a very good place.

Wednesday, November 19 (Moon in Leo to Virgo 8:13 p.m.)   Your good mood continues, but for different reasons. You and a neighbor get involved in a community project to help others. It appeals to the compassionate side of you and satisfies your need to touch the larger world.

Thursday, November 20 (Moon in Virgo)   Coming into the first of the holidays, guests may soon arrive at your place for Thanksgiving. Or you may soon head out of town. Whichever it is, don't stress about what you didn't get done. All that does is put you in a bad mood.

Friday, November 21 (Moon in Virgo)   There is a limit to your patience, and you may reach it. A neighbor or sibling pushes your buttons, and your response will determine the immediate future of the relationship. Best to keep your own counsel and deal with it all at a later time.

Saturday, November 22 (Moon in Virgo to Libra 3:20 a.m.)   With the moon in your fourth house, your mother or another nurturing female has advice and insights. If your mother has been visiting for the holidays, make her feel appreciated and loved. Take her out to a concert or an art exhibit.

Sunday, November 23 (Moon in Libra)   Mercury enters Sagittarius, joining Mars in your sixth house. This combination can be a powerhouse if used correctly. Rather than hammering away at how correct and right on the mark you are, use this energy to initiate change in your daily work and health routine. You have the energy to forge ahead.

Monday, November 24 (Moon in Libra to Scorpio 12:54 p.m.)   The moon enters passionate Scorpio, your fifth house. In romance, the Scorpio moon tends to be intense. You're able to get to the bottom line of a relationship. Get out and have some fun, Cancer.

Tuesday, November 25 (Moon in Scorpio)   You and your workout, running, or yoga partner suddenly discover you have more in common than you thought. This could be the beginning of an intriguing romance.

Wednesday, November 26 (Moon in Scorpio)   After retrograding back into Sagittarius, Pluto enters Capricorn and your seventh house. This transit lasts a very long time, so its influence on your partnerships will be subtle, but profound. Look for a dramatic shift in how you and your partner relate to each other.

Thursday, November 27 (Moon in Scorpio to Sagittarius 12:14 a.m.)   Uranus turns direct to Pisces. With this forward movement, you can expect unusual and exciting people to appear in your life. These individuals have insights or talents that help you in some way. And they definitely spice up your life. Happy Thanksgiving!

Friday, November 28 (Moon in Sagittarius)   The moon joins Mercury and Mars in Sagittarius. Your passions pick up, and you're a regular powerhouse of activity and vision. You spend time touching base with your clients and peers. You really do have the ability now to see the long-range picture.

Saturday, November 29 (Moon in Sagittarius to Capricorn 12:48 p.m.)   The moon joins Jupiter and Pluto in Capricorn, your seventh house. Anything you and your partner can imagine can be manifested. Pluto brings the power to do this, Jupiter brings the expansiveness and opportunities you so rightfully deserve, and the moon brings the emotional will and imagination to do what you need to do.

Sunday, November 30 (Moon in Capricorn)   A day for planning and strategy. You are intent on making an abstract idea grounded and practical for others. Jupiter brings in the opportunity you need and the moon shows you the way.

DECEMBER 2008

Monday, December 1 (Moon in Capricorn)   You and your business partner see eye to eye on the finer details of your short-range goals for your business. You're ready for an overseas expansion and want to be sure that you work into it in the right way.

Tuesday, December 2 (Moon in Capricorn to Aquarius 1:45 a.m.)   The moon joins Neptune in Aquarius, in your eighth house. This combination creates some emotional confusion around resources you share with others. Of course, the combination occurs once a month, so this is nothing new to you. But the concern itself may be new. Make no decisions until the moon is in your sign again.

Wednesday, December 3 (Moon in Aquarius)   You get together with friends this evening and involve yourself in a volunteer or charity project. It may be something as simple as raising money for your school or as complex as helping out at a nursing home, hospital, or another kind of facility.

Thursday, December 4 (Moon in Aquarius to Pisces 1:24 p.m.)   Your in-laws are talking about coming to visit you for the holidays. This could interfere with plans you already have, so you may have to be particularly tactful. Perhaps you can tack on a couple days during your vacation to swing by their place.

Friday, December 5 (Moon in Pisces)   Whenever the moon is in Pisces, forming such a beautiful angle to your sun, the day is usually pleasant, with some intriguing psychic events. The main thing to be aware of is the usual conflict between your head and heart. Blame the two fish,

303

the symbol for Pisces, who are swimming in opposite directions.

Saturday, December 6 (Moon in Pisces to Aries 9:45 p.m.)   With the moon entering Aries and Mars in fellow fire sign Sagittarius, you have plenty of get up and go, at least as it relates to your daily work and career. One feeds into the other.

Sunday, December 7 (Moon in Aries)   Venus enters Aquarius, joining Neptune in your eighth house. There's a tendency to idealize your romantic relationships. This isn't necessarily a bad thing, unless you allow it to victimize you in some way. If you're not involved at this time, you probably will be before this transit ends early next year. For any relationship that begins under this transit, strive to see the person as he or she is rather than how you would like that individual to be.

Monday, December 8 (Moon in Aries)   A boss has a special project for you. You get this job because your higher-ups have complete faith in your abilities. In fact, they may have more faith in your talents than you do. At any rate, you're in the driver's seat.

Tuesday, December 9 (Moon in Aries to Taurus 1:53 a.m.)   The Taurus moon is usually quite friendly for you. All that earth energy brings objectivity to your subjective world and practicality to your intuitive certainties; it helps you to funnel your considerable imagination into something that others will easily understand.

Wednesday, December 10 (Moon in Taurus)   In two days, the full moon in Gemini is going to illuminate something that is hidden in your life. You may have inklings already of what this issue or situation is. Pay close attention to events, conversations, and thoughts for clues about December 12.

Thursday, December 11 (Moon in Taurus to Gemini 2:34 a.m.)   Sit back and mull things over. Pick out one of the books you've been intending to read, get on the Internet and plan your Christmas vacation, or touch base with friends through e-mail.

Friday, December 12 (Moon in Gemini)   Mercury enters Capricorn, joining Jupiter and Pluto in your seventh house. Anything that occurs with your partner is exaggerated in one way or another. There's a full moon in Gemini, so something that's hidden in your life is illuminated.

Saturday, December 13 (Moon in Gemini to Cancer 1:41 a.m.)   The mix of planets could lead to some confusion. However, your saving grace is that the moon enters your sign, canceling most negative influences. Decorate your home for the holidays if you haven't done so already. Head out to shop this evening for holiday gifts. You feel like you have to catch up to those people around you who have finished their shopping already.

Sunday, December 14 (Moon in Cancer)   With the lights going up outside your house and the inside decorated and brightened with memories of holidays past, you're in a glorious mood. It's as if you feel you can do virtually anything and succeed. Try to carry this feeling forward into the rest of the month.

Monday, December 15 (Moon in Cancer to Leo 1:23 a.m.)   Once again, the stars are all over the place; the moon is the only entity in a fire sign. You may fret about all the money you've spent for the holidays. If there's absolutely no way you can cut back, take a little out of savings to get through the holidays.

Tuesday, December 16 (Moon in Leo)   If your plans for New Year's Eve are in flux, decide what you would like to do. Then make your plans. Chances are, your loved ones will come around to your way of thinking about the New Year's celebrations.

Wednesday, December 17 (Moon in Leo to Virgo 3:36 a.m.)
With the moon entering compatible earth sign Virgo,

you're the organizer for a community event or festivity. Or your community is involved in a charity function that goes off without a hitch.

Thursday, December 18 (Moon in Virgo)   With a week to go before Christmas, you and friends head out for some shopping. You'll have luck finding the right gifts for those on your list.

Friday, December 19 (Moon in Virgo to Libra 9:23 a.m.)   The moon enters Libra, your fourth house, so it will be another nice day if you can balance all the demands on your time and energy. One way to do that effectively is to spend a few minutes meditating so that you have a clearer sense of what's really important. Call it spiritual prioritization!

Saturday, December 20 (Moon in Libra)   Plans for Christmas and the rest of the holidays may be in flux. It's nothing serious. Neptune is forming a nice angle to the moon, though, so whatever you decide should meet your ideals.

Sunday, December 21 (Moon in Libra to Scorpio 6:37 p.m.)   On New Year's Eve, Saturn will turn retrograde, which could throw a wrench into your plans. Try to go with the flow. Understand that the purpose of Saturn retrograde is to prompt us to look inward for answers about duty and responsibility.

Monday, December 22 (Moon in Scorpio)   The moon is in your fifth house, bringing something quite nice to your love life. A special holiday gift, an insight, or a deeper commitment—all are possible. A Pisces, a Scorpio, or a Cancer individual plays a role.

Tuesday, December 23 (Moon in Scorpio)   As crazy as it might sound, you run out to do some real last-minute shopping. You know the perfect gift to get for your partner. You're pushing the envelope on this one, but go for it!

Wednesday, December 24 (Moon in Scorpio to Sagittarius 6:14 a.m.)   The moon in Sagittarius forms a harmonious angle with Venus in Aquarius. This combination should bring you creative insights and inspiration. Your only challenge is time.

Thursday, December 25 (Moon in Sagittarius)   Merry Christmas! Regardless of your plans for the day, remember that your family and friends are paramount to your happiness in life. Be grateful for them and don't hesitate to express that gratitude.

Friday, December 26 (Moon in Sagittarius to Capricorn 6:57 p.m.)   Once again, the moon joins Jupiter, Mercury, and Pluto in Capricorn, your seventh house. You're recovering from Christmas, but what a very nice recovery it is.

Saturday, December 27 (Moon in Capricorn)   Add Mars to the lineup of planets in Capricorn, in your seventh house. Five out of ten planets are clustered in your seventh house. This is sure to draw romance to you if you aren't already committed. And if you're in a relationship, things only get better!

Sunday, December 28 (Moon in Capricorn)   Today and yesterday should give you a flavor of what's coming up for you. Look at the pattern of events that have unfolded. Become your own oracle.

Monday, December 29 (Moon in Capricorn to Aquarius 7:44 a.m.)   The moon joins Venus and Neptune in Aquarius, your eighth house. This odd trio of planets triggers your inspiration, vision, and compassion. It also brings a new opportunity in romance, perhaps with someone you meet unexpectedly.

Tuesday, December 30 (Moon in Aquarius)   You're already in the 2009 groove, creating your resolutions for next year. Be sure to write everything down. Keep your goals realistic.

Wednesday, December 31 (Moon in Aquarius) Saturn turns retrograde. It's a weird way to end the year, but it could be worse. Take it all in stride. Tomorrow, you'll be glad that you did.

HAPPY NEW YEAR!

SYDNEY OMARR

Born on August 5, 1926, in Philadelphia, Pennsylvania, Sydney Omarr was the only person ever given full-time duty in the U.S. Army as an astrologer. He is regarded as the most erudite astrologer of our time and the best known, through his syndicated column and his radio and television programs (he was Merv Griffin's "resident astrologer"). Omarr has been called the most "knowledgeable astrologer since Evangeline Adams." His forecasts of Nixon's downfall, the end of World War II in mid-August of 1945, the assassination of John F. Kennedy, Roosevelt's election to a fourth term and his death in office . . . these and many others are on the record and quoted enough to be considered "legendary."

ABOUT THE SERIES

This is one of a series of twelve *Sydney Omarr® Day-by-Day Astrological Guides* for the signs of 2008. For questions and comments about the book, go to www.tjmacgregor.com.

Penguin Group (USA) Online

What will you be reading tomorrow?

Tom Clancy, Patricia Cornwell, W.E.B. Griffin,
Nora Roberts, William Gibson, Robin Cook,
Brian Jacques, Catherine Coulter, Stephen King,
Dean Koontz, Ken Follett, Clive Cussler,
Eric Jerome Dickey, John Sandford,
Terry McMillan, Sue Monk Kidd, Amy Tan,
John Berendt...

You'll find them all at
penguin.com

*Read excerpts and newsletters,
find tour schedules and reading group guides,
and enter contests.*

Subscribe to Penguin Group (USA) newsletters
and get an exclusive inside look
at exciting new titles and the authors you love
long before everyone else does.

PENGUIN GROUP (USA)
us.penguingroup.com